READING FRENCH

A GUIDE FOR STUDENTS OF RELIGION AND THEOLOGY

For my mothers,
who did not speak French

Reading French

A Guide for Students of Religion and Theology

Second Edition

K. Janet Ritch

CLEMENTS PUBLISHING / ÉDITIONS CLEMENTS
TORONTO

Reading French: A Guide for Students of Religion and Theology
Copyright © 2006, 2012 by K. Janet Ritch
Revised with formatting by Eric Mills Editing & Design, and English translations, 2012

First published 2006 by Clements Publishing Group Inc.
213-6021 Yonge Street
Toronto, Ontario M2M 3W2 Canada
Web: www.clementspublishing.com
E-mail: info@clementspublishing.com

The publisher and author acknowledge the following sources for permission to use the excerpts listed below:

Lise Baroni et al., *Voix des femmes; voies de passage* … (Montréal: Pauline, 1995), pp.112-13.

Catherine Rihoit for "Ah, si j'étais" in *Le Monde* (2 July 1982), reprinted *En bonne forme*, 4th ed. by S. Dietiker (Toronto: Heath & Co., 1988), p.303.

Lyse Roy for "Espace urbain et système de représentations. Les entrées du Dauphin et de François Ier à Caen en 1532" in *Memini* 5 (2001), pp.51-52.

Madeleine des Rivières for *Ozanam. Un savant chez les pauvres* (Éditions Bellarmin, 1984), pp. 27-28; 102-3.

Revue théologique de Louvain and Adolphe Gesché for "L'identité de l'homme devant Dieu", *Revue théologique de Louvain* 29 (1998) 3-4, reprinted in *Dieu pour penser. VII Le sens* (Paris: Éditions du Cerf, 2003), pp. 49-50.

Theoform for "La recluse de Montréal, Jeanne Le Ber" by Marie-Paul Dion in *Église et Théologie* 22:1 (1991), pp.50-51.

Library and Archives Canada Cataloguing in Publication Data

Ritch, K. Janet (Katharine Janet), 1955-
      Reading French : for students of religion and theology

Includes bibliographical references.
ISBN 978-1-894667-27-2

      1. French language—Textbooks for second language learners—English speakers. I. Title.

PC2120.R38R58 2012   448.2'421'088204   C2002-905209-2

Contents

3. REGULAR AND AUXILIARY VERBS: PRINCIPAL PARTS, PRESENT, PAST

4. CONTRACTIONS, PRONOUNS AND POSSESSIVE ADJECTIVES

5. VERBS: IMPERATIVE, FUTURE, IRREGULAR, MODAL

6. MORE IRREGULAR VERBS AND ASPECTS OF TIME

7. NEGATIVES AND RELATIVE PRONOUNS

8. VERBS: IMPERFECT, CONDITIONAL, IMPERSONAL...

9. OBJECT PRONOUNS AND VOCABULARY

13. THE CAUSATIVE AND *DEVOIR*

14. THE SUBJUNCTIVE: PRESENT AND PAST

15. THE SUBJUNCTIVE (CONT.): PAST, PERFECT AND PLUPERFECT

APPENDICES

Preface

The audience targeted by this book is first and foremost Christian, and secondly Canadian. Most Departments of Religious Studies or Schools of Theology have modern language requirements for students in Advanced Degree Programs. In Canada, where citizens should be sensitive to the French Canadian component of our culture, it is especially necessary to have a moderate understanding of the language and culture. Current textbooks which introduce students to a reading knowledge of French are usually designed for the Arts and Sciences. They may have a literary aspect, but they are most often oriented to science and technology, or business.

This textbook is designed to fill the gap for persons of religious persuasion. The exercises introduce vocabulary from the Christian liturgy, various translations of the Bible and French or Canadian religious history and theology. For research purposes, a comprehensive summary of French grammar and principles of translation are provided as aids to translation from French into English. This guidance is important for avoiding such pitfalls as *contresens* (understanding the exact opposite of what is written) and false friends (*les faux amis*). False friends are words similar in appearance, but quite distinct in meaning. Such treachery is marked by a superscript[FF] in this textbook and may be found listed in alphabetical order in Appendix III; e.g. *chair*[FF].

In the French language, much more than in English, there is a marked distinction between the written and the spoken word. This textbook necessarily focuses upon literary French, but it is hoped that some of the basics of pronunciation may be learned: first of all as a mnemonic device; and second to avoid giving offence, should the student ever be asked to pronounce a prayer or any other discourse before French speakers. Chapter Two, which deals with only the rudimentary principles of pronunciation, may be constantly revisited throughout the course, especially if the classes open with prayer.

The general method of translation which this book advocates is word-by-word translation, at first, until the basic grammar, vocabulary and its semantic range are appreciated. Translation hints are introduced on a regular basis to deal with those situations where the word-by-word method is hindered by differences in syntax and other complications. At the end of every third chapter is a list of Basic Vocabulary. Each list applies to the preceding three chapters, so that it may be consulted for help with translation exercises found therein. As a whole, the lists attempt to warn the reader of nouns, prepositions, common expressions, etc. which occur so often that they are worth memorizing or which are difficult to locate in a dictionary. Nevertheless, the reader must also become familiar with using the dictionary, whenever needed, for all the exercises given from the very beginning.

It is recommended not to attempt the translation of any given passage at the end of a chapter until the contents of the chapter have been thoroughly digested. The translations are always relevant to the grammar points raised in the chapter. When Biblical passages are presented for translation, they are drawn from either *La Bible de Jérusalem* (Paris: Desclée de Brouwer, 1975) or the *Traduction Œcumémique de la Bible* (TOB), a more recent French translation which aims to promote ecumenism (Paris: Éditions du Cerf, 1982 & 1988).

The seven appendices at the end provide an extra literary supplement for advanced practice (Appendix I), a verb chart as a mnemonic aid for memorizing tenses (Appendix II), a list of False Friends (Appendix III), verbs that are regularly found with prepositions before infinitives or objects (Appendix IV), a list of cardinal and ordinal numbers (Appendix V) and a summary of the grammatical vocabulary in English which is used throughout the book (Appendix VI). These lists and charts should be utilized whenever needed during the course of study. Sample English translations have been added to facilitate self-study (Appendix VII).

Everything in this textbook is designed to clarify the differences between the two languages in the simplest terms possible. Nevertheless, the French language is much more complex than it appears on the surface. Such a short book cannot hope to cover all the nuances of the language which arise in special contexts. Neither do any of the lists in it purport to be exhaustive. The text merely lays a foundation for comprehension and suggests methods, both tried and innovative, for dealing with the unknown. It is hoped that the guidance is sufficient to allow the reader, or student, of French to overcome all future obstacles. It will not have failed if the reader comes to appreciate the wealth of French thought and culture behind the words! Although no student can hope to become fluent in French after a thorough study of this textbook, at least he or she will have a reference work in English for easy access to the language, a minor contribution to the Canadian dream of becoming a bilingual country.

Finally, I would like to thank Anthony Calcagno, June Jodoin, Robert Taylor and Marie-Bethsabée Zarka for their encouragement, advice and sharp proof-reading eyes, as well as Fabienne Baider, Charlotte O'Donnell and Helen Smith for their help in the final stages, and Eric Mills for revising the layout. I would also like to express my appreciation to the Toronto School of Theology and the Northrop Frye Centre in Victoria College for their support of my work in general. The former furnished my direct audience, the students, who over the years have given me copious amounts of "critical" feedback. The students have thus compelled me to isolate and organize difficulties in order to treat them directly and more coherently. Above all, their keen interest, encouragement and patience while this book was being developed have supplied that most essential of ingredients: inspiration.

Enfin, je vous souhaite, mes chers lecteurs et lectrices,
bon courage.

1

BASICS:
PARTS OF SPEECH, GENDER,
NUMBER AND PHRASES

Please note that a "Basic Vocabulary" list for the following three chapters is found at the end of Chapter 3.

1. Dictionary Techniques

The methods presented below begin with the principle of word-by-word translation. One can loosen the translation only when the function of every word is understood in its proper context and the meaning is clear. The translation may then be polished into natural-sounding English, following the guidelines presented throughout this book.

Because many students in Canada today have not received sufficient training in basic grammar, this textbook uses grammatical terms cautiously, in an attempt to be as clear and jargon-free as possible. It must also be stated, however, that language cannot be discussed at all without a minimal understanding 4of grammar. The student is referred to Appendix VI, dictionaries and other aids if the terms used here are not fully understood.

2. Parts of Speech

To comprehend the context of a word, one must be able to distinguish nouns (n) from adverbs (adv), adverbs from adjectives (adj), etc. In English, we can recognize a regular adverb by the ending **-ly**. The equivalent in French is **-ment.** The latter ending also signifies a masculine noun, however, so that a clear understanding of normal syntax (word order) is essential for establishing the context of any given word.

The semantic field of any one French word can be as broad as or broader than any in English. Consider the adjective, adverb, pronoun (pron), or possible noun *tout*. The part of speech in question is just as important as the context. Of the four broad usages, the first has eleven sub-sections (*Collins Robert*). One has to run one's eyes over the semantic field to get an idea of which usage is relevant, and then run through the French expressions highlighted in bold to find the closest fit. *The Collins Robert* is especially helpful in giving French synonyms for every listed meaning, which help to orient the translator. Pronominal verbs (vpr) are always listed after their non-reflexive counterpart:

demander [d(ə)mãde] 1 vt a. (*solliciter*)... {a-i subsections}...
   2 se demander vpr (*hésiter, douter*) wonder {examples}.

If you cannot recognize the abbreviations which the dictionary uses to identify parts of speech, find a list of them inside the two covers, front and back (*Collins Robert French English / English French Dictionary*). They are listed according to the French syntax. Here are some of the essential abbreviations:

nm <u>or</u> nf	=	noun masculine <u>or</u> noun feminine
vi	=	verb intransitive (without a direct object)
vpr	=	verb pronominal (similar to a reflexive verb)
vt	=	verb transitive (takes a direct object)
vti	=	verb both transitive and intransitive

In *demander à qn de faire qch* (to ask s.o. to do sth.)

qn	=	*quelqu'un*	=	someone (s.o.)
qch	=	*quelque chose*	=	something (sth.)

There are many cognates (cousins) between French and English vocabulary: e.g. *théologie*, which one can learn to recognize without a dictionary. The first principle is to relax and recognize what you can. Get an idea of the subject of the whole passage before you attempt to tackle the details.

    One must also develop a keen appreciation of accents and gender. Sometimes, a word changes meaning entirely when an accent is added or the gender changes.

3. Accents

Accents distinguish:

i) one conjunction (conj.) from another:

ou	=	or
où (?)	=	where, when (or "where?", interrogative pron)

ii) one verb from another (here given in the infinitive forms):

pécher	=	to sin
pêcher	=	to fish

iii) one noun from another:

une tache	=	a stain
une tâche	=	a task

The circumflex accent (^) usually signifies an "s" which used to follow the vowel in Old French when the language was still developing from Latin. In time, the "s" dropped out of both pronunciation and the written form, but left a trace of its former presence in the circumflex accent. This can be demonstrated through the comparison of modern French spellings with Latin and English forms:

LATIN	**FRENCH**	**ENGLISH**
hospes	*hôte*	guest, host
hospitium	*hôpital*	hospital
insula	*île*	island
pascha	*Pâques*	Easter
	(NB adj. paschal)	

Note that *Bâle*, Switzerland, has retained the medieval spelling in English: Basle, which pronunciation has also modified to Basel. The three place-names are still in use.

4. Gender

In dictionaries, the feminine form of a noun is listed first in alphabetical order (*la* before *le*). Here are some examples of how gender effects the meaning of a word:

la critique (**f.**)	criticism
le critique (**m.**)	critic (person)
la politique (**f.**)	policy; politics
politique (**adj.**)	political
	as in *l'homme politique* (politician)
la poste (**f.**)	post office
le poste (**m.**)	position (employment)
la tour (**f.**)	tower
le tour (**m.**)	tour, turn
	e.g. *faire le tour de* = take a turn around
la voile (**f.**)	sail (and "sailing" by synecdoche)
le voile (**m.**)	veil (*du temple*: of the temple)

In French, the choice between two genders for every noun, masculine (**m**) and feminine (**f**), does not necessarily imply sexuality. A person (**une** *personne*) is always feminine, but an individual (**un** *individu*) is masculine; both *une personne* and *un individu* might refer to the same human being, whether male or female.

To post-modern English eyes, nevertheless, French appears to be a sexist language. For one thing, if there is a mixture of male and female objects or persons, the male gender predominates. For example, *elles* (they) designates a group of people entirely composed of women, but if just one member of the group is a man, the masculine pronoun *ils* (they) must be used. Furthermore, the indefinite pronoun *on* (one) or *l'on* (literary form, used after a vowel) contributes to this impression, since it is the Old French word for *l'homme* (man). Its use is very similar to the German pronoun *man* as it relates to the noun *der Mann* (man, husband): e.g. *man sagt = on dit* (one says = it is said).

We can give thanks that French has only two genders in comparison with the three of German. By contrast, English seems to be gender-deprived, or at least gender-challenged.

It is essential to recognize the gender of nouns, since pronouns, adjectives and past participles must agree with them in both number and gender. To comprehend fully how any French sentence is constructed, one must recognize these agreements (*les accords*).

5. Recognizing Gender without a Dictionary

Certain noun endings are sure indications of gender, especially when they are derived from Latin words. They are most often also recognizable in English as cognates because of the Latin root which both languages share.

A. FEMININE NOUNS ENDING IN *-IE* OR *-OIRE* (= -Y, -ORY ENGLISH)

LATIN	FRENCH	ENGLISH
theoria	*théorie*	theory
theologia	*théologie*	theology
energia	*énergie*	energy
geographia	*géographie*	geography
or		
gloria	*gloire*	glory
historia	*histoire*	history, story, etc.

B. FEMININE NOUNS ENDING IN *-TÉ* (= -TY ENGLISH)

LATIN	FRENCH	ENGLISH
libertas	*la liberté*	freedom (liberty)
honestas	*l'honnêteté*	honesty
veritas	*la verité*	truth (verity)
bonitas	*la bonté*	goodness (bounty)
qualitas	*la qualité*	quality

and other French words like *identité, obscurité, fragilité,* etc.

C. FEMININE NOUNS ENDING IN *-TION* (= ENGLISH)

LATIN	**FRENCH**	**ENGLISH**
natio	*nation*	nation
conversatio	conversa**tion**	conversation
inventio	*invention*	invention
quaestio	*question*	question
etc.		

D. FEMININE NOUNS ENDING IN *-URE* (= ENGLISH, USUALLY)

LATIN	**FRENCH**	**ENGLISH**
natura	*nature*	nature
structura	*structure*	structure
figura	*figure*	form (figure), face

E. MASCULINE NOUNS ENDING IN *-MENT*

gubernaculum	*le gouvernement*	government
	le parlement	parliament
	un appartement	apartment

N.B. These last sets of cognates do not have a clear and consistent relationship to the Latin. Notice also the minor orthographic differences between French and English.

F. MASCULINE NOUNS ENDING IN *-ISME* (= -ISM ENGLISH)

christianismus	*christianisme* (< 13th c.) Christianity	
	communisme	communism
	théisme	theism
	laïcisme	secularism

G. ENDINGS *-IC* (M) *-IQUE* (M & F) (= *-IC, -ICAL* ENGLISH)

English -ical always signifies an adjective, but -ic can function in this way as well. Nouns made from adjectives can be either masculine or feminine if they still relate to people.

Masculine	**Feminine**	**English**
apocalyptique	*apocalyptique*	apocalyptic(al)
public	*publique*	public (n.m.; adj.)
hystérique	*hystérique*	hysteric (n.m.f.)
		hysterical (adj.)

historique	*historique*	historic(al)
logique	*logique*	logic (n.f.)
		logical (adj.)
méthodologique	*méthodologique*	methodological
paranoïaque	*paranoïaque*	paranoiac (n.m.f.)
		paranoid (adj.)
pédagogique	*pédagogique*	pedagogical (adj.)
sceptique	*sceptique*	sceptic (n.m.f.)
		sceptical (adj.)

6. False Friends

False friends (*les faux amis*) look like English cognates but do not, in fact, carry the same meaning. False friends (*des faux amis*) may be represented by the sign [FF] as a warning.

actuel, actuelle (adj.)	current, present-day
réel(le)	actual
actuellement (adv.)	currently
en réalité	actually
conférence (n.f.)	lecture (possibly at a conference)
colloque, congrès (nm)	conference
demander (v.tr.)	to ask (to demand is too strong)
exiger (v.tr.)	to demand
éditeur (n.m.f.)	publisher (also applies to a woman)
rédacteur (n.m.f.)	editor
journal (n.m.)	newspaper; journal as "diary"
revue (n.f.)	journal (academic)
librairie (n.f.)	bookstore
bibliothèque (n.f.)	library
misère (n.f.)	poverty
misères (n.f.pl.)	misery, woes, worries
recherche de (n.f.)	search of/for
recherches (n.f.pl.)	research

In translation, it is advisable to choose the closest cognate to the recognizable noun, unless the apparent twins are false friends. For this reason, one must know one's false friends! See Appendix III for a more complete list.

7. Number

The "s" usually indicates plurality. However, the "x" often appears as a substitute, especially following a cluster of vowels: e.g.

Singular	**Plural**	**English**
château (n.m.)	châteaux	castle, castles
genou (n.m.)	genoux	knee, knees
jeu (n.m.)	jeux	game, games
niveau (n.m.)	niveaux	level, levels

but after -*ou* "s" is the norm:[1]

clou (n.m.)	clous	nail, nails

Some nouns which end with an "l", drop it and add a 'u' before an 'x':

animal (n.m.)	animaux	animal, animals
cheval (n.m.)	chevaux	horse, horses
journal (n.m.)	journaux	newspaper, newspapers
oeil (n.m.)	yeux	eye, eyes

If the singular noun ends in "s", "x" or "z", the plural form will appear exacty the same (i.e. there is no inflection).

le cas	les cas	the case, cases
le fil**s**	les fils	the son, sons (**s** pronounced)
but le fil	les fils	the thread, threads (**l** pronounced)
une foi**s**	deux fois	one time, two times (silent **s**)
but la foi	Ø	faith (no plural form)
le héros (Gk)	les héros	the hero, heroes
le discours	les discours	the speech, speeches
le poids	les poids	the weight, weights
le choix	les choix	the choice, choices
le nez	les nez	the nose, noses

---

1. There are seven exceptions to this rule, all masculine, where "x" follows "-ou" in the plural:
   genou (knee) : genoux   caillou (pebble) : cailloux   hibou (owl) : hiboux   pou (louse) : poux (lice)
   bijou (jewel) : bijoux   chou (cabbage) : choux   joujou (toy) : joujoux

In these cases, other words in the sentence like articles and adjectives indicate the number. Some nouns are used in the plural in French, whereas English convention prefers a singular equivalent (usually a collective noun).

FRENCH	**ENGLISH**
affaires	business, affairs
marchandises	merchandise
recherches	research[2]
en vacances	on holiday(s)

<u>Or vice versa:</u>

la politique	politics (<u>or</u> the policy)

8. Adjective-Noun Agreement

un cher ami	*une chère amie*[3]
a dear friend (male)	a dear friend (female)

A final "e" generally indicates the female gender. The feminine form of the adjective often doubles the final consonant of the masculine form before adding the "e", e.g. *canadien* (m), *canadienne* (f). The final "e" compels a French speaker to pronounce the final consonant, which might otherwise remain silent. In the example above, however, there is no obvious difference in pronunciation between *cher* and *chère*.

9. Syntax

Another principle of translation is the mirror-image effect between the two languages. Word order is often reversed. For example, most English adjectives precede the nouns, whereas French adjectives usually follow the nouns they modify. Only the most common, shortest adjectives go ahead of the noun in French. The mirror effect applies likewise to verbs and the adverbs which describe them.

Noun-adjective reversal:

C'est une **traduction excellente** de la Bible!
That's an **excellent translation** of the Bible!

---

2. *À la recherche du temps perdu* (*In Search of Lost Time*), Marcel Proust; note that French titles are not capitalized after the first word, unlike English.

3. The adjective *cher* means "dear" when it is placed before the noun. It means "expensive" if it follows the noun. Cf. Chapter 11, §108.

Verb-adverb reversal:
Elle **chante volontiers** avec la chorale le dimanche.
She **willingly sings** with the choir on Sundays.

Other consequences of this principle arise as one becomes more familiar with the French language. In the case of adjectives, however, there are some exceptions, easy to remember and relatively few in number.

10. Adjectives Placed Before the Nouns

Very short or common adjectives are placed before the noun. One might as well learn to recognize them immediately:

MASCULINE FORM	FEMININE FORM	ENGLISH
autre	autre	other
beau, bel*	belle	handsome, beautiful
bon	bonne	good
gentil	gentille	kind
grand	grande	big, tall
gros	grosse	thick, fat
haut	haute	high
jeune	jeune	young
joli	jolie	pretty
long	longue	long
mauvais	mauvaise	bad
meilleur	meilleure	better
nouveau, nouvel*	nouvelle	new
petit	petite	small
premier	première	first
vieux, vieil*	vieille	old
vrai	vraie	true

Note that the adjectives which end in vowels (marked above with an asterisk) receive an extra "l" when they precede a noun beginning with a vowel. This is for the purpose of pronunciation, since the added liquid consonant prevents elision with the following word. For example: *beau homme* becomes *bel homme* to introduce the consonant *l* between vowels −*eau* and *o*, when the *h* in *homme* does not sound. The added *l* prevents elision between the two words. Similarly for *Bel ami*, the title of a novel by Maupassant.

A few adjectives can be found both before and after the noun, but their meaning changes according to their position. These will be reviewed in Chapter Eleven. Other syntactical complications, related to inversions, are likewise treated in Chapter Eleven.

11. Deconstructing Compounds

Another trick for swift recognition of a French word might be termed, somewhat humourously, "deconstruction". One should be able to recognize prefixes which are usually borrowed from Latin or Greek ones and which contribute a relatively consistent meaning to any root to which they are attached. The easiest to recognize are the so-called privative prefixes which merely deprive the substance of its meaning or cancel it out.

Privative Prefixes (Préfixes privatifs)

Préfixes français	Prefixes	French	English
dé- ou *dés-*	=dis-(un-)	**dé**fait	**un**done
		désagréable	**un**pleasant
			or **dis**agreeable
in-	= in-	**in**complet	**in**complete
	un-	**in**connu	**un**known
im-	= im-	**im**possible	**im**possible
	un-	**im**pie	**im**pious,
			ungodly

Current French words are often amalgamations of smaller ones, sometimes from Old French: e.g.

afin que	=	*à + fin que* = to the end that **<** so that.
aujourd'hui	=	*au + jour + d' + hui* = on the day of today.
bientôt	=	*bien + tôt* = very soon < soon.
dorénavant	=	*d' + or + en avant* = from now on ahead
		< henceforth.
surtout	=	**sur + tout** = above all < especially.

Although such compounds may involve Old French words (e.g. *hui*), they are likelier to involve prepositions which are more easily recognized. The following list of essential prepositions should be memorized before complications arise, esp. for *à* and *de*.

12. Prepositions

à	to, at, in
après	after
avant	before (temporal)
avec	with
chez	at the house (people/nation) of; in the work of
contre	against
dans	in, into
de	of, from
derrière	behind
devant	before (in the physical sense)
en	in, to, into (from Old French: related to *dans*)
	in, by, while (before a gerund)
entre	between, among
hors, hors de	outside, out of
par	by, through
parmi	among
pour	for, in order to > to (before infinitive vb.)
sans	without
sous	under
sur	on, over (physical position), about (a subject)
vers	towards

A. THE PREPOSITIONS *À* AND *DE*

Of these prepositions, *à* and *de* (and *pour* to a lesser extent) are complicated by the relationships which they have with verbs. They sometimes serve as links between two verbs and this function overrides their semantic value. Sometimes, one can even ignore them in a translation. In the following example, the infinitive *chanter* already means "to sing". The *à* is therefore redundant and serves only to link the two verbs *commencer* and *chanter*.

Example

Il commence à chanter.
He is beginning to sing.

See Appendix IV for lists of verbs using *à* and *de* in this way. Most of the time, one can trust both *à* and *de* to reinforce their primary meanings (to, at, in & of, from respectively).

B. THE PREPOSITION À MEANING "FROM"

A few significant verbs regularly alter the meaning of *à* to mean "from". The essential verbs of this type are the following:

acheter à qn	to buy **from** someone
échapper à qn	to escape **from** someone
emprunter à qn	to borrow **from** someone

Examples

1. Par le moyen de la foi chrétienne, nous échappons **à** la mort.
   By means of the Christian faith, we escape **from** death.
2. La Bible emprunte cette phrase **à** Euripide.
   The Bible borrows this phrase **from** Euripides.

C. DATIVE OF PURPOSE

Sometimes *à* can mean "for" to represent a purpose when dependent upon certain verbs.

Example

3. Quelques évocations suffiront   **à** notre propos.
   A few recollections will suffice **for** our purpose.

13. Phrases

Prepositions lead to nouns in phrases. In other words, a phrase is composed of a preposition and an object of that preposition, which is always a noun or a pronoun.

Examples

… **sans** une nouvelle **idée**.

… without a new idea.

where **sans** is the preposition and the feminine noun **idée** is the object of this preposition **sans**. The indefinite article **une** and the adjective **nouvelle** agree with the feminine gender of **idée**. The grammatical unit with or without the embellishment of the adjective is called a "prepositional phrase", or "phrase" for short.

EXERCISE A

Translate the following phrases into English.

Note that English does not always translate the definite article. When the noun represents a general concept, the definite article "the" is unnecessary in English, whereas it serves a purpose in French as an indicator of gender: **e.g. la misère = poverty.** If there is no article in the French, often "a" or "an" works best in English.

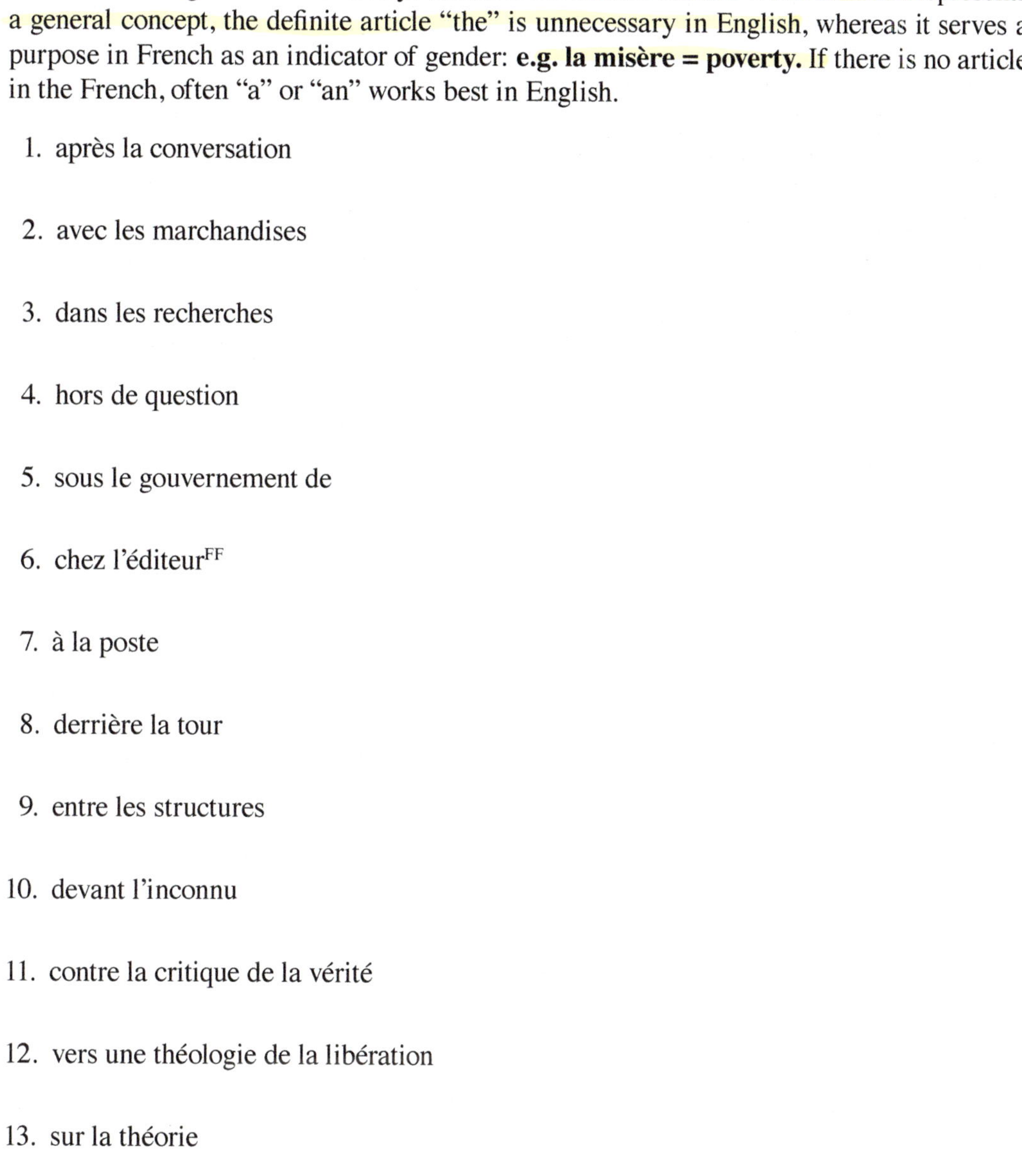

1. après la conversation

2. avec les marchandises

3. dans les recherches

4. hors de question

5. sous le gouvernement de

6. chez l'éditeur[FF]

7. à la poste

8. derrière la tour

9. entre les structures

10. devant l'inconnu

11. contre la critique de la vérité

12. vers une théologie de la libération

13. sur la théorie

14. sans énergie

15. sous les yeux de

16. hors contexte

17. par le critique

18. sous un gouvernement communiste

19. la question d'une amie

20. parmi les amis

21. à la nation

22. contre le laïcisme

23. devant le danger

24. avant la question

25. pour la conférence[FF]

26. à genoux

27. devant le château

28. avec les clous

29. dans le journal[FF]

30. vers la librairie[FF]

EXERCISE B

Translate the following, noting the gender and position of the adjectives.

1. une nouvelle édition
2. un individu charitable
3. un vieil homme
4. une personne généreuse
5. le nouveau style
6. la bonne adresse
7. une bibliothèque intéressante
8. une mauvaise attitude
9. une petite faute
10. un autre sujet
11. un long nez proéminent
12. une haute tour
13. un bon poème
14. la nouvelle théorie
15. un mauvais poème
16. un auteur intelligent
17. les yeux charmants
18. un vieil appartement
19. une femme fatale
20. Cher ami

2

PRONUNCIATION: ACCENTS, LIAISON AND ELISION

Pronunciation is a very delicate subject, since English Canadians have historically accepted Parisian French as the standard, with too little consideration for the French Canadian accent. Students, nevertheless, sometimes need to be able to hear the words in order to remember them. To simplify the task, this chapter will adopt the phonetic alphabet and standard pronunciation used in common dictionaries, such as the *Collins-Robert* and Harrap's, the International Phonetic Alphabet (IPA), *L'Alphabet Phonétique International* (API), but attempt to explain some of the basic distinctions found in Canadian French. The acceptance of Parisian French as a standard is equivalent to the acceptance of Received Pronunciation (RP), that spoken on the BBC (British Broadcasting Corporation), as a standard in English.

To English ears, French sounds very musical. There are several reasons for this. In general, English places emphasis and accentuation upon both words and syllables in ways which French does not. First, instead of throwing emphasis upon a word as it is articulated, as English speakers do, French speakers use certain stylistic turns of phrase to emphasize it.[1] For example:

> *C'est* la chanson *que* j'aime!
> It is the song that I love!
> *That*'s the song I love!

The song/*chanson* is emphasized in French by its placement between *C'est … que*, whereas English would emphasize the demonstrative *that*.

Second, English words have internal stress, which causes problems for French speakers who are not accustomed to it. A word like the English "inter′national," in which the primary accent falls upon -na-, is pronounced as if every syllable were equal in French. English speakers must really make an effort, therefore, to rid themselves of the desire to accentuate

---

1. Cf. Chapter 6, §52B for a more detailed explanation.

French words. Third, linkage between French words causes them to flow together in one melodic line.

In the following explanations, only the most common errors in pronunciation made by English speakers of French will be discussed. For clarity, phonetic symbols are always placed between square brackets [ ]. A word in parenthesis ( ) is a translation into English. Finally, this chapter is not meant to be perfectly grasped in the second lesson. It should be revisited throughout the course, if the students are at all interested in pronunciation.

14. Consonants

Most consonants are pronounced in French as they are in English. Only a few difficulties arise with "c", "qu-", "h", and final consonants, which tend to be silent.

A. [K] FOR "C", "Q", "QU" AND RARELY "CH" (NORMALLY SH [ʃ]).

i.   "c" before "a", "o", "u" and consonants other than "h"; e.g.
     canadien, capable, cousin, côté, client, croix, cuisine...

ii. The English tendency to pronounce a "w" for the "u" after a "q", as in **queen** [qwi:n] must be avoided; e.g.
     qui [ki], que [kə], quand [kã]...

iii. Normally "ch" is pronounced sh [ʃ] as in ar**ch**e [= ark, Eng.], except in certain, mainly ecclesiastical, terms which are based upon Greek; e.g. [k] in
     ar**ch**ange, ar**ch**étype, caté**ch**umène, **ch**rétien, **Ch**rist

B. [S] FOR "C" OR "Ç", AND "T"

i.   "c" [s] before "e" and "i"; e.g. **c**e (this), **c**élèbre, **c**ent, **c**iel (sky), **c**inq, **c**irconstance...

ii. "ç" [s] before "a", "o", and "u"; e.g. **ç**a, commen**ç**ons, fran**ç**ais, le**ç**on, re**ç**u (received)

iii. "t" [s] before "i", even when English speakers have a tendency to pronounce it as "sh" [ʃ] as in the last three cases below:
     démocratie, prophétie, patience, mention, nation...

C. SILENT "H" IN THE MIDDLE OF WORDS, AFTER A "T" AND AT THE BEGINNING OF MOST WORDS:

i.   Even if not pronounced, the "h" serves to divide the vowels on each side of it into separate syllables; e.g.
     bon~~h~~eur (happiness), ca~~h~~ier (notebook), tra~~h~~ison (betrayal)

ii. The "th" must not be pronounced as the English "th" sound <u>or</u> [ð], but the "h" must be discarded; e.g. ent~~h~~ousiasme, t~~h~~é (tea), t~~h~~éâtre, t~~h~~éorie.

iii. The initial "h" is always silent. Elision suggests that the word, in fact, begins with a vowel; e.g.

18

l'homme, j'hésite, l'hôpital, **h**ors d'haleine (out of breath)
but words of foreign origin (especially Germanic) forbid total elision; e.g.
la **H**ollande, de **H**ongrie, le **h**asard (chance), le **h**éros

D. The French [g] is pronounced as in English, except before the two vowels "e" and "i" when it is pronounced like the [ʒ] in je meaning "I" in English; e.g.
[g]: la gare (station), une fugue (in music)
[ʒ]: généreux (generous, adj.m.), Giverny (where Claude Monet painted his water lilies).

E. The uvular **[R]** is particularly characteristic of French. It comes naturally by imitation, once the speaker can feel the beauty of the language. One can begin to activate the uvula at the back of the throat, however, by gargling. Once the basic movement has been felt, inspiration may take over in a kind of Kierkegaardian "leap of faith".

15. Final Consonants

Convention usually holds that final letters are silent in French, especially final "e", "s", and the "r" in the first-conjugation infinitive which ends in "-er". The ramifications of this rule are most evident in conjugated verb forms. For example, because final consonants are usually silent, one can recognize no differences orally between:

je défends and *il défend* (I defend & he defends), where none of the final cluster -**nd(s)** is pronounced. Again there is no difference in pronunciation between the two verb forms:

je pense and *ils pensent* (I think & they think), where "s" is the last letter of the verb to be pronounced in both cases. Sometimes, especially in poetry, there is a slight lift (a light "uh") to mark the "e", known as the "schwa" [ə] or the unstable "e". **Note** that students often confuse the silent *-ent* ending in a verb with the [ã] sound which it can have in words like *souvent* (adv.). The latter *-ent* sounds like *-ant*, so that *souven*ant (remembering) and *souven*t both end with final syllables which sound the same. In contrast, the "-ent" in conjugated verbs like *ils pensent* remains silent.

grec and *grecque* (Greek as a masculine and feminine adjective) are pronounced [gRɛk] in both cases, except in poetry when the *-que* is pronounced as a schwa [kə].

However, there are many exceptions to the rule of silent final consonants and the convention is flexible enough to vary over time. For example, the Québecois have been less likely to pronounce final letters than the French, since they have held to their sixteenth-century legacy from France; e.g. *fleur de lys*; the final "s" is not always pronounced in Canada, whereas the French in France pronounce it nowadays to avoid confusion with *lit* (bed). In another case, the pronunciation varies according to usage; e.g. *plus*, where the "s" is pronounced to emphasize the meaning "more", but not pronounced when used in the expression of quantity *plus de qch* (more of sth.). Similarly, the "s" is pronounced in *tous* ("all" as a pronoun) but the final consonant "t" in *tout* (pron.) is not. Again, the final "st" in the proper name *Christ* was not originally pronounced, as it still is not in *Jésus Christ*, but the convention changed among preachers sometime in the seventeenth century, when the surname alone with the definite article, *le Christ*, began to be fully pronounced [kRist] by analogy with the Latin *Christus*.

One mnemonic device for remembering which final letters are likelier to be pronounced lies in the word **CaReFuL**, where the consonants are final; e.g.

C pronounced in ave**c** (with), par**c**, la**c**... or when final "q"
substitutes for the "c" [k]; e.g. *coq* (rooster), *cinq* (5).

R pronounced in fie**r** (proud), o**r** (gold, now) ca**r** (for), casto**r** (beaver) and after "e" in English loan words: e.g cance**r**. A major exception to this rule occurs at the end of the infinitive form of a first-conjugation verb; e.g. *demander* where the *-er* ending is pronounced exactly like *-é* (eh?).

F pronounced in neu**f** (nine, new), che**f** (leader), soi**f** (thirst)**... but not** in cle~~f~~ (key), cer~~f~~ (stag), and the plural forms of oeu~~f~~ (eggs), and boeu~~f~~ (oxen, beef).

L pronounced in i**l**, ma**l** (evil), cie**l** (sky, heaven), fi**l** (thread)...

16. Vowels

French vowels are much more difficult to deal with. To begin with, there are no diphthongs in standard French, i.e. a sliding from one vowel sound to another with no syllabic break. British English uses eight diphthongs. In the popular French Canadian language (*français canadien*), diphthongization occurs in such words as père, which could be pronounced [paɛr], [pa$_e$r] or [pa$_i$r], or even without the final R, [pa$_e$]. Another striking characteristic of Canadian French is the pronunciation of French "oi" as **[we]** as in moi **[mwe]**, toi **[twe]**, soi **[swe]**,[2] whereas Standard French is pronounced **[wa]** as in moi **[mwa]**, toi **[twa]**...

A. NASAL VOWELS

Standard French has four nasal vowels which present great difficulty to English speakers who have not been warned about them: [ã], [ɛ̃], [ɔ̃] and [œ̃]. They occur before either a single **n** or a single **m**, whether they are at the end of a word or precede a consonant. In all these cases, the **n** and the **m** are not pronounced, but the vowel is thrown up through the nose in a manner which must be learned through imitation.

---

2. Monique et Pierre Léon, *La prononciation du français*, 104.

No nasalization occurs if the **n, m** are doubled or followed by an "e"; e.g.

i. [ã] before **n** followed by unvoiced consonants; e.g.
a) s**ans** prep. (without) = s**ang** nm (blood) = [sã].
b) Loss of nasalization when the **n** is doubled (or < **mm**]
an [ã] n.m. (year considered quantitatively) ≠ année n.f. [ane] (year considered qualitatively).
évid**ent** [evidã] ≠ adj. (obvious) évidemm**ent** [evidamã] ≠ adv. (obviously).
Note that the doubled "mm" (above) blocks the nasal sound and forces pronunciation of the "m".
Jean [ʒã] (John) **Jeanne [ʒan]** (Jane) proper nouns.

ii. [ɛ̃] as in vin **[vɛ̃]** (wine) or saint **[sɛ̃]:**
a) in privative prefixes before consonants; e.g.
 injuste, **im**possible, **in**quiet (adj.).
but if the prefix precedes a vowel or a silent "h", there is no nasalization: **[in-]**
inacceptable, **in**-abituel (unusual). The "in-" here is pronounced as in English.
b) The same loss of nasalization occurs before **nn** or **e**; e.g.
chrét**ien [kRetjɛ̃]** adj. Christian ≠ chrétienne **[kRetjɛn]**.
cous**in [kuzɛ̃]** nm ≠ cousine nf **[kuzin]**.
exam**en** nm **[ɛgzamɛ̃]** ≠ examiner vtr. **[ɛgzamine]**.

iii. [ɔ̃] as in s**ont [sɔ̃]** v.i. (<they> are) and m**on**de **[mɔ̃d]** n.m.
The same rules apply; e.g.
bon **[bɔ̃]** adj. (good) ≠ bonne **[bɔn]**.
nom **[nɔ̃]** nm (name) ≠ nommer **[nɔme]** vtr. to name.

iv. [œ̃] as in the indef. art. m. **un[œ̃]** ≠ une **[yn]** f.
The same holds before **m** or **n** whether in the medial or final position; e.g.
h**um**ble **[œ̃bl(ə)]** adj. m & f, parf**um [paRfœ̃]** nm.,
l**un**di **[lœ̃ di]** nm (Monday).

B. THE SCHWA [ə] AND ITS LOSS WHEN "S", "T" OR "R" IS ADDED.

i. The schwa [ə] (Hebrew for "emptiness") is the unstressed vowel sound of the English "**a**" (uh) as in "**again**", or the vowel in "the", before words beginning with consonants.
In French, this sound is essential in very common monosyllabic words; e.g.
 le **[lə]**, de **[də]**, ne **[nə]**(negative particle), que **[kə]**;
 ce **[sə]** and refl. pron. me **[mə]**, te **[tə]**...
One must avoid the Spanish vowel "e" **[e]**, as in "day", which signifies plurality in French (*des*).

ii. With the addition of an "s" after "e", the schwa changes to **[e]**, as in the Canadian "eh?". The transformation of the vowel sound indicates plurality to the ear, not the "s" which remains unpronounced; e.g. le⃥ (m.& f.pl.), de⃥ (some), ce⃥ (these), me⃥ (my pl.)...
The same transformations take place within words; e.g.
"demander" with the schwa **[ə]** in 1st syll. ≠ **dés**accord
[dəmãde] = to ask   [dezakɔR] = disagreement

iii. The schwa changes to **[e]** with the addition of an "r" especially in -er (the infinitive ending of the first conjugation verb) or of a "t". The **t** and **r** are not pronounced any more than an **s** would be. Thus et (and) sounds the same as the final syllables of the following variety:
 et, des, demander (inf.) and deman**dé** (past participle)
In a poem, they would all rhyme with the Canadian "eh", eh?.
Orally and without a context, the last two are indistinguishable, although they function quite differently.

17. Accents

i. As just seen above, the "é" with an acute accent is pronounced **[e]**, as in English "say" [sei], or as the Canadian "eh" mentioned above.
ii. With a grave accent, "è" is pronounced **[ɛ]**, as in English "let". To the English ear, "è" sounds like "ai" or "aie" as in the homonyms demand**ais**, demand**ait** and demand**aient**. For example, été **[ete]** (summer) and était **[etɛ]** (was) are very similar in sound, but quite distinct in meaning.
iii. Other accents are used to distinguish homonyms from each other, as differing in both parts of speech and meaning; e.g.
 a (has) à (to, at, in)
 du (of the, from the) dû (past participle of devoir), etc.
The circumflex (^) was discussed in Chapter One as an aid to word recognition. It does not effect pronunciation, except in some dialects. Sometimes it indicates a collapse of syllables from the Latin root, not just a missing "s"; e.g. anima > âme (soul).

18. Mandatory Linkage

Final consonants were pronounced in Old French. When Middle French generally reduced them to silence, final consonants preserved their articulation when linked to a vowel or a mute "h" in the following word. The commonest sounds linking with vowels are **[z]** from "s", **[t]**, **[d]** (less often **[p]**) and **[n]**.

i.   Before a vowel, after articles (les, un), possessive adjectives (mon, ton...) and demonstrative adjectives (cet, cette, ces) and nouns or their adjectives, the "s" sounds as **[z]**, and the **[n]** and **[t]** sound the same as in standard English; e.g.
les‿amis, nos‿amis, un‿ami, mon‿ami, cet‿ami and des‿amis

ii.   The same holds true between pronouns and verbs; e.g.

nous‿avons (we have)   vous‿avez, (you have)
a-t‿-il? (has he?)   ont‿-ils? (have they?)
il en‿a besoin (he needs some)   il y en‿a! (there is some)

iii.   The letters "x" and "z" which substitute for "s", usually in adjectives, numbers or monosyllabic prepositions, are also pronounced **[z]** as in the English word "buzz"; e.g.

trois‿ordinateurs   three computers
de beaux‿yeux   beautiful eyes
chez‿eux   at their place

iv.   The letter "d" sounds as a **[t]** in most cases, with the exception of "un pied‿-à-terre" (base); e.g.

prend‿-il?   does he take?
quand‿il vient   when he comes
un grand‿enfant   a big child
l'homme dont‿il parle   the man of whom he speaks
un petit‿espoir   a little hope

v.   Other useful pronoun or prepositional linkages with conjugated forms of "être" or general expressions:

tout‿est possible   everything is possible
c'est‿une erreur   that's a mistake
ils sont‿assis   they are seated
je suis‿arrivé   I arrived
les‿États‿-Unis   the United States
de plus‿en plus   more and more

vi.   An example of **[p]** is optional:
trop‿heureux[3] [no h]   too happy

---

3. For more detailed lists of compulsory, forbidden and optional elisions, see Diane M. Dansereau, *Savoir dire: cours de phonétique et de prononciation* (Toronto: D.C. Heath and Company, 1990), pp. 24-32.

Exercise A

Pronounce and translate the following adjectives:

1. bon, bonne
2. bons, bonnes
3. public, publique
4. mauvais, mauvaise
5. grec, grecque
6. évident, évidente
7. favori, favorite
8. inquiet, inquiète
9. puissant, puissante
10. chrétien, chrétienne

Exercise B

Pronounce and translate the following verb infinitives:

1. écrire
2. appartenir
3. donner
4. venir
5. sortir
6. régner
7. garder
8. être
9. savoir
10. délivrer
11. croire
12. avoir
13. pardonner
14. offenser
15. sanctifier
16. accomplir

Exercise C

Pronounce the following inflected verbs and indicate with an **S** which pairs sound exactly the same:

1. donne, donné
2. garde, gardent
3. pense, pensent
4. accomplis, accomplissent
5. délivrez, délivré
6. examine, examiné
7. accompli, accomplis
8. règnent, régné
9. crois, croit
10. défends, défendent

Exercise D

Pronounce and translate each word:

1. tentation, tentations
2. monde humain
3. le, les
4. êtres humains
5. offense, offenses
6. ce, ces
7. de, des
8. siècle, siècles

Exercise E

Pronounce by omitting the "u" or the "h" and translate:

1. quiche	2. quatre
3. thé	4. Thomas
5. quand?	6. quoi?
7. théâtre	8. théologien, théologienne
9. théorie	10. quelqu'un
11. qui?	12. théologique
13. quel, quelle	14. quelquefois
15. théologie	16. thème
17. question	18. qualifier
19. thèse	20. que

Exercise F

Practice with pronouncing the French "oi" [wa], or [ɛ̃] nasalized before "n"; pronounce and translate:

1. gloire	2. toi
3. moi	4. loin
5. soit[4]	6. voie
7. soient[5]	8. soi
9. soin	10. histoire

---

4. *soit*: 3rd p. sg. subjunctive form of the verb *être*, to be.

5. *soient*: 3rd p. pl. subjunctive form of the verb *être*, to be.

19. Prayers

Practice elisions, nasals and schwas. An e highlighted in bold indicates the schwa [ə], a tie marks a linkage, and the phonetic symbols of difficult words are placed in the right margin.

PRIONS LE SEIGNEUR

A. NOTRE PÈRE

Notre Père, qui* e͡s͜ aux cieux,	[ki]*
que* ton nom soit† sanctifié,	[kə]* [tɔ̃][nɔ̃][swa]†[6]
que* ton† règne vienne,[7]	[kə]* [tɔ̃]†
que* ta volonté soit faite	[kə]*
sur la terre comme au ciel.	
Donne-nous͡s͜ aujourd'hui	
notre pain* de ce jour.	[pɛ̃]*
Pardonne-nous no͡s͜ offenses,	
comme nous pardonnon͡s͜ aussi*	[paRdɔ nɔ̃͡s͜ osi]*
à ceux qui nou͡s͜ ont ͜offensés.	
Et ne nous soumets pa͡s͜ à la tentation,	
mais délivre-nous du Mal.	

[pause pour les Catholiques]

Car c'est ͜ à toi† qu'appartiennent*	[twa]† [kapaRtjɛn]*
le règne, la puissance et la gloire*,	[glwaR]*
pour les siècles des siècles!	

Amen

---

6. Cf. n.4 above.

7. *vienne*: 3rd p. sg. subjunctive form of the verb *venir*, to come.

B. LA JOURNÉE CHRÉTIENNE

O Christ*, notre Seigneur et notre Dieu†,   [kRist]*[djø]†
tu es la voie*, la vérité et la vie: [vwa]*
hors* de toi, nous ne pouvons que† nous‿égarer;   ['ɔR]* [kə]†
sans toi*, nous ne comprenons rien†;   [sã][twa]* [Rjɛ̃]†
loin de toi*, nous ne pouvons vivre.   [lwɛ̃] [də] [twa]*
Veille* sur nos pensées, nos paroles et nos‿actes,   [vɛj]*[8]
garde-nous durant* cette journée[FF],   [dyRã]*
afin que* nos travaux soient†‿accomplis   [afɛ̃] [kə]* [swat]†[9]
pour la gloire de ton nom*   [glwaR] [də] [tõ] [nõ]*
et pour le salut du monde*.   [mõd]*
Amen.

---

8. *veille*: 2rd p.sg. imperative form of the verb *veiller*, to watch over.

9. *soient*: 3rd p.pl. subjunctive form of the verb *être*. The *t* is pronounced because of the following vowel.

C. SUPPLEMENTARY PRAYER: A LITANY

Je recommande à votre prière le peuple de Dieu partout dans le monde, notre ‿ évêque, cette ‿ assemblée et tous les ministres et les fidèles. Prions pour l'Église.

Lecteur:	**Seigneur**, en ta tendresse,
Peuple:	*Écoute nos prières*

Je recommande à votre prière la paix, la concorde entre les nations et le bien de tous les peuples. Prions pour la justice et pour la paix.

Lecteur:	**Seigneur**, en ta tendresse,
Peuple:	*Écoute nos prières*

Je recommande à votre prière les pauvres, les malades, les‿ affamés, les‿ opprimés et les prisonniers. Prions pour tous ceux qui sont ‿ en difficulté.

Lecteur:	**Seigneur**, en ta tendresse,
Peuple:	*Écoute nos prières*

Je recommande à votre prière ceux qui sont tourmentés par leur propre péché. Prions pour tous les pécheurs.

Lecteur:	**Seigneur**, en ta tendresse,
Peuple:	*Écoute nos prières*

Tous ensemble:
Rendons gloire à Dieu pour ceux en qui le Christ a été glorifié à chaque génération. Prions pour que nous‿ ayons, nous‿ aussi, la grâce de rendre gloire au Christ dans notre temps.

AMEN.

3

REGULAR AND AUXILIARY VERBS:
PRINCIPAL PARTS, PRESENT, PAST

20. Present Tense: The Three Regular Conjugations

	I. -er verbs donner (to give)	**II. -ir verbs** finir (to finish)	**III. -re verbs** perdre (to lose)
Roots:	**DONN**/-er	**FIN**/ -ir	**PERD**/-re
je	donne	finis	perds
tu	donnes	finis	perds
il, elle, on	donne	finit	perd
nous	donnons	finissons	perdons
vous	donnez	finissez	perdez
ils, elles	donnent	finissent	perdent

Note that in the third person singular, *il* and *elle* can also mean "it" (neuter) when they refer to inanimate objects or abstract ideas. The impersonal pronoun *on* literally means "one",[1] but it can also be translated as "we", "you" or "they" depending upon a perspective of inclusion or exclusion. It often arises when English would prefer the passive.

The II verbs also conjugate in an alternative manner which dispenses with *i* and *iss*, as in the verb *sortir* (to go out).

je sors	nous sortons
tu sors	vous sortez
elle, il, on sort	elles, ils sortent

---

1. Cf. Chapter One §4.

Other verbs in this category are *partir* (to depart), *servir* (to serve, etc.), *se repentir* (to repent), *sentir* (to feel, etc.), *dormir* (to sleep), *mentir* (to lie). With the one exception of *repentir*, the first three letters of the infinitives in this group, excluding the consonants *t, v* or *m*, constitute the root: i.e. *par, ser, sen, dor, men* and *repen*, before inflections are added.

Another group of **II verbs** reverts back to the endings of the first conjugation. Verbs like *souffrir* (to suffer), *offrir* (to offer), *ouvrir* (to open), *couvrir* (to cover) and their compounds add -e, -es, -e, -ons, -ez, -ent to the root: e.g. je souffre...

Because French does not distinguish the simple present from the progressive or continuous present, there are two possible translations for every French verb in the present tense. For example:

1. Je donne un exemple.
   a. I give an example.
   b. I am giving an example.

In this context, the second translation is more suitable than the first.

2. L'homme souffre!
   a. Man suffers! (Man = humankind)
   b. The man is suffering! (specific case)

The first translation of #2 suggests a general principle with no end or beginning. The second suggests a continuous action in the present time of a particular case with a beginning and an end.

21. Irregular Conjugations

Some verbs of the first conjugation (*-er*) double letters or modify vowels with accents for every person except *nous* and *vous*. Here are examples of the principal groups in this class:

	APPELER[2] (call)	**ACHETER[3] (buy)**	**ESPÉRER[4] (hope)**
je	appelle	achète	espère
tu	appelles	achètes	espères
il, elle, on	appelle	achète	espère
nous	appelons	achetons	espérons
vous	appelez	achetez	espérez
ils, elles	appellent	achètent	espèrent

Another sub-group of the third conjugation (-re) adds a *g* in the three plural persons, as for example *craindre* (to fear):

	CRAINDRE[5] (fear)
je	crains
tu	crains
il, elle, on	craint
nous	craignons
vous	craignez
ils, elles	craignent

22. Summary of Present Tense Endings

	I.	**II. & III.**
Singular	-e	-(i)s
	-es	-(i)s
	-e	-(i)t , *or* d
Plural	-ons	-(iss)ons
	-ez	-(iss)ez
	-ent	-(iss)ent

The *-s* always indicates the second person singular, an informal address to an intimate friend or a younger person. The three plural forms are fairly stable throughout the tenses: i.e. they don't often vary except in the letters which precede the recognizable endings, that is when the root changes.

---

2. Other verbs in this group which can double either *l* or *t* before the final *-e* (without *-r*) *or* *-ent* are: *jeter* (to throw), *épeler* (to spell), *projeter* (to project, plan), *rappeler* (to recall), *rejeter* (to reject).
3. Other verbs (including compounds) which add a grave accent when similarly conjugated in the present are: *geler* (to freeze), *mener* (to lead), *lever* (to raise).
4. Other verbs whose acute accent turns to grave, as indicated, are: *céder* (to yield), *considérer* (to consider), *interpréter* (to interpret), *préférer* (to prefer), *régner* (to rule), etc.
5. Other third conjugation verbs of this group are: *joindre* (to join) and *peindre* (to paint).

23. Postpositions: Translation Hint

English verbs often take "adverbial particles" which are required to complete the meaning of certain verbs. For example, "put on" (suggesting "clothes" or "a hat") is not the same as simply "to put". The French have invented a term to replace these "particles" by calling them "postpositions". The latter are words which are usually labelled "prepositions" (with nouns as their objects), but being placed after, and dependent upon, verbs, the term "postposition" suits them very well.[6] The prefix *post* is Latin for "after". A few examples in the vocabulary list at the end of Chapter 3 are:

demander:	to ask **for**
regarder:	to look **at**

Both "**for**" and "**at**" must be supplied by the English translator. Only rarely, does the same phenomenon occur in reverse, where a postposition in French must be cancelled in English: e.g.

*entrer **dans**:*	to enter (**in** is not required).

Exercise A

Translate the following sentences using the **Vocabulary Review** at the end of the chapter, supplemented by a dictionary if necessary.

1. Nous sortons.

2. La foi apporte la gloire.

3. Ils appellent les théologiens.

4. Je finis le journal[FF].

5. Nous donnons un choix.

6. Le fils demande[FF] la vérité.

7. Nous étudions la traduction.

8. Je perds la crainte de la confession.

---

6. Olorenshaw & Rogers, *Les 100 pièges de l'anglais* (Alleur, Belgium: Marabout, 1985), p.109 ff.

9. Tu demandes[FF] le salut?

10. Vous finissez la traduction.

11. Nous appelons l'amour comme témoin.[7]

12. Vous craignez Dieu, mais non pas[8] l'homme.

13 Je prends le journal[FF].

14. Le fils regarde la télévision sans intérêt réel.

15. Elle montre la faute au théologien.[9]

16. Le médecin enseigne la médecine.

17. Nous apprenons le français.

18. Le prêtre supporte[FF] la misère[FF].

19. L'argent aide à sortir de la misère[FF].

20. Un ami ne perd pas la foi.

24. Auxiliary Verbs: *avoir* and *être*

		être (to be)	Eng.	avoir (to have)	Eng.
je	(I)	suis	am	ai	have
tu	(you sg)	es	are	as	have
elle/il	(s/he)	est	is	a	has
nous	(we)	sommes	are	avons	have
vous	(you pl)	êtes	are	avez	have
ils/elles	(they)	sont	are	ont	have

---

7. *comme témoin*: as a witness. As a general rule, supply the indefinite article "a" when no other article or substitute is specified.

8. *non pas*: not. Cf. Chapter 7, §60 for a detailed description.

9. *au* : cf. Chapter 4, §30.

Avoir is certainly the more regular of the two. However, even *être* follows some of the regular pattern with -s, -s, -t endings in the singular and "-ont" for -ent in the plural. The final letter "s" also indicates the plural (instead of "z") in "êtes".

25. Past Participles

I. -er verbs	**II. -ir verbs**	**III. -re verbs**
Donner	Finir	Perdre
to give	to finish	to lose

ROOTS: DONN/-er **FIN/-ir** **PERD/-re**

Past participles:

donné (given)	fini (finished)	perdu (lost)
-é (= -ed/-en/-d/-t)	-i (= -ed/-en/-d/-t)	-u (= -ed/-en/-d/-t)

A. PAST PARTICIPLES USED AS ADJECTIVES:

Like adjectives, past participles agree in number and gender with the nouns they modify or describe:

une théorie donnée	une thèse finie	une foi perdue
(a given theory)	(a finished thesis)	(a lost faith)
les témoins donnés	les réformes accomplies	les païens perdus
(the given witnesses)	(the accomplished reforms)	(lost pagans)

Usually, the translation of past participles acting as adjectives follows the normal mirror pattern in syntax: i.e. reversal of placement. However, when a phrase depends upon the past participle, the past participle must remain in the French position.

Examples

1. Une théorie donnée par un philosophe...
   A theory   given   by a   philosopher...
       [*par un philosophe* = a phrase linked to *donnée*]

2. Un cours enseigné par un moine suffit.
   A course taught   by a   monk suffices.
       [*par un moine* = a phrase linked to *enseigné*]

B. PAST PARTICIPLES USED AS PREDICATE ADJECTIVES

Because the past participle works so well as an adjective, it can be placed after the verb "être" (the "predicate") when conjugated with specific persons in the singular and plural, like any other adjective. For example, we are accustomed to saying:

"The woman *is* **beautiful**." or "The woman *is* **intelligent**".

The adjectives "beautiful" and "intelligent" describe the woman. The verb *être* is conjugated in the third person singular of the present tense. The same structure occurs when the past participle is used as an adjective after the verb *être*. Following the rule of all French adjectives, such past participles are inflected to correspond with the number and gender of the subject which they describe (or modify).

Examples

1. Le philosophe   est beaucoup admiré.
    The philosopher is   much   admired.

2. Sa théorie est également   admirée.
    His theory is also/equally admired.

3. Les médecins sont occupés.
    The doctors   are busy.

Exercise B

Please use the list of Basic Vocabulary at the end of Chapter 3 and a dictionary to translate the following sentences or clusters of words (not all are complete sentences). **Note** that the past participle is related to the infinitive form of the verb (ending -er, -ir, -re) in the dictionary.

1. On prépare la fête de Pâques.

2. La puissance de Dieu est manifestée dans la Bible.

3. Le pain doré (<u>*ou*</u> pain perdu) est sur la table.

4. Le petit effort est apprécié par la vieille femme.

5. La misère[FF] absolue.

6. La traduction est finie.

7. La littérature française est variée.

8. En Europe, les cathédrales sont souvent gothiques.

9. La bibliothèque[FF] est climatisée.

10. Un peuple choisi.

26. Present Participles:

The French ending -**ant** on the root of any verb is equivalent to the English -ing: e.g. sing**ing**, runn**ing**, fly**ing**, etc. This form can be used as gerunds (verbal nouns) or gerundives (verbal adjectives). Unlike past participles, they do not usually agree in number and gender with the noun they modify, although agreement is possible when they are used truly as adjectives.

	I. -er verbs	**II. -ir verbs**	**III. -re verbs**
Roots:		a. **SORT**/-ir	
	DONN/-er	b. **FIN**/ -ir	**PERD**/-re
	donnant (giving)	sortant (going out)	perdant (losing)
		finissant (finishing)	

In French, these forms often follow the small preposition *en* which may be translated as "in", "by" or "while". The latter meaning may be strengthened by *tout* (all). The use of "en" plus a present participle forms a **participial phrase** which introduces a object. The following object can be any person or thing of any gender or number.

Examples

1.	en finissant	in (by, while) finishing
2.	[tout] en perdant	[all] while losing
3.	En considérant le problème, ils hésitent.	In considering the problem, they are hesitating.

Exercise C

Translate the following participial phrases and complete sentences, consulting a dictionary if necessary.

1. en finissant le travail[FF]

2. en parlant français

3. en donnant un exemple

4. en invoquant la foi

5. En abandonnant leur[10] travail, ils donnent un mauvais exemple.

6. En considérant la bonté en soi, il apprend à penser.

7. En offrant un choix, elle manifeste un sens de la liberté.

8. En ouvrant un oeil, elle regarde le théologien.

9. En étudiant, il rend la misère supportable.

10. Le professeur parle tout en regardant le pauvre Charles.

27. Auxiliary Verbs Used in the Compound Past (*Passé Composé*)

The two commonest but irregular verbs serve also as auxiliary verbs: **avoir** (to have) and **être** (to be). Here are their principal parts upon which the other tenses are built. **Note** that the future root has changed radically from the infinitive form in these irregular verbs.

A. PRINCIPAL PARTS

Infinitive	Present Participle	Past Participle	Future Root
avoir	ayant (having)	eu (had)	aura (will have)
être	étant (being)	été (been)	sera (will be)

---

10. *leur*: their (pl.poss.pron.).

B. TRANSLATION OF *AVOIR & ÊTRE* IN THE *PASSÉ COMPOSÉ*

The compound past (*passé composé*) denotes a completed action in the past. It is formed by using the present tense of the auxiliary verb (*avoir* <u>or</u> *être*) and the past participle of the main verb. This formal aspect is similar to the present perfect tense in English, but the translation should not be automatically accepted in these terms. For example, the English present perfect in "I have seen" connotes a relationship between the past and the present. The effect of the past action continues into the present. This is usually not the case with the French *passé composé* which is better translated into English as the preterite form of the verb. **Note** that the **preterite** can be either weak and regular (writt<u>en</u>, learn<u>ed</u>), or strong (irregular) and involving a radical change of the verb's root (s<u>aw</u>). Its use for translating the *passé composé* is to be **preferre**d in the hierarchy of choices.

I. AVOIR

In the following two translations, the first represents the literal translation, the second the preterite option which is usually preferable.

   1. **J'ai montré**   le livre à mon père hier.
   a. I **have shown** the book to my father yesterday.
   b. I **showed**   the book to my father yesterday.

The first choice (a) is the literal translation, but because the action is specified as having taken place yesterday (*hier*), "I have seen" sounds incorrect; the action has clearly terminated.

   2. **J'ai montré**   le livre à ton père.
   a. **I have shown** the book to your father.
   b. **I showed**   the book to your father.

In this case, because there is no adverb to specify a precise time or occasion in the past, either of the two choices is acceptable. In all cases, the context is significant. Do not automatically choose the literal translation (a); rather, try the preterite (b) before the present perfect (a).

II. ÊTRE

Verbs of motion or change form the *passé composé* in the same way, but using the auxiliary verb *être*. The English translation does not reflect the French change in auxiliary verb, however. The list of verbs which conjugate their compound tenses with *être* are arranged in six pairs of opposites as a mnemonic device.

aller*[11] (to go)	**venir*** (to come)
entrer (to enter)	**sortir** (to go out)
arriver (to arrive)	**partir** (to depart)
monter (to ascend)	**descendre** (to descend)
naître* (to be born)	**mourir*** (to die)
rester (to remain)	**tomber** (to fall)

Any compound of the above verbs is likewise conjugated with *être* for compound verbs in the past, e.g. *devenir* (to become) and *rentrer* (to come home again), etc. Pronominal verbs with reflexive pronouns also conjugate using *être* in the indefinite past (*passé composé*).[12]

   Note that the past participles of these verbs function almost like adjectives in reflecting the number and gender of their subject, simply because they are conjugated with *être*. In this way, the past participle resembles a predicate adjective (a.k.a. subjective completion) following *être*.

Examples

The preterite preference is here given first.

   1.   Je **suis allé** chez le médecin.
   a.   I **went** to the doctor's.
   b.   I **have gone** to the doctor's.

   2.   Elle est devenue riche.
   a.   She **became** rich.
   b.   She **has become** rich.

The literal translations, "I am gone..." and "She is become...", are now totally unacceptable. The auxiliary *être* replaces *avoir* in form but not in meaning. In English, one still thinks of this compound past tense in terms of *avoir*. **Note** the feminine *-e* on the past participle *devenu* in the second example.

---

11. The verbs marked with an asterisk are irregular. Cf. Chapter 5, §40 and Chapter 6, §49D.
12. Cf. Chapter 12, §113 for details.

III. CHOOSING BETWEEN *AVOIR* OR *ÊTRE*?

Some verbs oscillate between the two auxiliary verbs depending upon whether they are transitive or intransitive. When the verb is used as a transitive, it takes a direct object and is conjugated with *avoir*. When the verb is used without a direct object (one cannot answer the question "what?" after the verb), it is conjugated with *être*.

passer (v.tr.)   to spend (i.e. time)
passer par (v.int.)   to pass by

retourner (v.tr.)   to return, give back (something)
retourner (v.int.)   to return (from)

Another verb which can be conjugated with either *avoir* or *être* with no change in meaning is:

apparaître   to appear

Examples (a. intransitive, b. transitive)

1. a. Nous sommes passés par Paris.
      We passed through Paris.
   b. Nous avons passé trois jours à Paris.
      We spent three days in Paris.
      (We spent what? 'Three days' is the direct object.)

2. a. Êtes-vous retournés de la Chine?
      Have you come back from China?
   b. Avez-vous retourné le livre à la bibliothèque?
      Did you return the book to the library?
      (You returned what? 'The book' is the direct object.)

3. a. Jésus est descendu aux enfers.
      Jesus descended into hell.
   b. Il a descendu la croix.[13]
      He took down the cross.
      (He took down what? "the cross" is the dir. obj.)

---

13. Other verbs in this class, *monter, sortir* and *rentrer* (verbs of transition without direct objects), can also be used as transitive verbs (with direct objects) which require the use of the auxiliary verb *avoir* when they signify "to carry something up", "...out" or "...back in" respectively.

Exercise D

Translate the following sentences using the verbs given above, the prepositions and phrases given in Chapter One (pp. 15-30) and the vocabulary listed at the end of this chapter. Use the smoothest possible translations suggested above; i.e., the preterite.

1. Il a été hors de question de soupçonner l'église.

2. Je suis allée voir le prêtre.

3. Nous avons perdu les livres.

4. Elle est entrée avant.

5. Elles sont montées parmi les arbres.

6. Vous êtes restés[FF] dans la misère[FF].

7. Nous avons toujours donné un choix.

8. Nous avons perdu la traduction originale.

9. Le nouveau style est utilisé dans le journal[FF].

10. Ils sont venus[14] devant la nation.

11. Elle a donné un choix.

12. L'homme a défini une nouvelle théorie.

---

14. *venus*: past participle of *venir*, meaning to come. The *s* agrees with the plural subject, *Ils*, to which it is linked by a form of *être*.

28. Questions

A. There are three ways of asking a question in French. The first is a purely oral inflection, caused by raising the voice at the end of the sentence, as occurs sometimes in English as well. In France, this is the commonly preferred option.

Example

Tu viens demain?
You are coming tomorrow?

B. The same effect can be achieved by attaching "Est-ce que...?" (Is it that...) to the beginning of a sentence or the negative form "n'est-ce pas?" (is it not?) to the end. In oral Parisian French, the colloquial "quoi?" has replaced the second form, but polite company usually prefers the more formal "n'est-ce pas?".

Examples

1. **Est-ce que** vous comprenez?
   Do you understand?
2. Vous avez le droit de refuser, **n'est-ce pas**?
   You have the right to refuse, don't you?
3. Il est important, **n'est-ce pas**? / _ou_ quoi?
   It is important, isn't it? / _or_ right? eh?
4. Ils sont en cours, **n'est-ce pas**? / _ou_ quoi?
   They are in class, aren't they? / _or_ right? eh?

Note that English often uses the auxiliary verb "do" to aid the main verb in the composition of the question, as also that of emphatic or negative sentences.

C. The commonest method of asking a question using short verbs of frequent use is similar to the English way of reversing the word order: **Subject Verb** becomes **Verb Subject**. However, there is no auxiliary verb "do" in French to aid with this reversal. When the verb precedes the pronoun subject in French, a hyphen is placed between them.

Example

5. Avez-vous un crayon?
   a. Have you a pencil?
   b. Do you have a pencil?

Twenty-first-century English prefers the second option.

Est-ce que must be used for most verbs conjugated in the first person singular, with the exception of short verbs, commonly used as auxiliary verbs, such as the following:

Ai-je....?	Have I....?
Puis-je...?[15]	May I.....?
Sais-je...?	Do I know...?
Que sais-je?[16]	What do I know?
Suis-je...?	Am I......?

If, after the reversal, two vowels bump up against each other, a "t" is placed between them merely in order to prevent any elision.

Examples

   1. A-t-il son livre aujourd'hui?
   a. Has he his book today?
   b. Does he have his book today?

A noun subject is generally considered by the French too long and cumbersome to follow a verb. In this case, it remains in its normal first place position and a pronoun is used to form the question. In English, there would appear to be two subjects and it would be considered redundant. Therefore, one must use the noun subject in English and overlook the pronoun which refers back to it, whose function in French is merely to mark the question.

   2. Les recherches théoriques sont-**elles** utiles?
   a. Theoretical research, is **it** useful?
   b. Is theoretical research useful?

   3. Cet homme parle-t-il anglais?
   a. This man, does **he** speak English?
   b. Does this man speak English?

In both examples, there are two subjects in the first translation (a): research = it (elles); man = he. Such repetition is considered redundant in English and must be excluded.

---

15. One would expect "Peux-je", but the sound of "Puis-je" is preferred. In highly literary French, the form "Puissé-je" is occasionally found.

16. *Que sais-je?* is the title of a popular series of books which summarize given subjects. (It is also the motto of Michel de Montaigne, d.1592.) Each book in the series appears in the same condensed format, a more intellectual style of Coles Notes. For example, one book in the series is entitled *L'histoire du Canada.* This compact book summarizes everything that a French person should know about Canadian history and is periodically updated in new editions.

D. Interrogative Determiners

When interrogative determiners are involved, the word order follows the regular rules of inversion. For example, if *est-ce que* is combined with the determiner, there is no inversion. Here is a list of the commonest interrogative determiners:

i. Interrogative pronouns:

qui?	who?; (as an object of a preposition) whom?
que?	what; (as direct objects) that, which, whom?
quoi?	what?
lequel?	which one? (with gender and number agreement)
combien?	how many?

ii. Interrogative adverbs:

comment?	how?
où?	where?
pourquoi?	why?
quand?	when?

iii. Other determiners:

quel?	which? (adj. with gender and number agreement)
combien de?	how many? (expression of quantity)

Examples

1. Comment appelerez-vous votre premier enfant?
   What (*lit.* How) will you name your first child?

2. Où est-ce que vous avez trouvé ce passage?
   Where did you find this passage?

Exercise E

Translate the following sentences, noting that when a profession is linked to a person in French, no article is used (exceptionally). **Note** also that negative sentences are formed by placing **ne**...**pas** before and after the verb.

1. Suis-je théologien?

2. Est-ce que nous sommes artistes?

3. N'ai-je pas le droit d'être malade?

4. Pourquoi a-t-il un niveau intellectuel très élevé?

5. Combien de chrétiens ou chrétiennes sont-ils pratiquants?

6. Êtes-vous catholique ou protestant?

7. Ces musulmans, d'où viennent-ils?

8. Le prêtre a-t-il le pouvoir de pardonner?

9. À Noël, les chrétiens n'ont-ils pas une foi vivante?

10. Les confessions ne sont pas entendues aujourd'hui.

11. Nous avons souffert du matérialisme et du laïcisme.

12. Avez-vous trouvé la sortie dans le couloir?

13. À quelle heure partez-vous?

14. Et s'il est mort pour rien?

15. Êtes-vous souffrant?

16. Qu'est-ce que[17] l'amour? C'est une passion dangereuse.

17. A-t-on le droit de réussir sans faire[18] un effort?

18. Puis-je nommer le successeur?

19. Qu'est-ce qui[19] est préférable?

20. Qu'est-ce que vous pensez?

29. BASIC VOCABULARLY: Chapters 1-3

NOUNS

âme (f.)	soul
ami/e (m.f.)	friend
ange (m.)	angel
Dieu (m.)	God
femme (f.)	woman, wife
homme (m.)	man
mari (m.)	husband
la Pâque	Passover
à Pâques	at Easter
joyeuses Pâques	Happy Easter

---

17. *Qu'est-ce que*: what <is>; "is" is only implied in this exceptionally literary construction. Nevertheless, the same initial construction in Q.19 and Q.20, *Qu'est-ce qui* or *Qu'est-ce que*, still means "what", since the *Que* (or *Qu'* at the beginning) defines the question as concerning a "thing". The *que* at the end of the construction in Q.16 normally signifies the accusative (objective case). Literally, *qu'est-ce que* means "what is it that", whereas *qui est-ce que* means "who is it whom".

18. *sans faire*: without making; cf. Chapter 8 §78.

19. *Qu'est-ce qui*: what. The *Qu'* at the beginning determines that the interrogative subject is a thing (*Que* as "what) rather than a person ("who"), whereas the *qui* at the end indicates the nominative (subject) case; i.e. the thing or person normally performing the action of the verb. A final *que* here would signify the accusative (object) case; i.e. "what" *or* "whom". To mean *who*, this construction would have to *begin* with *Qui*.

le Noël	Christmas
à Noël	at Christmas
joyeux Noël	Merry Christmas
actualités[FF] (f.pl.)	current events
amour (m.)	love
argent (m.)	silver; money
bonté (f.)	goodness
choix (m.)	choice
Chrétien, Chrétienne (m.,f.)	Christian man, woman
christianisme (m.)	Christianity (a religious practice)
chrétienté (f.)	christendom
ciel (m.)	sky; heaven
confession (f.)	denomination; confession
droit (m.)	right, law
faute (f.)	fault, mistake
fils (m.sg. & pl.)	son/s
foi (f.sg. *only*)	faith
journal[FF], journaux (m.sg.,pl.)	newspaper; journal (= diary)
Juif, Juive (m.,f.)	Jewish man, woman
judaïsme (m.)	Judaism
laïcisme (m.)	secularism
médecin (m.)	doctor
misère[FF] (f.)	poverty
Musulman, Musulmane (m.,f.)	Muslim man, woman
niveau, niveaux (m.sg.,pl)	level/s
oeil, yeux (m.sg.,pl.)	eye, eyes
prêtre (m.)	priest
puissance (f.)	power
règne (m.)	kingdom (Lat. *regnum*)
revue[FF] (f.)	journal
salut (m.)	salvation, health; greeting (hello)
témoin (m.)	witness
théologien (m.)	theologian
traduction (f.)	translation

IMPORTANT PRONOUN

on / l'on (3 pers.)	one: *poss. trans.* they, you, we...

ESSENTIAL ADJECTIVES   Listed in §10 [Ch.1 above].

ESSENTIAL PREPOSITIONS   Listed in §12 [Ch.1 above].

ESSENTIAL VERBS

Auxiliaries
avoir	to have
être	to be

I.

demander[FF]	to ask (**for**)		donner	to give
montrer	to show		supporter[FF]	to endure
enseigner	to teach		regarder	to look (at)
étudier	to study		écouter	to listen (to)

II.

finir	to finish
sortir	to go out
agir	to act
souffrir	to suffer (pp. souffert)
ouvrir	to open (pp. ouvert)
couvrir	to cover (pp. couvert)

III.

perdre	to lose	
entendre*	1) to hear (*possibly* understand)	2) to intend, mean
rendre	1) to render, to make	2) to return

4

CONTRACTIONS, PRONOUNS AND POSSESSIVE ADJECTIVES

Please note that a "Basic Vocabulary" list for the following three chapters is found at the end of Chapter 6.

30. Contractions of Definite Articles

The two most commonly used prepositions contract or amalgamate with the masculine and plural definite articles:

i. à (to, at, in)

Masculine	à	&	le	<	**au**
Feminine					**à la** [mode]
Plural	à	&	les	<	**aux**

ii. de (of, from, some, or ϕ)

Masculine	de	&	le	<	**du**
Feminine					**de la**
Plural	de	&	les	<	**des**

The first is easier to translate than the second, insofar as there are fewer options from which to choose.

au (à + le) = to/in/at the   **du** (de + le) = of/from the
aux (à + les) = to/in/at the   **des** (de + les) = of/from the

31. The Partitive

A. The constructions **du**, **de la** and **des** can also mean **some**, in which case it is not always necessary to translate it. These forms constitute what is called the partitive article. In a suitable context, the translation "some" can also be entirely dropped from the English translation. For example:

Singular	**Plural**	**English**
du thé		some tea
de la patience		some patience
une théorie (a theory)	**des** théories	~~some~~ theories
une cathédrale (a cathedral)	**des** cathédrales	~~some~~ cathedrals
une confession[1] (a denomination)	**des** confessions	~~some~~ denominations

B. In a question or a negative sentence, "some" may be better translated as "any":

J'ai du thé.	Ai-je du thé?
I have some tea.	Do I have any tea?

C. If **des** precedes a short, common adjective before the noun, it changes to **de**, but still retains the partitive meaning:

Le prêtre a **de** jolis vêtements.
The priest has **some** pretty vestments.

Nous demandons **de** bons vins *or* **du** bon vin.[2]
We are asking for **some** good wines *or* some good wine.

Question and Answer
Avez-vous **de** l'argent?
Do you have **any** money?

Non, je n'ai pas **d'**argent.
No, I do not have **any** money.

The negative is made by surrounding the verb with **ne (n')** and **pas**. Just as *ne* loses its *-e* before a word beginning with another vowel, so does *de* before the *a* in *argent*.

---

1. *Confession:* Religious "denomination", but also "confession" in the sacramental sense (for some denominations).
2. **du** is now acceptable before an adjective preceding a noun in the singular.

Exercise A

For vocabulary, please refer to the list of Basic Vocabulary at the end of Chapter Nine and a dictionary.

1. de nouveaux développements

2. des poèmes lyriques

3. à la mode

4. des théories pratiques

5. Je ne connais pas de longues histoires[FF] intéressantes.

6. Je donne le livre au professeur.

7. La *Revue[FF] de la théologie actuelle*[FF] est tombée sous la chaise.

8. Je suis allé au magasin[FF].

9. Aux États-Unis on ignore[FF] souvent les principes politiques du Canada.

10. Au Canada le peuple est bilingue, en principe.

32. Relative Pronouns: *qui* & *que*

The relationship of the French relative pronouns *qui* and *que* to the two cases of subject (nominative) and object (accusative) may reflect Latin masculine inflections of the same pronouns:

Latin: quis[3] (nominative) quem (accusative)
French: qui que

In French, the two relative pronouns lose their association with gender (f.m) and function in a simplified manner only as two distinct cases: i.e.,

i. Nominative Case = subject

LATIN: *Benedictus* ***qui** venit in nomine Domini.*
FRENCH: Béni [soit] celui **qui** vient au nom du Seigneur.
ENGLISH: Blessed [is] he **who** comes in the name of the Lord.

ii. Accusative Case = direct object

LATIN: *Et vir **quem** ponebant quotidie ad portam templi...*
FRENCH: Et l'homme **que** l'on[4] déposait quotidiennement à la porte du temple...
ENGLISH: And the man **whom** they placed every day at the gate of the temple...
(Acts 3:2)

Consequently, the French *qui* and *que* are invariable (i.e. do not agree in number or gender with the nouns they modify). Both can signify either people or things. *Que* can also mean "that" in all the English senses. With the subjunctive form of the following verb, *que* also signals a translation "may" or "let". Only *que* can drop the vowel *e* before a following vowel in order to permit a liaison:

Summary:
Qui Who, which: subject of a subordinate clause.[5]
Que, qu' Whom, which: object of a verb in a subordinate clause.
That: subordinating conjunction; i.e.
Il dit **que**...: He says **that**...

---

3. *quis < qui* (Vulgate). The *s* drops off in later Latin
4. *l'on*: the addition of *l'* to *on* is purely to prevent elision. Without the extra consonant, the two vowels between *que* and *on* would collapse into *qu'on*. This is a particularly literary usage.
5. A subordinate clause is a sentence which depends upon another sentence for its complete meaning; it cannot stand alone.

Exercise B

Identify the relative pronouns and their antecedents (the nouns which they replace) before translating the following sentences.

1. Le journal[FF] qui est sur le bureau est un journal français.

2. La revue[FF] que vous demandez est dans le bureau.

3. Je cherche le livre que le professeur a recommandé.

4. La personne qui semble agitée est le président du colloque.

5. Le livre que je lis est intitulé *L'Art de fumer sans mourir*.[6]

6. L'homme qui entre est un professeur de littérature française.

7. Il présente[FF] la femme que vous regardez.

8. Le début de l'évangile selon saint Jean est un passage de la Bible qui est souvent cité.

9. L'avocat qui pose la question est mon ami.

10. L'espoir qu'on a perdu hier revient aujourd'hui.

---

6. *sans mourir*: cf. Chapter 3, n.18 and Chapter 8, §78.

33. Disjunctive Pronouns

Disjunctive pronouns are pronouns which have been disconnected ("disjoined") from verbs. They are used for emphasis in the nominative case or as objects of prepositions, and only replace people.

Subject Pronouns	Disjunctive Pronouns	English (s. or obj.)
je	moi	I or me
tu	toi	you
il	lui	he, it, him
elle	elle	she, her
on	soi	oneself or itself
nous	nous	us
vous	vous	you
ils	eux	them (m.)
elles	elles	them (f.)

34. Possessive and Demonstrative Adjectives

A. Possessive Adjectives

Since possessive adjectives in French act truly as adjectives, the gender which they express does not refer to the gender of the possessor or owner. Instead, the adjective agrees in number and gender with the object possessed, like any other adjective.

Person	Masculine	Feminine	Plural	English
1st sg.	mon	ma	mes	my
2nd sg.	ton	ta	tes	your
3rd sg.	son	sa	ses	his, her, its
1st pl.	notre	notre	nos	our
2nd pl.	votre	votre	vos	your
3rd pl.	leur	leur	leurs	their

Exercise C

Translate the possessive pronoun as representative of the subject of the sentence in each case. One can assume that the subjects constitute the referents of the following possessive adjectives. Since there is some ambiguity in these possessives (i.e. *son* may mean either "his" or "her"), the French speaker would add "à lui" to confirm the former and "à elle" for the latter.

1. Elle a son livre.

2. Elle aime son ennemi.

3. Il a sa thèse.

4. La mère a donné son pardon à son fils.

5. Nous avons notre foi.

6. Edouard? Je suis sa soeur.

7. Elles sont leurs guides.

8. Nous sommes leurs amis.

9. Ils sont vos ennemis.

10. Marie? Où est son frère?

Exercise D

Translate a mixture of disjunctive pronouns and possessive pronouns.

1. Je pense à mon frère. Je pense à lui.

2. Je pense à ma soeur. Je pense à elle.

3. Je souffre sans toi.

4. Il travaille[FF] pour nous.

5. J'ai chanté avec eux hier.

6. Je n'ai pas de livres, moi.

7. Appelles-tu Paul ou moi? Lui?

8. Mon mari et moi, nous pensons voyager cette année.

9. La crainte de Dieu est le commencement de la sagesse.

10. Les familles ici sont pauvres. Je prie pour elles.

11. Non pas à nous, ô Éternel, non pas à nous, mais à ton nom nous donnons la gloire (Ps. 115:1).

12. Nous avons besoin d'eux[7] pour terminer le travail.

13. Selon eux, l'homme propose, Dieu dispose.

14. Le coeur a ses raisons que la raison ne connaît point.[8] (Pascal)

15. Selon lui, elle apprend vite.

B. DEMONSTRATIVE ADJECTIVES

Demonstrative adjectives (this, these) follow a pattern similar to the definite article:

	Masculine	**Feminine**	**Plural**
Definite Article	le	la	les
Demonstrative Adj.	ce, cet	cette (this)	ces (these)

Strictly speaking, *ce* means "this" (not "that"), although sometimes "that" seems to be more appropriate in English. If the French really mean "that", however, they add *-là* to the noun being pointed out: e.g. **cet homme-là** (that man)! The "t" in "cet" prevents an elision between "ce" and "homme" (in which the "h" is not pronounced), just as the "l" does in "ce bel homme-là" (that handsome man).

---

7. *avoir besoin de*: to (have) need (of)

8. *point*: *pas*, where *point* is more emphatically negative.

56

35. Another Pronoun: celui

Celui with its feminine and plural forms is a pronoun meaning "that" or "those". The antecedent (the noun it replaces) is usually ahead of it in the same sentence, and it is often followed by **de** (of).

Examples

1. I know my **response**, but not the **response** of my wife.
2. I know my **response**, but not **that** of my wife.
    [Je sais ma **réponse**, mais non pas **celle** de ma femme.]

In the second case the pronoun **that** replaces the second **response,** which the speaker does not want to repeat.

The French Forms

	Singular	**Plural**
Masc.	celui	ceux
Fem.	celle	celles
English	that, the one	those, the ones

A. *Celui & de*

Since the use of this pronoun, in any of its forms, with *de* (of) usually denotes the possessive case, English always has the option of using the genitive "'s" (non-existant in French).

Examples

3. Moi, je n'entre pas dans **l'église** catholique, mais dans **celle** des Protestants.
    I am not entering the Catholic Church, but that of the Protestants
    (*église* is a feminine noun represented by *celle*).

4. Nous étudions **le livre** saint des Chrétiens et **celui** des Juifs.
    We are studying the holy book of the Christians and that of the Jews
    (*livre* is a masculine noun represented by *celui*).

5. Ma **grand-mère** et **celle** de Jeanne ont le même âge.
    My grandmother and that of Jean are the same age.
    My grandmother and Jean**'s** are the same age.

B. *Celui & qui, que*

Celui qui: The one who; He who (subject of the verb)
Celui que: The one whom; He whom (object of the verb)

Note that the first option in both cases ("the one") avoids sexist language, even if it is rather formal for our time. This usage follows the principle that the masculine form is universal.

Examples

1. Béni soit **celui qui** vient au nom du Seigneur (cf. p.66).
    Blessed be **the one who** comes in the name of the Lord.
    or May **the one who** comes in the name of the Lord be blessed.

2. **Celui qui** clôt scs lèvres passe pour intelligent (Prov.17: 28).
    He who closes his lips passes for <being> intelligent.
    He that shutteth his lips is esteemed a man of understanding (KJV).

3. Ceux que tourmentent des esprits impurs sont guéris (Luc 6: 18).
    Those whom unclean spirits torment are healed.

36. The Latter, The Former: *celui-ci & celui-là*

By deconstructing two common words, one discovers the consistent meaning of -ci (here) and -là (there).

Voici: Here is; Here are.... (*lit.* See here: voi[s] + ci).
Voilà: There is; There are...(*lit.* See there: voi[s] + là).

Consequently:
celui-ci: this one here < the latter.
celui-là: that one there < the former.

Note that celui-ci (this one here) is used first in French, although its translation into English (the "latter" one closer to the speaker) follows "the former" in English.

Examples

1. Voilà le prince et le paysan. Celui-ci est pauvre; celui-là est riche.
    There are the prince and the peasant. The latter is poor; the former is rich.
    (normally reversed in English)

2. Quelle église vais-je choisir? Celle-ci ou celle-là?
    Which church am I going to choose? This one or that one?

    (*église* = f.)

3. Dans celle-ci la chorale chante tout le temps; dans celle-là jamais!
    In the latter the choir sings all the time; in the former never!

Exercise E

1. J'ai ton livre et celui de Jean.

2. Ta mère et celle de Marie fêtent leur anniversaire aujourd'hui.

3. Ces événements et ceux d'hier sont incroyables!

4. Nous étudions le règne d'Henri VIII et celui d'Élisabeth I.

5. Nous considérons ces circonstances et celles d'hier.

6. Mon avocat et celui de ma femme sont des amis.

7. Le jeune enfant de Nazareth, à sa douzième année, se rend[9] enfin au Temple de Jérusalem.
   Celui-ci est le centre du monde pour les Juifs (cf. Aron, p.127).

8. Ces enfants-là ont besoin d'un père.[10]

9. Nous contestons la vérité de son discours et celle de sa réponse aux questions.

10. Les Sadducéens ne partagent pas la répugnance des Palestiniens pour la langue
    et pour la culture hellénique: celle-ci est méprisée par les Juifs au temps de Jésus
    (cf. Aron, p.134).

---

9. *se rend*: goes (*lit.* renders himself).

10. Cf. note 7 ahead.

37. Reading the Bible: The Psalms

Exercise F

Identify the number and gender (if applicable) of the words highlighted in bold: adjectives (possessive and demonstrative) and pronouns (disjunctive and relative), in the following psalm extracts. Then translate the highlighted words within the textual context.

1. Pourquoi **ces** nations en tumulte,
   ces peuples **qui** murmurent en vain?

   Puis [Yahvé] dans **sa** colère il parle,
   dans **sa** fureur il parle fort:
   "C'est **moi qui** ai sacré **mon** roi
   sur Sion, **ma** montagne sainte."

   Yahvé m'a dit: "Tu es **mon** fils,
   moi, aujourd'hui, je t'ai engendré.
   Servez Yahvé avec crainte,
   baisez **ses** pieds avec tremblement...

   (From Ps. 2: 5-12)

2. Yahvé, **mes** oppresseurs sont nombreux
   contre **moi**, **qui** disent de **moi**:
   "Point de salut pour **lui** en **son** Dieu!"

   Mais **toi**, Yahvé, **ma** gloire...
   Et **moi**, je me couche et m'endors,
   je m'éveille: Yahvé est **mon** soutien.
   Je ne crains pas **ces** gens par milliers
   qui forment un cercle contre **moi**.
   　　Dresse[11]-**toi**, Yahvé!
   　　Sauve[12]-**moi**, **mon** Dieu!
   Tu frappes... **mes** ennemis,...
   　　À Yahvé, le salut!
   　　Sur **ton** peuple, **ta** bénédiction!   (From Ps. 3)

---

11. *Dresse-toi*: 2nd person imperative form of a 1st conjugation pronominal verb meaning "draw yourself up" (stand up, arise). Notice the form *dresse* which normally suits the 1st or 3rd person singular, rather than the 2nd p. (tu dresses: you draw up).
12. *Sauve-moi*: 2nd person imperative (save) and dir. obj. again.

Exercise G

Add forms of "à", "de" and their contractions to all the highlighted adjectives and pronouns in Exercise F for analysis and translation:

1. Fils **d'**homme, jusqu'où irez-vous dans l'insulte **à ma** gloire,
    dans l'amour **du** néant et la course **au** mensonge?   (Ps. 4: 3)

2. Écoute **ma** parole, Yahvé,
        discerne **ma** plainte...
    C'est **toi** que je prie, Yahvé!
        Au matin tu écoutes **ma** voix;
    au matin je me prépare pour **toi**...
    Et **moi**, par la grandeur **de ton** amour,
        j'accède **à ta** maison;
    vers **ton** temple sacré je me prosterne,
        pénétré de ta crainte.
                                    (Ps. 5)

5

VERBS:
IMPERATIVE, FUTURE, IRREGULAR, MODAL

38. Imperatives

The imperative verb is used to give orders or commands. There are three possible forms of the imperative in French: the second person singular (informal) form, the first and second plural (formal) forms. The imperative is always recognizable by the lack of the personal pronoun with the verb, just as in English; we normally say "Go!" rather than "You go!"

Implied		**I.**	**II.**	**III.**
tu	[to a child or a familiar]	Demande (Ask...)	Finis (Finish...)	Perds (Lose...)
nous	[let us...]	Demandons (Let us ask)	Finissons (Let us finish)	Perdons (Let us lose)
vous	[to an elder or a group]	Demandez	Finissez	Perdez

Note that all the endings suit the appropriate person with which they are commonly associated, except the first, informal imperative of the first conjugation. One would expect *Demandes!* rather than *Demande*! The *s* is dropped in the familiar imperative only in the first conjugation.

Exercise A

1. Demandez à Philippe s'il a gardé sa foi.

2. Finissons en une heure!

3. Ne perds pas[1] la clé!

4. Rentre avant minuit!

5. Sors avec ta soeur!

6. Pense à moi demain.

7. Ne souffre pas sans eux.

8. Priez pour que Dieu aide[2] son fils.

9. Pose la question à Martin.

10. Prions ensemble.

39. The Real Future Tense

The future is the easiest tense to learn, because one simply adds the present endings of the verb *avoir* to the infinitive of the verb in question. Only *avons* and *avez* must drop the first syllables to form the future endings of *nous* and *vous*. The infinitive of the third conjugation drops the final "e" before adding the endings.

Because the infinitive is the root of the future conjugation, there is always an "*r*" found before the endings. This phenomenon occurs even in irregular verbs.

____

1. *ne...pas*: cf. Chapter 7 for use of the negative.
2. *aide*: 3rd p. subjunctive after *pour que* (so that): may help.

		I.	II.	III.
	AVOIR (present) (for endings)	**DEMANDER** (I will ask) (etc.)	**FINIR** (I'll finish)	**PERDRE** (I'll lose)
je	**ai**	demander**ai**	finir**ai**	perdr**ai**
tu	**as**	demander**as**	finir**as**	perdr**as**
il/elle	**a**	demander**a**	finir**a**	perdr**a**
nous	av**ons**	demander**ons**	finir**ons**	perdr**ons**
vous	av**ez**	demander**ez**	finir**ez**	perdr**ez**
ils/elles	**ont**	demander**ont**	finir**ont**	perdr**ont**

Exercise B Practice with the future, imperative & pronouns.

Translate the following from the Book of Daniel 12: 2-4, using the vocabulary provided below and a dictionary, if necessary.

La résurrection et la rétribution

Un grand nombre de ceux qui dorment au pays de la poussière s'éveilleront, les uns pour la vie éternelle, les autres pour l'opprobre, pour l'horreur éternelle. Les doctes resplendiront comme la splendeur du firmament, et ceux qui ont enseigné la justice à un grand nombre, comme les étoiles, pour toute l'éternité.

Toi, Daniel, serre ces paroles et scelle le livre jusqu'au temps de la Fin. Beaucoup erreront de-ci de-là, et l'iniquité grandira.

VOCABULARY

Verbs

errer	to stray
s'éveiller	to wake up
resplendir	to shine
sceller	to seal
serrer	to lock away

Nouns

opprobre (m)	opprobrium, disgrace
les doctes (m.pl)	the learned

Pronouns

les uns ... les autres	some ... others

40. Irregular Verbs: *aller, faire, savoir, venir...*

The root changes in irregular verbs for the singular and third person plural forms. The first and second plural forms (*nous, vous*) generally revert to the regular root. Some irregular verbs have similar patterns, such as *venir* and *tenir*. *Faire* is the most irregular, but it resembles *savoir* in the singular.

	ALLER (to go)	**FAIRE** (do, make) (cause to)	**SAVOIR** (to know how)	**VENIR** (to come)	**TENIR** (to hold)
je	vais	fais	sais	viens	tiens
tu	vas	fais	sais	viens	tiens
il	va	fait	sait	vient	tient
ns	**allons**	faisons	**savons**	**venons**	**tenons**
vs	**allez**	faites	**savez**	**venez**	**tenez**
ils	vont	font	**sav**ent	viennent	tiennent

The bold letters highlight the forms which revert to the root (i.e. all-, sav-, ven-, ten-). The first three verbs often combine with the infinitives of other verbs. Each of them has its own peculiar usage. *Faire*, for example, becomes a **causative verb** in combination with an infinitive, but it is also used as "do" or "make" much more often than in English.

41. The Immediate Future (*le futur immédiat ou proche*): *aller*

The immediate future tense, which is more common in oral than in written French, uses the **progressive (or continuous) present** tense of *aller* before the infinitive in the English translation: i.e. *Je vais* = **I am going (to)**..., <u>not</u> I go (to)...

1. Nous **allons demander** une explication.
    We are going to ask for an explanation.

2. Ils **vont lire** le quatrième chapitre.
    They are going to read the fourth chapter.

42. Introduction to The Causative: *faire*[3]

The first two examples below use *faire* as the main verb, meaning either "do" or "make". It is a much more common verb in French than in English, as in #2 below where one would normally "write" a cheque in English. There are three standard options of equal value for the causative in #3 which are treated in greater detail in Chapter 13.

1. Il **fait** ses devoirs après le dîner (does).
    He does his homework after dinner.

2. Elle **fait** un chèque à donner au propriétaire (makes).
    She makes out a cheque to give to the owner.

3. Nous **faisons connaître** les signes (causative).
    a. We cause the signs to be known.
    b. We have the signs made known.
    c. We make the signs known.

43. The Usage of *connaître* and *savoir*

Savoir often includes the English idea of "how to", but not always.

1. Je **sais chanter**, mais je ne **sais** pas **déchiffrer** la musique.
    I know how to sing, but I don't know how to sight-read music.

2. Tu **sais parler** aux enfants, mais Dieu **sait** leurs chemins.
    You know how to speak to children, but God knows their paths.

If the knowledge is intimate and demonstrates a real acquaintance with a person (people), place, subject or emotion, the verb used is *connaître*.

3. Il connaît la faim.
    He knows hunger.

---

3. Cf. Chapter 13 for an in-depth study of the Causative.

44. Modal Verbs

Modal verbs (a term borrowed from German) describe the circumstances of an action, such as compulsion (*devoir*) or ability (*pouvoir*), or the subjective attitude of the speaker, such as wishing (*vouloir*). They often combine directly with the infinitive of the following verb, as in §§41-43 above.

	VOULOIR	**POUVOIR**	**DEVOIR**
	(to wish)	(to be able)	(to have to, ought)
je	veux	peux	dois
tu	veux	peux	dois
il	veut	peut	doit
ns	**voulons**	**pouvons**	**devons**
vs	**voulez**	**pouvez**	**devez**
ils	veulent	peuvent	doivent

Note that *devoir* means "to owe" when not used as a modal verb.

Examples

1. Je veux fumer, mais je ne peux pas.
   I want to smoke, but I cannot.

2. Vous pouvez lire jusqu'à dix heures.
   a. You can (are able to) read up until ten o'clock.
   b. You may read up until ten o'clock.

3. Ils doivent partir avant minuit.
   They have to leave before midnight.

4. Je dois une explication de ma conduite à mon professeur.
   I owe my teacher an explanation for my conduct.

Exercise C

Translate using a dictionary, if necessary:

1. Si vous pouvez trouver le temps, allez voir ce film.

2. Nous voulons considérer la question en détail.

3. Je vais lire ce livre demain.

4. Elle fait une salade pour ce soir.

5. Il sait philosopher.

6. Nous devons partir tout de suite.

7. On doit connaître les noms des étudiants.

8. Elle ne peut pas devenir prêtre dans l'Église Catholique.

9. Elles doivent étudier les grands philosophes.

10. Je veux perdre la crainte de la mort.

11. Nous allons continuer après le repas.

12. Nous savons qu'il ne vient pas.

45. Summary: Principal Parts of these Verbs

Infinitive \	Pres. Part.\	Past Part.\	Future Root
faire	faisant	fait	fer-
aller	allant	allé	ir-
savoir	sachant	su	saur-
venir	venant	venu	viendr-
tenir	tenant	tenu	tiendr-
vouloir	voulant	voulu	voudr-
pouvoir	pouvant	pu	pourr-
devoir	devant	dû	devr-

The chart provided in Appendix 2 allows the student to lay out these principal parts in relation to the verb tenses which they govern. It is a good exercise to copy and complete the charts for all the regular conjugations and irregular verbs.

46. Reading the Bible: Proverbs, Commandments, Beatitudes

Exercise D

Read the following selections from the Book of Proverbs (Prov. 1:1-14) and analyze the verbs highlighted in bold. Even if you cannot translate a verb, at least identify the infinitive form of it. Then check a dictionary for the meaning.

I. Proverbes de Salomon fils de David, roi d'Israël:
   pour **connaître** sagesse et discipline,
     pour **pénétrer** les discours profonds,
   pour **acquérir** une discipline **avisée**
     - justice, équité, droiture -
   pour **procurer** aux simples le savoir-faire,
     au jeune homme le savoir et la réflexion,
   pour pénétrer proverbes et sentences[FF] obscures,
     les dits des sages et leurs énigmes.
   La crainte de Yahvé, principe de savoir:
     les fous **dédaignent** sagesse et discipline.
Écoute, mon fils, l'instruction de ton père,
   ne **méprise** pas l'enseignement de ta mère...
Mon fils, si des pécheurs **veulent** te **séduire**,
   n'y **va** pas!
S'ils disent: "**Viens** avec nous, **répandons** le sang,
   sans raison,...
comme le shéol, **avalons**-les tout vifs,
   tout entiers...
Nous **trouverons** mainte chose précieuse,
   nous **ferons** tous bourse commune!"

Exercise E

With the help of a dictionary, where necessary, analyse and translate the highlighted verbs in the following well-known passages, the Ten Commandments and the Beatitudes:

1. Tu n'**auras** pas d'autres dieux devant moi. Tu ne **feras** aucune image sculptée, rien qui **ressemble** à ce qui **est** dans les cieux, là-haut, ou sur la terre, ici-bas, ou dans les eaux, au-dessous de la terre.

2. Tu ne te **prosterneras** pas devant ces dieux et tu ne les **serviras** pas, car moi Yahvé, ton Dieu, je **suis** un Dieu jaloux qui **punis** les fautes des pères sur les enfants, les petits-enfants et les arrière-petits-enfants pour ceux qui me haïssent, mais qui fais grâce à des milliers pour ceux qui m'aiment et gardent mes commandements.

3. Tu ne **prononceras** pas le nom de Yahvé ton Dieu à faux...

4. Tu te **souviendras** du jour du sabbat pour le **sanctifier**...

5. **Honore** ton père et ta mère...

6. Tu ne **tueras** pas.

7. Tu ne **commettras** pas d'adultère.

8. Tu ne **voleras** pas.

9. Tu ne **porteras** pas de témoignage mensonger contre ton prochain.

10. Tu ne **convoiteras** pas la maison de ton prochain. Tu ne convoiteras pas la femme de ton prochain, ni son serviteur, ni sa servante, ni son bœuf, ni son âne...

(L'Exode 20:3-17)

Heureux ceux qui **ont** une âme de pauvre, car le Royaume des Cieux **est** à eux.

Heureux les doux, car ils **posséderont** la terre,

Heureux les **affligés**, car ils **seront consolés**.

Heureux les **affamés** et assoiffés de la justice, car ils **seront rassasiés**.

Heureux les miséricordieux, car ils **obtiendront** miséricorde.

Heureux les cœurs purs, car ils **verront**[4] Dieu.

Heureux les artisans de paix, car ils **seront appelés** fils de Dieu...

Heureux êtes-vous quand on vous **insultera**, qu'on[5] vous **persécutera**...

(Matt. 5: 3-11).

---

4. *verront*: will see (from *voir*; cf. Chapter 6, §49B).

5. *qu'on*: when they. Instead of repeating *quand*, in a complex sentence, *que* or *qu'* replaces it the second time. This can occur with any type of subordinating conjunction (e.g. *si, jusque...*).

47. Exercise F: Extract from *Le Petit Prince*

This exercise emphasizes the distinction between grammatical gender and the sexual gender of the referent. *Faites attention!*

Dédicace
À LÉON WERTH

Je demande pardon aux[6] enfants d'avoir dédié[7] ce livre à une grande personne. J'ai une excuse sérieuse: cette grande personne est le meilleur[8] ami que j'ai au monde. J'ai une autre excuse: cette grande personne peut tout[9] comprendre, même les livres pour enfants. J'ai une troisième excuse: cette grande personne habite la France où elle a faim[10] et froid. Elle a bien[11] besoin d'être consolée. Si toutes ces excuses ne suffisent pas, je veux bien dédier ce livre à l'enfant qu'a été autrefois cette grande personne[12]. Toutes les grandes personnes ont d'abord été des enfants. Je corrige donc ma dédicace:

À LÉON WERTH QUAND IL ÉTAIT[13] PETIT GARÇON

48. Five Dialogues in the Form of a Catechism

In a classroom situation with a group of students, these dialogues can be used as a mnemonic aid (*aide-mémoire*) and for practice with pronunciation. The students should divide into pairs and designate to each an **A** or **B** role. Each will be responsible for pronouncing and understanding their part. After their oral presentation, they should be able to translate their part without consulting any notes in English.

---

6. Cf. Chapter 1, §12B (*acheter à*) for this class of preposition.

7. *d'avoir dédié*: *d'* (de) depends upon *pardon* as with the vb. *pardonner de* (to forgive for).

8. *le meilleur*: the best (superlative).

9. *tout*: everything (direct object of the verb *comprendre* which requires adjustment of the syntax).

10. *a faim*: < *avoir faim*: "to have hunger", translated "to be hungry". The same phenomenon (substituting "to be" for "to have") occurs again for *froid*.

11. *bien*: really (adv. which intensifies the verb with which it is associated).

12. *qu'a été autrefois cette grande personne*: the subject (*cette grande personne*) comes at the end of this subordinate clause and should be moved up to the position immediately following *qu'* in the English translation. The relative pronoun *qu'* (really *que*) is not the subject, which would have to be *qui* to constitute the subject. This inverted word order only arises in literary French (cf. Chapter 11, §109).

13. *ÉTAIT*: 3rd p.sg. of the verb *être* in the imperfect tense: was (cf. Chapter 8, §70).

Vocabulary:

également	also (= *aussi*)
non plus	either (cf. Ch.7 §47F)
pas du tout	not at all
tout/toute	all; every

I. DIALOGUE SUR L'EXISTENCE DE DIEU

A. Je crois que Dieu existe!

B. Dieu, qui est-il?

A. Vous ne connaissez pas Dieu?

B. Non! Pas du tout! Est-ce que c'est le nom d'un de vos amis ou le nom d'une déité païenne?

A. C'est le nom du Créateur du ciel et de la terre! Dieu est, en réalité, trois personnes: le Père, le Fils et le Saint Esprit.

B. Comment? Dieu, est-il une personne ou trois personnes?

A. Dieu est à la fois une personne et trois personnes.

B. Mais, c'est impossible!

II. DIALOGUE SUR LES ATTRIBUTS DE DIEU

A. J'entends dire que vous ne croyez pas que Dieu existe?

B. Je ne crois pas que Dieu existe parce que je ne le[14] connais pas. Dites-moi alors quelque chose sur lui.

A. Sans avoir vu Dieu, je crois en lui, mais je vais le[15] décrire par ce qu'il n'est pas.

B. Comment? Dieu, est-il quelque chose de négatif?

---

14. *le*: him (direct object, placed before the verb in French), <u>or</u> possibly it. Cf. Chapter 9, §81.
15. See note 13 above.

A.   Pas du tout! Il n'est pas imparfait comme nous.

B.   Alors, il doit être parfait! Mais est-il beau et bon?

A.   Oui, il est toute beauté et toute bonté! Il ne peut pas être laid ou mauvais. Il ne peut pas mentir non plus.

B.   Il doit comprendre également toute vérité absolue.

A.   Vous comprenez bien maintenant.

III. DIALOGUE SUR LA MAISON DE DIEU

A.   Si Dieu existe, où habite-t-il?

B.   Dieu? Dieu existe partout, mais il habite, en particulier, dans nos coeurs.

A.   Comment peut-il exister dans mon coeur? Est-il invisible?

B.   L'amour, est-il invisible? Non, pas tout à fait. On voit l'amour dans le visage d'une personne ou dans leurs gestes. On voit l'amour de Dieu dans la nature, peut-être.

A.   Si Dieu est l'amour qui réside dans nos coeurs, pourquoi y a-t-il tant d'édifices où il est censé habiter? On les appelle les églises, n'est-ce pas?

B.   Oui! En quelque sorte, ces églises sont les maisons de Dieu.

A.   Dieu, est-il à la fois dans l'église et dans mon coeur?

B.   Oui, mais il est aussi partout. Il habite également dans l'esprit et dans la conscience.

IV. DIALOGUE SUR LES PERSONNES DE DIEU

A.   Dieu, est-il une personne comme nous?

B.   Oui et non. Il est la personne de Jésus Christ qui est né sous la forme d'un être humain, mais Dieu le Père est une autre personne de la divinité.

A.   Dieu le Père est toujours masculin! Est-il humain?

B.   Non, il est divin. Cela veut dire qu'il est éternel, sans commencement et sans fin. Par contre, Jésus est à la fois humain et divin. Il est mort par crucifixion!

A.   Vous avez mentionné aussi le Saint Esprit. Est-il une personne humaine ou divine?

B.   Le Saint Esprit est une personne divine. Il représente l'Amour de Dieu comme une sorte de feu.

A.   Un feu? N'est-ce pas dangereux?

B.   Oui et non! Quand il brûle, il affine nos coeurs comme l'or.

V. DIALOGUE SUR LA FOI

A.   La foi, est-elle une personne humaine ou divine?

B.   La foi n'est pas du tout une personne comme les trois personnes divines qui constituent Dieu. La foi est un attribut tout à fait humain.

A.   La foi, doit-elle habiter dans mon coeur?

B.   Si la grâce est entrée dans votre coeur, vous aurez également la foi.

A.   Mais cette grâce, d'où vient-elle?

B.   La grâce est divine et vient uniquement de Dieu.

A. Quel est le rapport entre la grâce divine et la foi humaine alors?

B. La grâce nous[16] aide à avoir confiance en Dieu. C'est une sorte de renforcement spirituel qui nous donne la force de travailler pour le Royaume de Dieu dans ce monde. La foi nous donne[17] l'espoir de recevoir cette grâce comme un don.

---

16. *nous*: us (dir. obj. of the verb); cf. Chapter 9, §85.
17. See note 15 above; grammatically, *nous* is the indir. obj. in this case.

6

MORE IRREGULAR VERBS
AND ASPECTS OF TIME

49. Principal Parts of Common Irregular Verbs

The irregular verbs can be learned in groups which resemble one another.

A. The *-ire* Group

Infinitive	Pres. Part.	Past Part.	Future Root	English
dire	disant	dit	dir-	say, tell
écrire	écrivant	écrit	écrir-	write
lire	lisant	lu	lir-	read
rire	riant	ri	rir-	laugh

All of these verbs use the **-s, -s, -t** endings in the present tense singular (e.g. *j'écris, tu lis, il dit*). The plural forms use the root with the middle consonant found in the present participle (e.g. *nous écrivons, vous lisez, ils rient*). Only *dire* constitutes an exception in the second person plural (*nous disons, vous dites, ils disent*), in a way similar to *faire*.[1]

B. The *-oir/-oire* Group

Infinitive	Pres. Part.	Past Part.	Future Root	English
boire	buvant	bu	boir-	drink
croire	croyant	cru	croir-	believe
recevoir	recevant	reçu	recevr-	receive
voir[2]	voyant	vu	verr-	see

---

1. For the present tense of faire, see Chapter 5 §40.

2. Do not confuse the verb *voir* (to see) with the adverb *voire* (indeed, truly). The final -e makes all the difference!

All of these verbs are conjugated in a fashion similar to the above group (*je bois, tu crois, il/elle voit* with the consonant found in the present participle for the first two plural forms: *nous buvons, vous croyez*). Characteristically, the third person plural forms revert to the root of the infinitive. The *y* reverts to *i* because the semi-consonant is no longer needed to break two syllables: e.g.

ils/elles　　　　*boivent*　　　　*croient*　　　　*reçoivent*　　　　*voient*

Note that *recevoir* is not conjugated like *voir* as one would expect. The singular forms use "reç-" as their root (e.g. *je reçois, tu reçois, il/elle reçoit*) **Note** also that the *ç* occurs in all persons of the present tense, except the first and second plural (*nous recevons, vous recevez*), in order to retain the **[s]** sound before the vowel "o". In this way, the first and second persons plural stand out from the other persons in a fashion characteristic of irregular verbs.[3]

C. Mettre & Prendre

Infinitive	Pres. Part.	Past Part.	Future Root
mettre	mettant	mis	mettr-
to put	putting	put	will put

Other verbs that follow this pattern are *admettre* (to admit), *permettre* (to permit), *promettre* (to promise), *remettre* (to put back). Similarly:

Infinitive	Pres. Part.	Past Part.	Future Root
prendre	prenant	pris	prendr-
to take	taking	taken	will take

Present Tenses:	**Mettre**	**Prendre**
je	mets	prends
tu	mets	prends
il/elle	met	prend
nous	mettons	prenons
vous	mettez	prenez
ils/elles	mettent	prennent

Other verbs that follow this pattern are *comprendre* (to understand) and *surprendre* (to surprise).

---

3. See Chapter 5, §40 (faire, aller, savoir, venir and tenir) and §44 (the modal verbs).

D. Most Irregular Verbs

Inifinitive	Pres. Part.	Past Part.	Future Root	English
naître	naissant	né	naîtr-	be born
suivre	suivant	suivi	suivr-	follow
vivre	vivant	vécu	vivr-	live, experience
mourir	mourant	mort	mourr-	die

The two middle verbs here follow the basic pattern of **Groups A & B** above (*je suis, tu vis, il/elle vit, nous suivons, vous vivez, ils/elles suivent*). **Note** that *je suis* may mean "I am" <u>or</u> "I follow" <u>or</u> "I am following" depending upon the context. **Note also** that the past participles in English do not all fit easily into the "-ed" pattern; e.g., born, as opposed to followed, lived (or experienced), and died in the above list.

The present tenses of *naître* and *mourir* are the most irregular:

	NAÎTRE	**MOURIR**
je	nais	meurs
tu	nais	meurs
il/elle/on	naît	meurt
nous	naissons	mourons
vous	naissez	mourez
elles/ils/on	naissent	meurent

Even here, there is some regularity within the irregularity, once one knows that *meur* is an alternative root of *mourir*. **Note** that these two verbs are conjugated with *être*.[4] The past participles, therefore can be either adjectival (subjective completion: i.e. "he is dead" as contrary to "he is alive")[5] or main verbs as in the following examples.

Examples

1.   Je **suis née** en 1975.
     I **was born** in 1975 (<u>not</u>: I am born in 1975).

2.   Il **est mort** de bonne heure hier.
     He **died** early yesterday (<u>not</u>: He is dead early yesterday).

---

4. See Chapter 3, §27B, II.

5. See Chapter 3 §25.

50. Aspects of Time

The following adverbs and temporal prepositions are worth memorizing since they are used frequently:

aujourd'hui	today
bientôt	soon
de bonne heure	early
d'abord	at first, first of all
déjà	already
demain	tomorrow
désormais	henceforth, from now on
dorénavant	henceforth, from now on
encore	still, yet
encore une fois	again
enfin	finally, at last
hier	yesterday
jusqu'à (prep.)	until
longtemps	<for> a long time
maintenant	now
partout	everywhere
pendant (prep.)	during
durant "	"
presque	almost
quelquefois	sometimes
parfois	at times
souvent	often
tard	late
tôt	early
toujours	always, still
tout de suite	immediately
vite	quickly, fast

Exercise A

Use the list of adverbs above together with the verbs just studied to translate the following:

1. Ils sont morts hier.

2. Elle est déjà morte.

3. Ils sont morts pendant la deuxième guerre mondiale.

4. Suivez-moi, s'il vous plaît.[6]

5. Nous boirons et vivrons jusqu'à la fin.

6. Ils boivent souvent.

7. J'écris quelquefois au frère de Jacques.

8. Je lirai vos lettres à Paul désormais.

9. D'abord, verrez-vous le film?

10. Nous verrons le film bientôt.

11. Parfois il dure longtemps.

12. Quand on a vécu une guerre, on n'oublie pas vite.

---

6. The polite expression *s'il vous plaît* literally means "if it pleases you" or "if it is pleasing to you". The verb plaire, meaning "to please" is conjugated like *naître* without the doubled "ss" in the plural. Its past participle is *plu* like that of *boire, croire, lire, vivre*. The verb *connaître* falls somewhere between *naître* and *plaître*. It doubles the "ss" in the plural (*nous connaissons*), but uses the -u form of past participle for *connu*.

13. En écrivant à Pierre aujourd'hui, je suis mon habitude.

14. Ils riront longtemps.

15. Elles écrivent souvent, presque toujours, à sa famille.

16. Enfin nous lisons le passage qui nous[7] est venu à l'esprit.

17. Il dira demain s'il pourra venir dorénavant.

18. Nous ne buvons pas pendant les lectures[FF].

19. Il mourra demain.

20. Le pécheur recevra le fruit (ou le salaire) de son péché.

51. Articles With Days and Dates

There is no French way to say "on the" or "in the" apart from the definite article (except for *en* with *l'an* (in the year...). Such use of the article can also suggest repetition, which can be translated as "every".

Examples

le deux avril	on the second of April
le lundi	on Mondays, every Monday
le matin	in the morning(s), every morning
tous les matins	every morning
la nuit	at night, in the night, every night
le soir	in the evening, every evening

---

7. *nous:* to us (indirect object pronoun; cf. Chapter 9, §84). In this case, it designates the possession of *l'esprit,* whereas English would say the equivalent of: *qui est venu à notre esprit.* In English, "our" (*notre*) is not even necessary.

The following three alternative forms for day, morning and night refer to these times in the qualitative, not quantitative sense:

la journée	the day
la matinée	the morning
la soirée	the evening

Exercise B

Translate using the vocabulary at the end of the chapter and a dictionary.

1. Elle est née le deux avril en l'an 2000.

2. Le soir les étudiants vont à la bibliothèque.

3. On peut faire la grasse matinée le samedi.

4. C'est la fête de saint Jean-Baptiste le 24 juin.

5. Il joue au hockey le matin.

6. Ce jour-là une idée géniale nous[8] est venue.

7. Cette inspiration soudaine a éclairé l'esprit.

8. Le matin du 3 avril nous sommes allés au marché.

9. À partir de lundi, nous allons recommencer.

10. Le travail[FF] sera fini le 15 mai.

---

8. Cf. Note 7 above.

52. Impersonal Expressions: il y a, c'est

A. Il y a + noun (at the beginning of a sentence)

Il y a is translated "there is" or "there are" (both singular and plural) according to whether the noun which follows the verb is singular or plural.

Examples

1. **Il y a** une idée importante dans la philosophie de Kierkegaard.
    There is an important idea in Kierkegaard's philosophy.

2. **Il y a** plusieurs idées important**es** dans sa philosophie.
    There are several significant ideas in his philosophy.

A synonym for *il y a* which reflects English usage more accurately, but which is seen much more rarely in French, is *Il est*: There is. The translation is much more often the impersonal *It is*.

B. *C'est & ce sont*

The construction using the demonstrative pronoun "*Ce*" (this) plus the third person singular or plural of *être* is slightly deceptive, since *ce* is rarely translated as "this" in this context. It is usually translated as "It" and sometimes as "That" or even a personal pronoun like "He" or "She".

C'est... = **It's**... Sometimes the stylistic circumlocution that arises from its use with *que* can be omitted in English.

The plural form is used when the noun following the verb is plural and is usually translated as "They" or "Those".

Ce sont = There are, Those are, They are (and possibly **These are**)...

Examples

1. **C'est** Jacques Cartier **qui**, en 1534, a revendiqué le Canada.
    a. **It is** Jacques Cartier **who**, in 1534, claimed Canada.
    b. Jacques Cartier claimed Canada in 1534.

2. **C'est** une question difficile **que** vous me posez.
    a. **That is** a difficult question **which** you are asking me.
    b. You are asking me a difficult question.

Note that in both cases, one can begin the sentence with the real subject of the subordinate clause, before *qui* or after *que*, and omit *C'est* or *Ce sont* altogether. These forms are used in French for stylistic emphasis, which English can accomplish by merely inflecting the voice (as in #2 above).

Exercise C

1. C'est moi qui ai fait cette faute.

2. Il y aura trois jours de paix cette fin de semaine.

3. C'est toi qui lis toujours, pas elle.

4. Ce sont elles qui ont revendiqué le droit de voter.

5. Il y a un chien devant la maison.

6. C'est le début du passage que nous signalons comme important.

7. Ce sont eux qui connaissent l'histoire du Canada.

8. Il y a eu une semaine de tranquillité avant la débâcle.

9. C'est une politique qui peut sauver le pays.

10. Si nous insistons sur ce point, c'est pour suggérer une juste compréhension du pardon.

53. Ago: *il y a* and a Quantity of Time

Near the end of a sentence, just before some temporal quantity, *il y a* means **ago** as in:

> *il y a deux jours*
> = two days **ago**

Note the same mirror effect between the two languages as discussed in Chapter 1, insofar as the *il y a* crosses over to "ago" at the end. We could call it the "chiasmus" effect.

Examples

1. Nous avons vu le médecin **il y a** cinq minutes.
   We saw the doctor five minutes **ago**.

2. Nous avons été à Avignon **il y a** quinze jours.
   We were in Avignon a fortnight **ago**.

Note that "a fortnight" is the two weeks which follow a specific day (also counted). This expression along with *quinze jours* are still used in England and France respectively.

54. The English Present Perfect: *il y a...que, depuis*

A. *Il y a* + time + *que* (introducing a verb)

Literally, this pattern follows that of **C** above, but the translation is smoother if the *il y a* becomes "for" and falls to the end of the sentence before the temporal signifier. The French verb in the **present tense** is translated into the **English present perfect**. The second translation below is preferable to the first.

Example

1. **Il y a** deux heures **que** j'<u>attends</u>.
   a. There it is two hours that I <u>have been waiting</u>.
   b. I have been waiting **for** two hours.

In this example, "*j'attends*" constitutes the main subject and verb, even if they appear to be in a subordinate clause following "*que*". For a smoother translation, begin after the *que*, add "for" and the duration of time to avoid the circumlocution of "*il y a... que*" altogether. Synonyms of *Il y a* which entail the same transformation from the French present tense to the English present perfect are:

Voici... que	Here it is... that	
Voilà... que	There it is... that	
Cela* fait...que	That makes... that	*Ça is used orally.

B. Depuis

Similarly, the **present tense** of a verb is translated into the **English present perfect** after the preposition *depuis* which varies in meaning according to the time specified:

depuis   for (before an expanse of time)
             since (from one point in time)

Examples

2.   Ça fait cinq heures que nous **sommes** ici.
  a. That makes five hours that we **have been** here.
  b. We **have been** here for five hours.

3.   Nous **sommes** ici <u>depuis</u> cinq heures.
      We **have been** here <u>for</u> five hours.

4.   Philippe **est** chez nous <u>depuis</u> samedi.
      Phillip **has been** with us <u>since</u> Saturday.

Exercise D

Practice with "il y a" and "depuis" as indicators of time.

1. Il est arrivé il y a deux heures.

2. Il y a trois mois que nous lisons ce passage.

3. Cela fait quatre jours qu'elle lit ce journal[FF].

4. Elle a commencé à étudier il y a quatre jours.

5. Voilà une heure que nous attendons!

6. Ils sont déjà partis il y a une heure.

7. Cela fait un an qu'elle ne suit pas de régime[FF].

8. Il y a des théories irrésolues prônées par ce professeur.

9. Elles ne travaillent pas depuis l'été.

10. Elle est sortie tôt le matin.

11. Ils ont vécu il y a cinq cents ans.

12. Il y a presque cent cinquante ans que le Canada existe.

13. Il est au Canada depuis la Première Guerre Mondiale.

14. Il y a des hypothèses pour expliquer ce phénomène.

15. Êtes-vous malade depuis hier?

55. Impersonal Expressions: alone, or with *à* or *de*

Impersonal expressions use either *il* or *ce* with *est* to make an impersonal comment on any given situation. **Note** that *ce* is translated into English no differently than *il* (= "it"). In French, one prefers *ce* for an impersonal expression to avoid the possible confusion between two meanings for *il*: "he" and "it".

Examples

1. Il est peu probable qu'il vienne[9]!
    It is unlikely   that he will come!

2. C'est dur quand même.
    It is hard even so.

If the adjective which completes the impersonal expression is followed by an infinitive, one of the two common prepositions *à* or *de* will link it to the infinitive.

A. *À*

When the following infinitive has no direct object, *à* is used and the infinitive may be translated as a passive one. The passive construction, however, is not obligatory.

Examples

3. C'est un livre à lire.
    It's a book to be read.

4. C'est une chanson à chanter.
    It's a song to be sung.

5. C'est un film à voir.
    It's a film to be seen.

6. Le professeur est difficile à comprendre.
    The teacher is difficult to understand.

B. *De*

If the infinitive which is dependent upon the impersonal expression carries its own objects, *de* is used. This linkage is treated no differently than *à* above. Neither *à* nor *de* have any real meaning of their own, since the French infinitive includes the differentiated English particle "to" [do sth.].

Examples

7. Il est difficile de comprendre ce passage.
    It is difficult to understand this passage.
8. Il est important d'étudier vos verbes.
    It is important to study your verbs.

---

9. *vienne:* subjunctive form (cf. Chapter 14 for the use of the subjunctive with impersonal expressions).

Exercise E

1. C'est à elle de choisir la traduction préferable.

2. Ceci est l'énumération des actions à accomplir.

3. La fonction du silence sera à[10] analyser en détail.

4. Il est juste de dire que la Bible peut faire allusion à une époque fixée par Yahwé pour l'accomplissement d'un but précis.

5. Hier, j'ai commencé à douter.

6. Voilà une semaine que nous ne pouvons pas penser à autre chose.

7. À partir de la semaine prochaine je serai prêt à voyager.

8. Il n'est pas encore temps de rassembler les troupeaux.

9. Il commence à lire lentement.

10. Nous parlerons à haute voix.

56. Nicene Creed

Exercise F

Analyze the present, past and future tenses of all the regular and irregular verbs in the Creed (*Symbole*) before translating it. Translate the reflexive pron. in *s'est fait* as "made himself"... or "was made" (passive).

---

10. *être à:* to have to be.

Le Symbole de Nicée

       Nous croyons en un seul Dieu,
       le Père tout-puissant,
       créateur du ciel et de la terre,
4   de l'univers visible et invisible.

       Nous croyons en un seul Seigneur, Jésus Christ,
       le fils unique de Dieu,
       né du Père avant tous les siècles.
8   Il est Dieu, né de Dieu,
       lumière née de la lumière,
       vrai Dieu, né du vrai Dieu.
       Engendré, non pas créé,
12   de même nature que[11] le Père ;
       et par lui tout a été fait.
       Pour nous hommes, et pour notre salut,
       il est descendu du ciel ;
16   Par l'Esprit Saint il a pris chair[FF] de la Vierge Marie,
          et s'est fait homme.
       Crucifié pour nous sous Ponce Pilate,
       il a souffert sa passion, et fut mis au tombeau.
20   Il a été ressuscité le troisième jour,
          conformément aux Écritures,
          et il est monté au ciel :
       il est assis à la droite du Père.
24   Il reviendra dans la gloire
          pour juger les vivants et les morts,
          et son règne n'aura pas de fin.

       Nous croyons en l'Esprit Saint, qui est Seigneur
28   et qui donne la vie,
      Il procède du Père et du Fils.
      Avec le Père et le Fils, il reçoit même adoration et même gloire, il a parlé par les
      prophètes.
32   Nous croyons en l'Église, une, sainte, catholique et apostolique.
      Nous reconnaissons un seul baptême pour le pardon des péchés.
      Nous attendons la résurrection des morts,
      et la vie du monde à venir. Amen.

---

11. *même... que*: same... as (comparative construction; cf. Ch.10).

57. BASIC VOCABULARLY: Chapters 4-6

NOUNS

chose (f.)	thing
colère (f.)	anger
compréhension (f.)	understanding
crainte (f.)	fear
croyance (f.)	belief
église (f.)	church
ennemi/ ennemie (m.f.)	enemy
esprit (m.)	spirit, *mind*[FF]
l'Esprit Saint	the Holy Spirit
l'Évangile	The Gospel (Lat. *Evangelium*)
événement (m.)	event
fois (f: sg,pl.) [nb. la foi]	time/s [nb. faith]
une fois	once
à la fois	at the same time, simultaneously
gloire (f.)	glory
livre (m.)	book
matin (m.)	morning
miséricorde (f.)	mercy
pardon (m.)	forgiveness; sorry! (colloquial)
péché (m.)	sin
politique (f.)	politics, policy
semaine (f.)	week
soir (m.)	evening
soutien (m.)	support

RELATIVE PRONOUNS

qui	who, which (nominative case)
que, qu'	whom, which (accusative case)

PREPOSITIONS

à partir de (prep.)	from, beginning with
depuis (prep.)	since; for (quantity of time)
en (prep.)	in (year, etc.);
	in, by, while (vb. -ing)
jusqu'à	until

pour (prep.)	for (& n) *or* for (vb -ing)
	to, in order to (& inf)
selon	according to

ADJECTIVE

saint/e (m./f.)	holy (Lat. *sanctus*)

ESSENTIAL ADVERBS

Listed in §50.

il y a	ago
quand même	even so, all the same
peut être	perhaps

ESSENTIAL VERBS

appeler	to call, name	aller	to go
assister[FF] (à)	to be present (at)	faire	to do, make, cause
écouter	to listen to	suivre	to follow
essayer (de)	to try (to)	tenir	to hold
frapper	to hit; strike (*fig.*)	venir	to come
parler (de)	to speak (about)	devenir	to become
penser (à)	to think (about)	dire	to say, tell
trouver	to find	écrire	to write
travailler[FF]	to work	lire	to read
		rire	to laugh
		boire	to drink
		croire (en)	to believe (in)

choisir	to choose
connaître	to know, to be acquainted with

mourir	to die	recevoir	to receive
naître	to be born	voir	to see
vivre	to live; experience	savoir	to know (how)

mettre	to put	
prendre	to take	
apprendre	1) to learn	2) to teach (à qn)
comprendre	1) to understand	2) to comprise, include

il y a	there is; there are		
c'est	it's, it is	ce sont	there are

93

MODAL VERBS

devoir	must, to have to, ought; owe (not modal)
pouvoir	can, to be able to, may
vouloir	to wish to, to want to

7

NEGATIVES AND RELATIVE PRONOUNS

58. Alternative Negative Terms

There are ten alternative ways to express a negative idea. Like the basic ***ne...pas*** which surrounds the verb or its auxiliary, all of these alternatives can be so positioned. However, they can also float around in the sentence, causing some confusion to the uninitiated.

A. Examples of the Regular Construction

1. Je **n'ai pas** de livres!
   I do not have any books!

2. Je **n'ai pas** eu l'occasion de l'essayer.
   I have not had the chance to try it <u>or</u> I did not have ...

3. Je **ne** suis **pas** allé chez le médecin.
   I have not gone to the doctor <u>or</u> I did not go to the doctor.

4. Je **ne** peux **pas** aller chez le médecin.
   I cannot go to the doctor.

In the first example above, the negative forms **ne...pas** surround the main verb *avoir* as conjugated in the first person singular. In the second, the same verb acts as an auxiliary verb and the main verb, *avoir*, as its past participle *eu*. In the past (*passé composé*) tense, the negative always surrounds the auxiliary verb, as seen also in the case of *être* in the third example. Modal verbs, because they act like auxiliary verbs, also attract the **ne...pas** negative forms to their sides.

B. The Ten Alternatives

For the alternative forms, one can always recognize the fixed position of *ne*. The second part of the pair is more flexible. Sometimes, this second part wanders to a position of stress, either at the beginning of a sentence, or before certain words which require emphasis.

	point	not (emphatic)
	rien	nothing, not...anything
	plus	no longer
	que	only, not...but/except
	personne	nobody, not...anyone
	jamais	never, not...ever
ne [+ verb]	guère	hardly, scarcely
	ni...ni (correlatives)	neither...nor
	aucun, aucune (m. & f.)	no + noun, not...any
	nul, nulle (m. & f.)	no + noun, not...any

C. Examples of Regular Positioning with Translations

In the following translations, the majority of sentences furnish two possible translations. The first option places the negative meaning in the negative particle (*pas* or its equivalent) which functions as a pronoun, direct object of the verb; the second option makes the verb itself negative and converts the negative particle into an affirmative meaning (as below). Negative verbs are commonly expressed as contractions in English (e.g. don't, doesn't, can't, etc.), but these have been avoided below for the sake of clarity.

1   Je **n'**ai **rien** à dire.
  a. I have <u>nothing</u> to say.
  b. I do <u>not</u> have <u>anything</u> to say.

2.   Il **n'**a **plus** d'eau.
  a. He has <u>no more</u> water.
  b. He <u>no longer</u> has <u>any</u> water.

3.   Ils **n'**ont **qu'**une solution.[1]
  a. They have not <u>but</u> one solution.
  b. They have <u>only</u> one solution.

---

1. "They have not but one solution" belongs to Shakespeare's epoch!

4. Elle **ne** voit **personne** sur le balcon.
   a. She sees <u>nobody</u> on the balcony.
   b. She does <u>not</u> see <u>anyone</u> on the balcony.

5. Nous **n'allons jamais** à ce marché.
   a. We <u>never</u> go to this market.
   b. We do <u>not ever</u> go to this market.

6 Vous **ne** pouvez **jamais** apprécier mon point de vue.
   a. You can <u>never</u> appreciate my point of view.
   b. You cannot <u>ever</u> appreciate my point of view.

7. Je **n'ai guère** commencé à travailler.
   I have <u>scarcely</u> begun to work.

8. Nous **n'avons ni** la patience **ni** le courage.
   a. We have <u>neither</u> the patience <u>nor</u> the courage.
   b. We do <u>not</u> have <u>either</u> the patience <u>or</u> the courage.

9. Je **n'ai aucune** idée!
   a. I have <u>no</u> idea!
   b. I do <u>not</u> have <u>any</u> idea!

10. Il **n'a nul** intérêt à ce sujet.
   a. He has <u>no</u> interest in this subject.
   b. He does <u>not</u> have <u>any</u> interest in this subject.

D. Examples of Irregular Positioning with Translations

Notice that the *ne* remains before the verb, but is rarely translated. The negative emphasis is communicated by the second half of the negative when placed at the beginning.

1. **Rien n'est** arrivé!
   <u>Nothing</u> happened!

2. **Personne ne** me comprend.
   <u>Nobody</u> understands me.

3.　　**Jamais** il **n'**acceptera cette décision.
　　　　<u>Never</u> will he accept this decision.

4.　　**Aucune** des deux personnes **ne** sait la réponse.
　　　　<u>Neither</u> of the two people　　knows the answer.

59. Only or Anything But/Except: *ne... que*

In the example below, the *que* wanders as well, but this time towards the words it seeks to emphasize further on in the sentence. The translation ("only") requires some adjustments of the word order, especially to bring the direct object of the verb ("common words") closer to the verb ("find") by displacing the phrase (*dans le dictionnaire*). In each case, however, the "only" or "but" directly precedes the direct object which receives the emphasis ("common words"). When an English negative is used, it is sometimes necessary to add an "anything".

　1.　Je **ne** trouve dans le dictionnaire **que** les mots communs.
　　　a. I find <u>only</u> common words in the dictionary.
　　　b. I do <u>not</u> find <u>anything but</u> common words in the dictionary.
　　　c. I do <u>not</u> find <u>anything except</u> common words....

Translation Hint: Whenever a *ne* arises without a *pas* immediately following its verb, suspend judgement on its negative value until the complementary negative particle in the same clause has been located. If *que* (only) is the complement, the verb is not really negative. Only two other cases might arise which could account for a *ne* lacking a negative value: COPS (§63) and the peonastic *ne* in subordinate clauses (§132).

　2.　On <u>ne</u> peut expliquer l'absence de Dieu dans le monde <u>que</u> par la présence accablante du mal humain.
　　　One can <u>only</u> explain the apparent absence of God in the world by the overwhelming presence of human evil.

Exercise A

　1. Rien. Personne. Depuis deux jours que je suis revenue chez moi, rien ne se passe, personne ne vient.[2]

　2. Il n'est jamais libre le soir, ni le weekend, ni en vacances.

---

2. The first three sentences of Exercise A are adopted liberally from the work of Madeleine Chapsal, *Une soudaine solitude* (Paris: Librairie Arthème Fayard, 1995).

3. Ami adorable, toujours souriant, serviable, prêt à aider, donnant sans jamais demander de l'aide.

4. Ne blâme pas avant d'avoir examiné, réfléchis d'abord, puis exprime tes reproches (Ecclésiastique [Ec.] 11:7).

5. On dit, «Donne à l'homme pieux et ne viens pas en aide au pécheur,» mais nous sommes tous des pécheurs.

6. Elles ne souffrent la faim ni la fatigue et n'abandonnent jamais leur tâche (Ec. 16:27b)

7. Aucune n'a jamais heurté l'autre et jamais elles ne désobéissent à sa parole (Ec. 16:28).

8. Nos pères ont péché: ils ne sont plus; et nous, nous portons leurs fautes (Lm 5:7).

9. Des esclaves dominent sur nous, nul ne délivre nos enfants de leur main (Lm 5:8).

10. Jésus dit, «Personne n'a condamné la femme» et Marie-Madaleine se met d'accord avec lui en disant, «Personne». Jésus parle de nouveau et dit, «Va et ne pèche plus» (cf. Jn 8:10-11).

60. The Use of *non* for *ne*

The particle *non* is the traditional word for "no" and "not" which may be found alone, in place of "pas" or beside "pas" for emphasis.

Examples

1. Il s'arrête **pas** loin de là. Il s'arrête **non** loin de là (Flaubert, *Éducation sentimentale*)[3]
    He stops **not** far from there.

2. Il s'arrête, **non pas** inquiet, mais curieux[FF] (G. Bernanos).
    He stops, **not** worried, but careful.

3. **Non plus** simplement une idée intellectuelle de Dieu, mais bien plus une expérience vivante.
    No longer simply an intellectual idea of God, but much more a living experience.

---

3. Examples 1 & 2 here are cited in *Le bon usage,* 2nd ed. André Goosse (Louvain-la-Neuve: Duculot, 1993) p. 971.

61. Either/Neither: *non plus* to reinforce, not create a negative.

If the expression *non plus* follows a negative verb (*ne...pas*), it is not equivalent to *ne* [verb] *plus* ("no longer"). When the previous sentence is likewise negative, the effect is equivalent to the English *either*. For example, one person says "I am not going swimming today" and the other answers "I am not going **either**" (= *non plus*) or "Neither am I".

Example

1. On <u>ne</u> tirera <u>pas</u> **non plus** la conclusion que la dialectique de la mort et de la vie est une dialectique fermée.[4]
   a. One would <u>not</u> draw the conclusion **either** that the dialectic between life and death is a closed dialectic.

   > *or*

   b. **Neither** would we draw the conclusion that the dialectic...
Note the position of "either" after the direct object ("the conclusion") in 1.a above. English has a strong tendency to aim the action of a verb directly at the object without tolerating any obstacle between the verb and its direct object. A translator does well to facilitate this urge by removing obstacles to this path! A direct object which is a pronoun, instead of a noun, cannot cause any trouble, since it necessarily precedes the verb.

Exercise B

Sometimes, the alternatives listed above are combined for even more interesting results. See what you can do with the following. **Hint:** To avoid double negatives in English, choose one negative meaning and convert the other negative particles into their affirmative meanings.

1. Je ne pense qu'à sa visite.

2. Mon ami ne vient jamais plus à l'université.

3. Cet égoïste ne donne jamais rien à personne.

4. Elle habite un appartement qui n'offre guère de confort.

5. Je ne reverrai jamais plus Pierre.

6. On ne donne plus au mot "charisme" le sens de talent exceptionnel que quelqu'un a reçu à sa naissance.

---

4. *tirera*: will draw; the future can become a conditional (cf. Ch.8, §74).

7. En histoire des idées et des mouvements religieux, rien n'apparaît jamais sur une terre entièrement vierge.

8. Du point de vue chrétien, il ne peut y avoir qu'une théologie du scandale irréductible de la croix: celle qui comprend la croix comme une crise (Hans Urs von Balthasar).

9. Il ne veut qu'aller au cinéma quand elle veut lire.

10. Le soir il n'y a plus personne à l'université.

62. Correlative Conjunctions

The negative use of *ne...ni...ni* (neither...nor) introduces the principle of correlative conjunctions. Affirmative ones are even simpler than *ni...ni* since they do not have to be related to a *ne*. Here is a list of common correlatives:

FRENCH		**ENGLISH**
et...	et...	both ... and
ou...	ou...	either... or
soit...	soit[5]...	be it.... be it (either...or)
ou bien...	ou bien...	or rather or (more emphatic)
ou alors...	ou alors...	or then or (")
plus...	plus...	the more... the more
de même que...	de même	in the same way as... so

Examples

1. L'événement a eu lieu soit bien, soit mal.
   a. The event took place, be it well or badly.
   b. The event took place for better or worse.

2. Plus ça change, plus c'est la même chose.
   The more it changes, the more it is the same thing!

3. De même que chaque mot prononcé évoque un aspect de Dieu...., de même chaque instant du jour se sanctifie (Aron, 76-77).
   Just as each word <when> pronounced evokes an aspect of God, so each instant of the day is sanctified.

---

5. *soit*: subjunctive form of *être*; cf. Chapter 14, §128.

Exercise C

The following sentences have been adapted from *Le bon usage* (§1030-1033, pp.1563-70).[6]
This exercise is meant to illustrate the wide range of literary usage possible.

1. Rien, ni les vieux jardins reflétés par les yeux, ni la clarté de cette lampe ne retiendra
   ce coeur (Mallarmé, *Poésies*).

2. Il faut[7] ou croire, ou nier, ou douter (Pascal, *Pensées*).

3. Il est accompagné et de sa soeur et de sa mère (Gambetta).

4. Il n'a ni père ni mère.

5. Il ne boit ni ne mange.

6. Je ne veux, ni ne dois, ni ne peux obéir.

7. Il ne parle à personne ni de ses affaires, ni de ses projets.

8. Personne n'est si éloquent ni si profond.

9. Il n'y a là rien d'étonnant ni de rare.

10. Ni la douceur ni la force ne peuvent rien.

63. COPS

COPS is a mnemonic device to help you remember four common verbs whose negative
can exclude *pas* and still signify the negative: i.e.; *ne* by itself can be negative before the
following four verbs:

Cesser	to cease, desist
Oser	to dare
Pouvoir	to be able
Savoir	to know

---

6. See n.2 for the complete bibliography.
7. *Il faut*: It is necessary (impersonal expression from *falloir*).

The omission of *pas* is optional because these verbs are used so often. Nevertheless, all four verbs are often found with *pas* as well as with any of its replacements.

Example

Je **ne** sais quoi dire.
I **do not** know what to say.

64. The Relative Pronoun as Object in a Phrase: *qui*

In Chapter Four, the relative pronouns *qui* and *que* were introduced in simplified terms (§32). Please remember that *qui* can be either a person or a thing when it is the subject of the sentence (nominative case). However, if it follows a preposition,[8] it must always be translated as a person, *whom* (object of the preposition).

Examples

1. Je ne sais jamais **à qui** je dois rendre la clé.
   I never know **to whom** I ought to return the key.

2. **À qui** penses-tu?
   Of whom are you thinking?

3. **Avec qui** travaillent-ils?
   With whom are they working?

4. Il a été prêtre sous la papauté **de qui**?
   He was a priest under **whose** papacy?

65. Combinations and Usage of *lequel, laquelle*

Lequel is a combination, in itself, of the definite article plus *quel*. Both parts reflect the number and gender of their antecedent (the noun to which they refer): e.g.

lequel, laquelle, lesquels, lesquelles = which?, whom, which.
(m.sg.)   (f.sg)   (m.pl)   (f.pl)

The antecedent can be either a person or a thing. All four forms are regularly used as either subjects or objects of the verb in interrogative sentences: e.g.

---

8. See the list of common prepositions in Chapter One (§12).

1. Il y a deux sortes d'espoir: celle qui est finie et celle qui est infinie.
   Laquelle avez-vous?
   There are two kinds of hope, the kind which is finite and that which is infinite.
   Which (kind) do you have?

In this example, the antecedent is *sortes*, as reflected by *celle* (one of the kinds) and *Laquelle*. Because these pronouns have the advantage of specifying the gender and number of the noun to which they refer, they are sometimes preferred over *qui* as objects of prepositions (whom, which), especially when the antecedent to which they refer is potentially ambiguous. In the following examples, the main clauses will be underlined and the subordinate ones bracketed off to distinguish them.

Note that, unlike *qui* as object of a preposition, these pronouns can still replace objects as well as persons.

2. L'ami de Georges et l'amie de Jeanne [avec **laquelle** nous avons parlé hier] sont déjà partis.
   George's friend and Jane's friend [with **whom** we spoke yesterday] have already left.

In this case, the antecedent *l'amie* is distinguished from the male friend by the feminine singular gender of the pronoun *laquelle*. We only spoke with Jane's female friend yesterday, excluding George and his friend. The same sentence might be modified in the following manner:

3. L'ami de Georges et l'amie de Jeanne [avec **lesquels** nous avons parlé hier] sont déjà partis.
   The friends of George and Jane [with **whom** we spoke yesterday] have already left.

When combined with the prepositions *à* and *de*, *lequel*, *laquelle*, *lesquels* and *lesquelles* contract whenever the articles contract: e.g.
to whom/which = *auquel* (m.sg.), *auxquels* (m.pl.), *auxquelles* (f.pl.)
of whom/which; from whom = *duquel*, *desquels* (m.), *desquelles* (f.)

Examples

4. Notre nouveau texte [**auquel** il se réfère] est une amélioration.
   Our new text [**to which** he is refering] is an improvement.

Texte is clearly a masculine noun, reflected by both the adjective *nouveau* and the relative pronoun *auquel* which both refer to it.

5.   Les personnes [**desquelles** ils parlent] sont arrivées.
     The people   [**of whom** they are speaking] have arrived.

Clearly *personne* is a feminine noun, since both the pronoun *desquelles* and the past participle *arrivées* (conjugated as expected with *être*) are feminine (and plural). A possible substitution or synonym for *desquelles* is *dont*.

66. Dont

Dont = *de* + relative pronoun; a simplified synonym for *de qui, duquel, de laquelle, desquels, desquelles*.

One must be aware of all the diverse meanings of *de*! The most obvious use of *de* is in the possessive (= of). In this case, the clearest translation of the relative pronoun *dont* is "whose". Some English speakers prefer not to use "whose" unless a human being is actually doing the possessing. In this case, they would choose 1a or 1b below.

1.   La lettre [**dont** l'adresse est fausse] n'arrivera jamais.
   a.   The letter [of which the address is incorrect] will never arrive
   b.   *or*   [the address of which is incorrect]
   c.   The letter whose address[9] is incorrect will never arrive.

In the above sentence, the thing possessed ("l'adresse") is right beside *dont* ("whose"). Sometimes the thing possessed by the relative pronoun *dont* is separated from it by an entire, or almost complete, subordinate clause. In the English translation, it is best to bring the thing possessed together with *dont* (whose), as preferred in 2b and 3b below.

2.   Cette harmonie [**dont** les savants attribuent **l'invention** à Mozart] est magnifique.
   a.   This harmony, [**of which** scholars attribute **the invention** to Mozart] ....
   b.   This harmony, [**whose invention** scholars attribute to Mozart], is magnificent.

3.   Le compositeur [**dont** ils célèbrent **l'anniversaire**] est Mozart.
   a.   The composer [**of whom** they are celebrating **the birthday**] is Mozart.
   b.   The composer [**whose birthday** they are celebrating] is Mozart.

____

9. *whose address*: the address of which. Similarly in 2b. below, "whose invention" should be "the invention of which", if the English relative pronouns "who" and "whose" are restricted to people as referents. Nevertheless, because the proper circumlocution is rarely used today, even in writing, it seems awkward.

67. Common Verbs Followed by *De*

Some very useful verbs to memorize which arise frequently with *dont* are:

avoir besoin de	need (to have need of)
avoir envie de	desire (to have a fancy for)
avoir peur de	fear (to have fear of)
il s'agit de	it concerns (it is a question/matter of)
faire la connaissance de	become acquainted with
parler de	talk about

Because English uses the more direct expressions above, there is no need to translate the "of", even within *dont*. Cf. 1b and 2b below.

Examples

1. L'examen [**dont** j'ai peur] aura lieu demain.
    a. The exam [**of which** I have fear] will take place tomorrow.
    b. The exam [**which** I fear] will take place tomorrow.

2. La personne [**dont** il s'agit] est absente.
    a. The person [**of whom** it is a question] is absent.
    b. The person [**whom** it concerns] is absent.
        or (even)
    c. The person [concerned/in question] is absent.

Exercise D

1. Je cherche le texte que le professeur a recommandé.

2. Les étudiants qui étudient régulièrement vont certainement réussir.

3. L'ami à qui j'écris est à Paris en ce moment.

4. Je ne peux pas acheter les livres dont j'ai envie.

5. L'homme avec qui j'ai parlé dans le train est archéologue.

6. Ne prenez pas les papiers dont nous avons besoin.

7. Le professeur nous[10] a expliqué la méthode avec laquelle il a étudié l'art préhistorique de cette région.

8. Pierre est un ami avec qui je ne peux travailler facilement.

9. Je désire le livre dont j'ai lu la critique[FF] dans le journal[FF].

10. Proust est un auteur dont on reconnaît facilement le style.

11. Le cours de français est un cours auquel les étudiants vont avec plaisir.

12. Les professeurs doivent parler des livres auxquels les étudiants s'intéressent.

13. Le château de Fontainebleau, auquel le professeur d'histoire a fait allusion, est au sud de Paris.

14. Stephen Hatfield est un compositeur dont les Canadiens admirent le génie.

15. Les catastrophes dont on a peur n'arrivent[FF] que rarement.

16. Voici un livre dont je n'aurai plus jamais besoin.

17. Voici un document dont l'authenticité n'est pas encore certaine.

18. Les films dont on parle souvent ne sont pas toujours bons.

19. J'ai lu le livre de Camus dont le professeur a parlé en classe.

20. N'achetons que les livres dont nous avons besoin.

---

10. nous: to us (indirect object of the verb *expliquer*). Cf. Chapter 9, §84.

68. The Relative Pronouns with *ce*

These pronouns are used when there is no explicit antecedent to refer to things abstract or concrete.

ce qui = that which (subject of a subordinate sentence), what
ce que = that which (direct object of the dependent clause), what
ce dont = that of which, what
tout ce qui = all that which *or* all that[11]

The simplified translation, "what" does not always work, but it is likelier to provide a smoother translation in the last case (*ce dont*).

Examples

1.   **Ce qui** rend ce passage difficile, **c'est** le mot en latin.
   a.   **That which** renders this passage difficult [it] is the word in Latin.
   b.   **What**   renders this passage difficult is the Latin word.

Note that the *c'* ("it" before "is") at the beginning of the second half of the sentence is redundant in English translation. This often occurs in sentences beginning with *ce qui*.

2.   **Ce que** tu penses est extraordinaire.
   a.   **That which** you are thinking is extraordinary.
   b.   **What** you are thinking is extraordinary.

3.   **Ce dont** ils ont besoin ne se trouve pas ici.
   a.   **That of which** they have need is not (found) here.
   b.   **What** they need is not (found) here.

4.   **Tout ce qui** est offense à la dignité de l'homme est infâme.
   All that is offensive to human dignity is loathsome.

---

11. For a more detailed analysis of *tout* in all its manifestations, see Chapter 9.

Exercise E

1. Je sais ce que vous voulez dire.

2. Nous savons ce que le médecin dira.

3. Il sera au courant de ce qui se passe dans la rue.

4. C'est Jacques Cartier qui, en 1534, a revendiqué la possession du Canada au nom de la France.

5. Ce qui rend la défaite de Montcalm si tragique, c'est la blessure mortelle qu'il a reçue[12] le 13 septembre 1759.

6. Ce dont nous faisons profession, c'est la vérité.

7. Ce que les théologiens enseignent ne va pas pour autant à l'encontre de la logique.

8. Ce qui va d'emblée au coeur du problème peut choquer.

9. C'est là ce qu'il y a d'extraordinaire.

10. Ce qui est frappant, c'est le manque de compassion au sein du gouvernement actuel[FF].

11. Ce que j'aime dans la vie, c'est dormir (Saint-Exupéry).

12. Ce qui m'émeut[13] si fort de ce petit prince endormi, c'est sa fidélité pour une fleur, c'est l'image d'une rose qui rayonne en lui comme la flamme d'une lampe, même[14] quand il dort (Saint-Exupéry).

---

12. *reçue*: without the feminine inflection (*-e*), the past participle would be *reçu* from *recevoir*.
13. *m'émeut*: moves me.
14. *même*: even (cf. Chapter 9).

69. Reading: Analysis of *Dominus Jesus*

Exercise F

Translate the following extract (with modifications) from *Le Monde* (6 September 2000), a Parisian newspaper. Vocabulary is provided for the words highlighted in bold. Other words can be found in the following list of Basic Vocabulary for Chapters 7 to 9 (§95). Note that Cardinal Ratzinger was not yet Pope Benedict XVI in the year 2000.

Stylistic Note: French and English conventions concerning punctuation and capitalization do not always agree. The run-on sentence, using commas in French where English would require full stops, is not acceptable in English. Minor adjustments must therefore be made to conform with English conventions. Secondly, French makes less frequent use of capital letters than English does. Nouns in the title of a book, for example, are not capitalized in French after the first word. In the passage below, the French adjectives for Catholic and Christian, Buddhist and Orthodox are not capitalized either, whereas English prefers the capital for distinguishing such key words. Finally, repetition is considered a weakness in English, where French requires it. In lists, for example (e.g. "du relativisme, du subjectivisme..."), only the first "of the" is required in English. Furthermore, English usually terminates a list with an "and" before the last element to lend the sentence a sense of finality. Sometimes the "and" must be supplied.

Dominus Jesus
Vatican, le 5 septembre 2000

Le cardinal allemand Josef Ratzinger, préfet (depuis 1981) de la Congrégation pour la Doctrine de la Foi, est l'auteur de ce document **approuvé** par le pape. Réaffirmant la supériorité de la religion catholique, le document est une douche froide pour tous ceux qui **font profession** d'oecuménisme - le rapprochement entre les confessions chrétiennes séparées - et **de** dialogue avec les religions non chrétiennes.

Au pape appartiennent les gestes symboliques, **les baisers** de **paix** avec les "*frères séparés*" protestants, anglicans ou orthodoxes, les visites dans les synagogues ou mosquées, **les poignées de main** aux bouddhistes ou hindouistes. Au cardinal Ratzinger, "gardien" de la doctrine, le devoir de "défendre" la foi catholique, selon lui **menacée** par les dangers du relativisme, du subjectivisme et d'une fausse conception du pluralisme.

Le cardinal Ratzinger réaffirme la plénitude de la révélation chrétienne:

"Les mots, les oeuvres et l'existence historique de Jésus ... portent en eux le caractère complet et définitif des voies du salut de Dieu." Il ajoute que **seuls** l'Ancien et le Nouveau Testament sont *"des textes inspirés"*. **Seul** le christianisme mérite d'être **qualifié de** *"foi"*, les autres confessions étant de simples *"croyances"* qui, si elles peuvent être des trésors de sagesse, ne **relèvent** que **de** la **seule** *"expérience religieuse"*.

Selon le cardinal, Jésus-Christ n'est pas *"une figure historique particulière"*, à l'image d'un Bouddha, d'un Socrate ou d'un grand "sage" de l'humanité. Il est *"l'unique médiateur entre Dieu et les hommes et le sauveur universel"*. Il n'y a pas d'**autre** voie de salut **que** le christianisme. C'est une vérité *"définitive"*. *"La volonté salvifique de Dieu est manifestée et accomplie, une fois pour toutes, dans le mystère de l'Incarnation, de la mort et de la Résurrection du Fils de Dieu."* Toutes les autres expériences du divin *"ne peuvent **tirer** leur sens et leur valeur que de celle du Christ. Elles ne peuvent pas être considérées comme parallèles et complémentaires."*

VOCABULARY

autre ... que	other than
baiser (nm)	kiss
poignée de main (nf)	handshake
seul (adj)	only, alone

Verbs

font profession de	make profession of = profess
relever de	to arise from, to be a matter/product of
tirer	draw
approuvé, menacée (pp.)	(as both vb. and adj.); cf. Ch.3 §25.
qualifié de (pp.)	qualified as, styled

8

VERBS:
IMPERFECT, CONDITIONAL, IMPERSONAL...

70. Imperfect Tense

Take the root of the present participle of any verb and add endings similar to those of the present tense (2nd and 3rd conjugations for the singular), but with an *ai* added before the regular singular and third person plural endings. In the first and second plural forms, the extra vowel is *i*.

Être (inf.: to be), **Étant** (pres. part. being)

j'	**étais**	I used to be, I was
tu	**étais**	you...
il, elle, on	**était**	
nous	**étions**	
vous	**étiez**	
ils, elles	**étaient**	

Again, the correct translation depends upon a hierarchy of choices depending upon the context. The following order of choices is recommended for regular verbs, such as *demander* (to ask):

je demandais

a. **I was asking** = continuous or progressing action in the past
b. **I used to ask** = habitual action in the past
c. **I asked** = background information

The above hierarchy of choices must be adjusted for five cases. The last choice above (c) becomes first choice for the following verbs:

avoir	**j'avais**	I had (possibly: was having)
être	**j'étais**	I was (possibly: was being)
comprendre	**je comprenais**	I understood
savoir	**je savais**	I knew
vouloir	**je voulais**	I wanted (possisbly: was wanting)
pouvoir	**je pouvais**	I could

Examples

The context dictates which translation is best suited to it.

1. Nous demandions la réponse avant la question.
   We were asking for the answer before the question.

2. Nous allions au parc le dimanche.
   We used to go to the park on Sundays.

3. Elle arrivait au bout de son discours.
   She was arriving/arrived at the end of her speech.

In both 1 and 2 above, the simple past (asked, arrived) is as possible as the first option. The "was/were -ing" option is preferable in most cases in order to maintain the nuance of an action which is ongoing. However in #3, "arrived" sounds better.

71. Conditional

The same endings placed on the future root produce the conditional tense, best translated by "**would**". Since the future tense is usually built upon the infinitive, look for the infinitive form first, which must include "**r**". The same sentences above in the conditional would be:

1. Nous **demander**ions   la réponse avant la question.
   We would ask for   the answer before the question.

2. Nous **ir**ions   au parc   le dimanche.
   We would go   to the park   on Sundays.

3. Il **arriver**ait   au bout de son discours.
   He would arrive   at the end of his speech.

In the first two examples above, only the "**i**" following the infinitive distinguishes the conditional from the future tense.

114

72. Conditional of *pouvoir*

The one exception to the translation rule of using "would" for the conditional in English, arises with *pouvoir*. The possibility of translating this verb "Would [you] be able" is unnecessarily cumbersome. "**Could**" is simpler:

Examples

4. **Pourrais**-tu fermer la porte?
   a. Would you be able to close the door?
   b. **Could** you close the door?

5. **Pourriez**-vous venir demain?
   a. Would you be able to come tomorrow?
   b. **Could** you come tomorrow?

73. Conditional of *devoir*

Although the conditional form of *devoir* could be translated "would have to", this is not always an option. It is easier just to think "should" for any occurrence of a conditional form of this verb.

Examples

1. Il devrait s'intéresser à leur discours.
   He should be interested in their speech.

2. Nous devrions prêter attention à ce nouvel appel.
   We should pay attention to this new appeal.

74. The Future as Conditional

A simple future may express a present fact which the author considers probable, as if he or she were placing him- or herself at the moment when the opinion is verified. Such a future opinion which seems probable is best translated by the conditional in English and is found most often in cases of *avoir* and *être* (as in the first example below):

1. Pour qui donc a-t-on sonné la cloche[FF] des morts? Ah! mon Dieu, ce **sera** pour Mme Rousseau (Proust, *À la recherche du temps perdu*).
   For whom then has the bell tolled? Oh! my God,
   that **would be** for Mrs. Rousseau.

2. On **préférera** penser que l'auteur de 2 Thess. ignorait[FF] le grec littéraire.
   One **would prefer** to think that the author of 2 Thess. was unfamiliar with literary Greek.

75. Compound Tenses

When the imperfect, future or conditional is used in the auxiliary verb (être, avoir), translate the verbs literally, word by word, by considering the tense of the auxiliary verb before adding the past participle.

Note that this rule of translation must treat the auxiliary verb *être* with verbs of motion as if it were "have" in English. The tense of *être* (translated "have") should still be considered before the past participle.

Examples

1. J'**avais** <u>posé</u> la question trop tard.　　　(imperfect of aux. *avoir*).
   I **had** <u>asked</u> the question too late.

2. Il **était** <u>allé</u> au parc.　　　(imperfect of aux. *être*).
   He **had** <u>gone</u> to the park.

3. Vous **aurez** <u>payé</u> cher votre visite.　　　(future of aux. *avoir*).
   You **will have** <u>paid</u> dearly for your visit.

4. Nous **serons** <u>partis</u>!　　　(future of aux. *être*).
   We **will have** <u>left</u>!

5. Elle **aurait** <u>eu</u> mal à la tête!　　　(conditional of *avoir*).
   She **would have** <u>had</u> a headache!

6. Ils **seraient** <u>arrivés</u> aujourd'hui　　　(conditional of *être*).
   They **would have** <u>arrived</u> today.

116

Exercise A

1. Je voulais poser une question au médecin.

2. J'allais répondre à votre question.

3. Que ferais-tu à ma place? Moi? J'irais au Québec.

4. Nous voudrions commencer par considérer le rapprochement comme une solution tout à fait raisonnable.

5. Malgré les inconvénients[FF], les personnes âgées diraient que la vieillesse apporte la sagesse.

6. Pourrions-nous recommencer? Cela serait préférable!

7. Nous ne pouvions guère apercevoir au loin le clocher.

8. Or Jésus aimait Marthe et sa soeur et Lazare; et quand il avait appris que celui-ci était malade, il a demeuré deux jours encore dans le lieu où il se trouvait (Jean 11:6).

9. "Notre ami Lazare repose, mais je vais aller le[1] réveiller" (Jean 11:11).

10. "Seigneur, s'il repose, il sera sauvé." Jésus avait parlé de sa mort, mais les disciples ont cru qu'il parlait du repos du sommeil (Jean 11:12-13).

---

1. *le*: him; direct object of the verb *réveiller* (cf. Ch.9).

76. Special Cases: More Impersonal Verbs

A. To be necessary: *falloir*

Falloir is used only in the third person singular like a modal verb, in its simplest form, leading into an infinitive. When it is necessary for someone or something (an agent) to do something, then *il faut* is followed by *que* and the following verb is conjugated in the subjunctive mood.[2]

il faut [faire qch.]: it is necessary [to do sth].
il fallait: it used to be/was necessary (ongoing necessity)
il a fallu: it was necessary
il faudra: it will be necessary
il faudrait: it would be necessary
il aura fallu: it will have been necessary
il aurait fallu: it would have been necessary.

Examples

1. Il faut étudier.
    a. It is necessary to study (literally).
    b. Studying is necessary.

2. Il faut étudier la liste des candidats.
    a. It is necessary to study the list of candidates.
    b. The list of candidates must be studied.

In the first example above, the infinitive is converted into a "gerund" (a "verbal noun" which looks like a present participle, but acts as a noun), i.e. "studying", and becomes the subject of the sentence. The change from "It is necessary" to "must" in the second example allows a smoother translation, but requires a passive infinitive ("be studied"): i.e. The direct object ("list of candidates") becomes the subject of the sentence and the impersonal pronoun *il* can be discarded. However, it is simpler to maintain the impersonal construction in some complex sentences; e.g.:

3. Il faudrait étudier la liste des candidats.
    a. It would be necessary to study the candidates' list.
    b. One would have to study the list of candidates.
    c. The list of candidates would have to be studied.

The choice of translation for #3 depends solely upon the context or the aesthetic taste of the translator.

---

2. Cf. Chapter 14, §134 for the use of *il faut que* with the subjunctive mood.

B. *se trouver:* **to be found**, often translated as merely "to be".

4.　Le manuscrit se trouve à Ottawa.
　　The manuscript is (found) in Ottawa.

Note that the reflexive pronoun is translated as a passive verb.

C. *Il reste:* **There remains**

Because the *il* of this impersonal verb is a false subject, one must seek the real subject after the verb, and discard the *il*. The first option below is too awkward.

5.　Il reste trois livres à lire.
　a.　There remain three books to be read.
　b.　Three books remain to be read.

Note that the infinitive after the preposition *à* is translated as if it were passive. This is a common occurrence.

Note also that *il* means "there" in this construction as may sometimes occur with *être* as well: e.g.

6.　Il était une fois....
　　There was once *or* There once was...

D. arriver can mean "to arrive" *or* "to happen".

7.　Cela nous arrive tout le temps.
　　That happens to us all the time.

77. To Have Just: *venir de*

It is easy to mistake *venir de* (to have just) for *venir* (to come) + *de* (from), but the context should make it clear which meaning is intended. **When *venir de* is followed by an <u>infinitive verb</u>**, it means either "has"/"have just" or "had just". For this idiom (*venir de*), the **<u>present tense</u>** in French is translated as "has/ve just" and the infinitive becomes a past participle (which results in the **<u>English present perfect</u>**).

Examples

1.　Je viens du Canada.
　　I come from Canada.

2.　Je **<u>viens de rentrer</u>** de la Chine.
　　I **<u>have just returned</u>** from China.

In the second example, the real verb is *revenir* (to return) in the **infinitive**, which is translated as a **past participle**. The first conjugated verb, *viens de*, acts as an auxiliary verb, helping the other more significant verb.

When **venir de** is put into the imperfect tense, it is translated as the pluperfect (a double past) in English.

3.   Il **venait d'entrer**.
     He **had just** **entered**.

SUMMARY

FRENCH
present tense & infinitive
       viennent de terminer
imperfect tense & infinitive
       venaient de terminer

ENGLISH
"have just" & past participle
       have just finished
"had just" & past participle
       had just finished

Exercise B

1. Nous venons d'arriver.

2. Nous venions d'arriver.

3. Ils viennent de recevoir leur diplôme.

4. Ils venaient de recevoir leur diplôme.

5. Venez-vous d'apprendre à lire?

6. Le médecin, venait-il d'écrire un livre?

7. M. et Mme. Stuart viennent d'Écosse.

8. Elle vient de naître il y a dix minutes!

9. Il venait de naître quand elle est morte.

10. Le livre d'art que je viens de recevoir est un cadeau de ma collègue.

78. Prepositions with Infinitives

A preposition which is followed by an infinitive is often translated as a present participle in English.

Examples

1. Il lit **sans comprendre** ce qu'il lit!
    He is reading **without understanding** what he is reading!

2. Il faut prier **avant d'agir**.
    It is necessary to pray **before acting.**

3. Nous parlions de la nécessité **de lire**.
    We were talking about the necessity **of reading**.

The same rule applies for past infinitives.

4. Elle commence à lire **après être entrée** dans la salle.
    a. She begins to read **after having entered** the room.
    b. She begins to read **after entering** the room.

Modern usage simplifies the French past infinitive to the present, as in 4b. **Note** that *pour* makes an exception to this rule when it is translated as "to" <u>or</u> "in order to" before an infinitive. e.g.,

5. Nous chantons **pour faire** plaisir.
    We are singing **to give** pleasure.

but

6. Il n'est là que **pour prendre** plaisir à la musique.
    a. He is there only **for taking** pleasure in the music.
    b. He is only there **to take** pleasure in the music.

Exercise C

1. Elle aurait lu le journal[FF] avant de partir.

2. Je ne sortirai pas avant d'avoir demandé pardon à ma femme.

3. Ils rencontreront une autre difficulté.

4. En considérant le problème, ils hésitent sans vraiment se décider.

5. Il se trouvera en Angleterre avant la nouvelle année.

6. Il faut rester[FF] trois jours après avoir rencontré le président.

7. Nous venions de dire la même chose.

8. Après avoir lu le texte, j'ai changé d'avis.

9. Il reste un peu de nourriture dans le sac.

10. Il est trop tard pour commencer à lire ce soir.

11. Il a fallu arrêter son discours.

12. Il était une fois un peuple superstitieux qui refusait toute croyance en Dieu.

13. Il reste[FF] deux phrases[FF] à traduire.

14. On écoute sans rien[3] comprendre.

15. Il aurait fallu s'interésser à la théologie.

---

3. *rien*: anything (direct object of *comprendre*). In translation, one jumps over *rien*, translates *sans comprendre* as a unit and then returns to *rien*.

79. Conditional Sentences: *si*

A. Protasis and Apodosis Clauses

Conditional sentences typically include the word **if** since it is necessary to introduce the condition. If the tense of the verb which follows after **if** (*si*) in the conditional half of the sentence (the protasis clause) is expressed in the imperfect, it might best be translated with the simple past in English, but might more literally be translated "were to". In the consequent clause (the apodosis clause), the present conditional presents the idea of a possibility in the immediate future, where the future auxiliary **will** becomes **would**:

Examples

1. **Iriez**-vous à Paris, **si** vous en[4] **aviez** l'occasion?
   Would you **go** to Paris, **if** you **had** (were to have) the chance?

2. Je **voudrais bien** venir, **si** j'**étais** en bonne santé.
   I **would love** to come, **if** I **were** in good health.

3. **Si** tu **venais**, elle en **serait** contente.
   If you **came** (were to come), she **would be** happy about it.

The protasis clause can sometimes be omitted when the condition is understood between interlocutors.

4. **Iriez**-vous à Paris?   Je **voudrais** aller à Paris!
   Would you **go** to Paris?   I **would like** to go to Paris!

Such conditional sentences do not necessarily have to include a conditional verb, if the idea is a simple future possibility.

5. Si je m'endors, je ne serai pas malade!
   If I go to sleep, I will not be ill!

B. Polite use of the conditional (*politesse*)

To avoid the brusque sound of the imperative, the French couch requests in the conditional or, more rarely in modern times, the subjunctive. Instead of boldly stating: "Close the door", they prefer to say: "Would you close the door". In English, we would add a "please": e.g.

6. Non "Fermez la porte" mais, "Voudriez-vous fermer la porte?"
   Not "Close the door" but, "Would you [please] close the door?"

---

4. *en*: of it *or* for it (really pleonastic; unnecessary to translate).

C. Compound sentences

In the case of a pluperfect protasis, the past conditional is translated **"would have"**.

Examples

1. **Si j'avais** étudié le document, j'**aurais** su la réponse.
   If I **had** studied the document, I **would have** known the answer.

2. **Si** je m'**étais** endormie, je n'aurais pas été malade!
   If I **had** gone to sleep, I **would** not **have** been sick!

Note that *si* can also mean "**whether**", as well as "if" or "so", but this usage is not related to the conditional.

Summary of the sequence of tenses (to be)

	protasis	apodosis
Si	PRESENT	FUTURE
If	I am (je suis)	I will be (je serai)
	IMPERFECT	CONDITIONAL
If	I were (j'étais)	I would be (je serais)
	PLUPERFECT	PAST CONDITIONAL
If	I had been (j'avais été)	I would have been (j'aurais été)
If	I had gone (j'étais allé/e)	I would not have stayed (je ne serais pas resté/e)

Exercise D

1. Si vous étiez venus, j'aurais été heureuse.

2. Pourriez-vous garder le journal[FF] d'aujourd'hui?

3. S'il avait dit quelque chose, j'aurais entendu.

4. Si j'avais été prêt à mourir pour la paix comme Gandhi, mes prières auraient été exaucées.

5. Le philosophe jurait qu'il n'écrirait plus.

6. Si la femme avait parlé, elle aurait été abandonnée.

7. S'ils devenaient riches, ils feraient le tour du monde.

8. Si j'étais à Paris, je visiterais Montmartre.

9. Les églises protestantes savaient qu'elles seraient exclues!

10. Nous voudrions regarder votre livre.

11. Si je pouvais m'endormir, je ne serais pas malade!

12. Je savais qu'il réussirait.

13. Si vous veniez, j'en[5] serais heureuse.

14. Je voudrais terminer avant midi.

---

5. *en*: about it <u>or</u> of it.

80. Readings by Catherine Rihoit and Madeleine des Rivières

Exercise E

The following poem is adapted from one written by Catherine Rihoit, novelist and linguistics professor at the Sorbonne in Paris. Originally published in *Le Monde* (2 July 1982), it also appeared in *En bonne forme*, 4th ed., p.303. In order to establish a familiar tone, the author uses *pas* alone to mean *ne...pas*.

Ah, si j'étais!...

Si j'étais Marilyn, je serais très belle mais si fragile!

Si j'étais Dieu, je serais bien embêtée...

Si j'étais une fleur, ça ne serait pas le myosotis.

Si j'étais Groucho Marx, je serais assez contente. Jerry Lewis aussi, ça pourrait aller aussi.

Si j'étais Mme Curie, je serais sur les timbres-poste.

Si j'étais Voltaire, je serais sur les billets de banque.

Arrêtez, je n'en peux plus!

Si j'étais un homme, je pourrais pas être une femme.

Si j'étais Calamity Jane ou Anny du Far West, j'aurais des beaux pistolets, ah là là!

Si j'étais Jeanne d'Arc, je m'occuperais de mes moutons, au lieu d'aller causer à ces Anglais qui ne méritent pas tant, ah non!

Si j'étais Mitterand, je serais pas allée au Panthéon.[6]

Si j'étais jeune, je referais pas les mêmes bêtises. J'en[7] ferais d'autres.

Si j'étais pêcheuse de perles, je les[8] garderais pour moi...

Si j'étais W.C. Fields, j'aimerais bien les petits enfants.

Si j'étais Chandler, ah, si j'étais Chandler[9], je boirais moins pour écrire plus, nom de Dieu!...

Si j'étais un rêve, je me réveillerais...

Arrêtez, je n'en peux plus!

---

6. Mitterand was televised walking alone in the Panthéon, the French Hall of Fame, on the night of his election as president. He was criticized for taking an ego trip.

7. *en*: of them (pronominal adverb translated after the verb in English, and at the end of the sentence; cf. Ch.9 §89). Here, it can be omitted.

8. *les*: them (direct object pronoun translated after the verb in English; cf. Ch.9 §81).

9. Chandler is an American detective author.

Exercise F

Translate the following passage from *Ozanam: un savant chez les pauvres* by the Canadian historian Madeleine des Rivières, pp.27-28. Footnotes 10 and 11 from the same source are to be translated as well. Note the differing principles of punctuation in French.

Frédéric Ozanam (1813-1853) founded the first chapter of the St. Vincent de Paul Society when he was twenty years old (1833) in response to a challenge raised by a fellow student at the Sorbonne, now the Université Paris IV in France. At this time, France was still suffering the aftershocks of the French Revolution. During a Saturday morning debate sponsored by the History Department, the fellow student taunted Ozanam with the failure of the Catholic Church to alleviate the poverty of low-income people and challenged him to do something about it personally. Despite his time-consuming studies in law, history and languages, Ozanam inspired a group of like-minded students to, initially, distribute their own scholarship money to the poor. Since then, the movement has spread all over the world with so much support that such a radical sacrifice of personal finances is no longer deemed necessary.

L'Apprentissage
Paris 1831-1833

... [Il y a un an que Louis-Philippe règne en France.] Un grand nombre de royalistes sont encore convaincus qu'il a usurpé le trône **aux dépens du** petit fils de Charles X, le duc de Bordeaux. ... Des émeutes sporadiques éclateront à Paris comme en province **au cours des** années qui suivront. La Congrégation, organisation religieuse controversée qui regroupe les chrétiens **les plus** déterminés - pas nécessairement **les plus** authentiques-, vient d'être **dissoute**. La religion catholique n'est plus la religion d'État. Les Chambres renoncent à assurer la sécurité du clergé. Des prêtres **ont été mis** à mort. **Certains** parmi **les plus** courageux continueront cependant d'afficher clairement leurs croyances.

Les grands écrivains sont **à l'oeuvre**. Balzac **rédige** sa *Comédie humaine*, Hugo vient de terminer *Notre-Dame de Paris*, Lamartine, le poète, opte pour la politique, alors que Chateaubriand, fatigué et ruiné, abandonne celle-ci pour écrire ses *Mémoires*. C'est la période où George Sand publie *Lélia* et vit ses grandes passions successives avec Sandeau, Musset et Chopin. Liszt et Berlioz, ces immortels de la musique sont **au**

faîte de leur gloire. Montalembert[10] et Lamennais[11] viennent de fonder, en 1830, le journal[FF] *l'Avenir* qui instaurait un catholicisme libéral, favorable à la séparation de l'Église et de l'État. L'éloquence et l'écriture ont une importance primordiale au XIXe siècle, ne **l'oublions** pas, ce sont les clous d'or qui fixent les idées. Il y a **même**, à la Sorbonne, ô paradoxe! une chaire d'éloquence sacrée!

Vocabulary

Compound prepositions

With compound prepositions, one looks for the middle term in the dictionary:

aux **dépens** de (+ *le*)	at the expense of (**dépens** n.m.pl. = expenses)
au **cours** de (+ *les*)	in the course of (**cours** n.m. = course)
à **l'oeuvre**	at work (**oeuvre** n.f.= work)
au **faîte** de	at the pinnacle of (**faîte** n.m. = summit)

Verbs

dissoute (pp.f.) < dissoudre (inf.) <	to dissolve
<u>but</u> *dissous* (pp.m.)	dissolved
rédiger	to draw up, write
ont été mis	were (*ont été*) put

Other parts of speech

même (adv.)	even
Certains (pron.)	Certain others (= *prêtres*)
les plus ... (superlative adj)	the most + adj.[12]
l'oublions	le < l': it (dir. obj.)

---

10. Charles Forbes, comte de Montalembert, publiciste et homme politique français (1810-1870). Collaborateur de *l'Avenir*. Apôtre du catholicisme libéral.

11. Félicité de Lamennais (1782-1854), écrivain et penseur français. Fondateur de *l'Avenir*. Partisan de l'humanitarisme démocratique.

12. For more details on superlative adjectives, see Chapter 10 §98.

9

OBJECT PRONOUNS AND VOCABULARY

81. Direct Object Pronouns

A. Forms of the Direct Object Pronouns

Direct object pronouns are simply the definite articles without the nouns they are meant to accompany. Instead of accompanying the noun to show number and gender, they actually replace the noun, still revealing that same noun's number and gender. For those unfamiliar with the romance languages, however, the placement of these pronouns before the conjugated verb may seem odd. Furthermore, the singular forms of **le** and **la** lose their vowels before a word beginning with a vowel: i.e. **l'**. In this case, the indication of gender is lost.

Examples

1. Nous lisons **un livre** de théologie. Nous **le** lisons.
   We are reading a theological book. We are reading **it**.

2. J'étudie **la** philosophie. Je **l'**étudie actuellement.
   I am studying philosophy. I am currently studying **it**.

B. Placement of Direct Object Between Modal Verb & Infinitive

When the main verb is aided by a modal verb, the direct object pronoun directly precedes the main verb, not the latter. In these cases, the direct object receives the action of the infinitive.

3. Elle doit lire **cette édition**. Elle doit **la** lire.
   She ought to read this edition. She ought to read **it**.

4. Je veux étudier **la théologie**. Je veux **l'**étudier.
   I want to study theology. I want to study **it**.

129

C. The Neutral Form of *le* (direct object)

Just as the subject pronoun *il* can mean "it", so can *le*, e.g.:

5. Vous avez raison, je le reconnais.
  a. You are right, I recognize it.
  b. You are right, I admit.
  c. I admit that you are right.

Quite often, this *le* is pleonastic or redundant in English as in the smoother b translation above. In c, "that" might represent it.

Finally, a pleonastic *l'* may also appear with *on* either for literary effect or in order to prevent an elision after a word which ends in a vowel, e.g. *que*. In the following sentence, *l'* prevents elision between two vowels without any meaning of its own; it also reflects the Old French etymology of *l'on* as *l'homme*.

6. Il a fallu vivre comme **l'**on pouvait.
  a. It was necessary to live as **one** could.
  b. We had to live as we could *or* They had to live as they could.

82. Special Case: *l'emporter sur*

The direct object *le* (< *l'*) in the idiom *l'emporter sur* is literally translated "carry it away over". When a smoother translation is found, like "get the best of", "win out over" or, even better, "outweigh", a translation for *le* is no longer necessary.

1. Le bon **l'**emportait sur le mal.
  a. The good carried **it** away over the evil.
  b. The good outweighed the evil.

2. Le dernier argument **l'**emporte sur les autres.
  a. The last argument carries **it** away over the others.
  b. The last argument wins out over the others.

83. Agreements (*les accords*) with Direct Objects

In the compound past tense of the auxiliary verb *avoir*, (*passé composé*; e.g. il a vu: he saw) there is an **agreement** in gender and number between the direct object and the past participle when the **direct object is placed before the verb**. The placement before the verb occurs with the use of both direct objects and relative pronouns.

1.　J'ai vu **les livres** hier. Je **les** ai vu<u>s</u> hier.
　　I saw the books yesterday. I saw **them** yesterday.

2.　Les livres [**que** j'ai vu<u>s</u> hier]* ont disparu.
　　The books [**that** I saw yesterday]* have disappeared.

The subordinate clause "que j'ai vus hier" might stand alone as an independent clause as in #1 above, which amounts to the same meaning. Therefore, *que* represents the noun just as much as *les* does. They are just different kinds of pronouns (standing in place of the nouns) relating to *les livres*.

3.　Nous avons lu **cette traduction** hier. Nous **l'**avons lu<u>e</u> hier.
　　We read this translation yesterday. We read it yesterday.

4.　La traduction **que** nous avons lu<u>e</u> hier est bonne.
　　The translation **that** we read yesterday is a good one.

84. Indirect Objects (Invariable)

There are only two indirect objects to represent singular or plural. Gender is not represented. The placement is before the verb, again, but if both a direct object and an indirect object accompany the verb, the direct object precedes the indirect one.

lui (sg.): to him, to her, to it
leur (pl.): to them

Note that *leurs* does not exist as an indirect object pronoun placed before the verb. This *leurs* is a possessive adjective necessarily accompanying a plural noun: e.g. **leurs voisins**: their neighbours. The **indirect object *leur* can never be plural.**

Examples

1.　Il parle **au professeur**.　　　　Il **<u>lui</u>** parle.
　　He is speaking **to the teacher**.　　He is speaking **<u>to him</u>**.

2. Elle écrit **à ses amis.**   Elle **leur** écrit.
    She is writing **to her friends.**   She is writing **to them**.

3. Elle écrit **une lettre <u>à une amie</u>.**   Elle **la <u>lui</u>** écrit.
    She is writing **a letter <u>to a friend</u>.**   She is writing **it <u>to her</u>**.

85. Conjunctive pronouns

A. Direct and Indirect Objects

The conjunctive pronouns (*me, te, se, nous, vous, se*) can be either direct objects or indirect objects, but they are always placed before all the other pronouns in front of the verb, whether they signify a direct or an indirect meaning. These forms are the same as the reflexive (or pronominal) pronouns. In the reflexive sense (when the subject and object are the same), *se* means **him-/her-/oneself** or **themselves**.[1]

After a command, the conjunctive pronouns become disjunctive pronouns and follow the verb in the imperative, but are attached to it by a hyphen. When the command is in the negative, the object pronouns precede the verb in the regular order.

Examples

1. Elle **me** voit (*me* as direct object).
    She sees **me**.

2. Ils **m'**écrivent une lettre (*me* as indirect object).
    They are writing a letter **to me** *or* They write **me** a letter.

3. Ils **<u>me</u> l'**écrivent (*me* is an indirect object, but comes first).
    They are writing **it <u>to me</u>**.

4. Écrivez-**la-moi.** Non, ne **me** l'écrivez pas.
    Write **<u>it to me</u>**. No, do not write **it to me**.

Conjunctive pronouns always precede the other object pronouns, whether they represent a direct or indirect object.

---

1. See Chapter 12 for a more detailed analysis.

B. Impersonal Expressions

Some impersonal expressions are personalized by adding a conjunctive pronoun, functioning as an indirect pronoun, to certain verbs. The commonest verbs to be used in this way are *convenir, manquer, plaire, sembler.*

Examples

  5.   Votre coupe me plaît.
    a. Your haircut is pleasing to me.
    b. I like your haircut.
  6.   Votre robe vous va bien.
        Your dress suits you.

  7.   Il me manque trois dollars.
    a. It is lacking to me three dollars.
    b. I am short $3.00.

  8.   Il me semble bizarre de nier l'existence d'un Créateur.
        It seems strange to me to deny the existence of a Creator.

  9.   Il me vient de temps en temps une idée géniale.
    a. It comes to me from time to time a brilliant idea.
    b. A brilliant idea occurs to me every now and them.

10. Il m'a coupé les cheveux.
    a. He cut the hair for me.
    b. He cut my hair.

86. Summary of Personal Pronouns

Subject Pr./ Nominative	Object Pr./ Accusative	Indirect Object Pr./ Dative	Conjunctive Dir. *or* Indir.
je	me	me	me
tu	te	te	te
il/elle/on	le, la	lui	se
nous	nous	nous	nous
vous	vous	vous	vous
ils/elles	les	leur	se

Exercise A

1. Il donne les livres à Pierre et moi. Il nous les donne.

2. Je raconte l'histoire à Françoise. Je la lui raconte.

3. Quand ils auront les résultats, ils me les rapporteront.

4. Malgré sa vieillesse, il l'emporte sur ses ennemis.

5. On vous croit sincère quand vous les trompez.

6. Elle donne les livres aux citoyens. Elle les leur donne.

7. Nous rappelons ici la vision théologique de saint Irénée. Nous la rappelons ici
   Rappelons-la ici.

8. La mission de l'Église dérive de sa nature, telle que[2] le Christ l'a voulue.

9. Le Concile Vatican II nous a rappelé le mystère de la dignité sacerdotale, prophétique
   et royale de tout le[3] Peuple de Dieu.

10. La responsabilité pastorale de l'Église? Chaque prêtre l'exerce au sein d'une Église
    particulière.

11. Donnez-lui l'occasion de l'exercer, s'il vous plaît!

12. Il a montré que cette tradition était beaucoup plus[4] répandue aux origines du
    christianisme qu'on ne[5] pourrait le penser à première vue.

---

2. *telle que*: cf. below, §92.
3. *tout le*: cf. below §93.
4. *plus...qu'*: more than (comparative construction; cf. Ch. 10).
5. *ne*: this *ne*, with no *pas*, is pleonastic (superfluous) and not negative.

87. Pronominal Adverb: *y*

The pronoun *y* replaces **à + noun object** (thing, only rarely a person). It also indicates the place to which someone goes or where someone is. Possible translations are: *there, to it, on it, in it, at it*, etc. If one or more human beings were involved, the indirect pronouns *lui* and *leur* could be used instead.

Examples

1. Je vais **à Paris**. J'**y** vais.
    I am going **to Paris**. I am going **there**.

2. Souvent femme varie,/ Bien fol est qui s'**y** fie. (Victor Hugo)
    Woman often changes, / He is a real fool who trusts **in her**.[6]

88. Common Verbs Followed by *À*

Any verb whose meaning requires *à* to link it to its object or another verb will use the pronominal adverb *y* as object pronoun, whether animate or inanimate, whether direct or indirect object in English. See Appendix IV for a complete list of verbs regularly associated with *à* and more specialized lists in Chapter 1 §12B-C and Chapter 12 §114.

avoir à	to have to (necessity)
être à	belong to; to have to be (necessity)
être habitué à	to be accustomed to
penser à	to think about
renoncer à	to renounce [sth.= à + indirect object], to give up
se fier à	to trust in
s'intéresser à	to be interested in
servir à	to be useful for, to serve as
tenir à	to be anxious/keen to; hold to

Examples

1. Je suis à vous dans un instant.
    a. I am yours in a moment.
    b. I will be with you in a moment.

2. Il serait à refaire, à créer à neuf.
    It would have to be redone, to be created anew.

3. Je suis habitué à **y** penser.
    I am accustomed to thinking **about it**.

---

6. *se fier à qn* = to trust in someone.

Exercise B

1. Vas-tu à Montréal? Tu n'as qu'à m'y attendre.

2. J'y serai ce soir.

3. S'il te plaît, réponds à ma question. Moi? J'y répondrai.

4. Si vous voulez renoncer à vos vacances, renoncez-y.

5. Alors les épines d'une rose, à quoi servent-elles[7]? Ça ne sert à rien (Saint-Exupéry).

6. Je pense comme je respire, sans y penser (Aymé).

7. Depuis longtemps il tient à le lire. Il y tient depuis longtemps.

8. Me posez-vous une question sur l'exclusion des femmes de l'hiérarchie ecclésiale? Nous y sommes habituées.

9. M'accompagnerez-vous? Si vous y tenez.

10. Les choses sont intéressantes dans la mesure où nous nous y intéressons.

89. Pronominal Adverb: *en*

The pronoun *en* replaces **de + noun object** (person or thing). Given the wide variety of meanings for "de," some possible translations are *some, any, of it, of them, from it, etc.* Place the translation of *en* at the end of the English sentence. See Chapter 7 § 67, Chapter 12 §114, and Appendix IV for lists of verbs associated with *de*.

---

7. servir à: to be useful (*or* good) for.

Examples

1. Avez-vous **des timbres**?   **En** avez-vous?
   Have you **any stamps**?   Have you **<u>any [of them]</u>**?

2. Il revient **de Paris**.   Il **en** revient.
   He is returning **from Paris**.   He is returning **<u>from there</u>**.

For a list of verbs which are commonly used with *de*, see Chapter 7, §67.

Exercise C

1. Avez-vous assez d'argent? Oui, j'en ai assez.

2. Le maître a envoyé les ouvriers à la vigne et puis il en a trouvé d'autres (cf. Matth.20).

3. Il est intelligent et il en est fort fier.

4. Des philosophes du dix-neuvième siècle? Elle m'en a beaucoup parlé.

5. Elle est membre de la Société des Théologiens, mais il n'en fait pas partie.

6. Nous avons les textes alors qu'ils en ont besoin.

7. N'en parlons plus!

8. Quand le savant entre, nous avons peur de lui.

9. En 1530, Holbein se convertit[8] à la religion réformée en demandant[FF], comme en témoignent les registres du recrutement, "une meilleure explication de la Sainte Communion avant de s'engager[9]."

10. Son activité esthétique triomphe de cette latence mélancolique tout en en gardant la trace.[10]

---

8. *se convertit*: converted (simple or literary past of a pronominal verb; cf. Ch.12 for details).

9. *s'engager*: committing himself (following *avant de*). Note that *s'*<*se* here is a reflexive pronoun which, in other contexts, could mean "herself" or "themselves".

10. Sentences 9-10, Julia Kristeva, *Le soleil noir*. Kristeva is a Bulgarian who escaped communism in the sixties to study psychoanalysis, among other disciplines, in Paris, France.

90. Summary of the Order of Pronouns Before the Verb

Conjunctive (direct & indirect)	**Dir.obj.**	**Indir. obj.**	**Pron.Adv.**
me	le	lui	
te	la	leur	**y** **en**
se	les		
nous			
vous			

The same order is respected for imperative verbs, but they must follow, not precede the imperative form. For example, we know from chapter one that *demander à qn de faire qch* is the French structure for "to ask someone to do sth.", meaning that the person asked is expressed in the indirect object case. In English we ask someone, but the French equivalent for ***demander à qn*** in English is to ask **to** someone. Consequently, the third person pronouns for the someone asked would be ***lui, leur***.

Examples

1.   Demande-le-lui!
   a. Ask it to him! (familiar, singular address)
   b. Ask him it!

2.   Demandons-le-lui!
      Let us ask him it!

3.   Demandez-le-leur!
   a. Ask it to them! (formal, plural address)
   b. Ask them it!

4.   Intéressons-**nous**-y!
   a. Let us interest ourselves in it.
   b. Let's get interested in it! (***nous* is not a subject pronoun**)

Exercise D

1. Il nous donne des soucis. Vous en donne-t-il?

2. Ne lui en donnez pas!

3. J'ai besoin des timbres. Oui, il m'a dit que tu en as besoin.

4. Il n'y a pas d'argent. Non, il n'y en a pas.

5. Si tu as trouvé de l'argent, donne-le-lui.

6. Quelle est la conclusion que vous avez tiré de la discussion? Ne me la cachez pas!

7. La dame demande[FF] le livre récemment édité[FF]. Envoie-le-lui!

8. Le document intégral est arrivé hier. Nous vous le préparons.

9. Pensez-y.

10. Les directeurs de sa thèse (il y en a deux) ne sont pas au courant de la situation. Expliquez-la-leur, s'il vous plaît.

91. Special Cases: *même* and *propre*

même (adv.) even (with verb) e.g. Elle l'a même vue!
She even saw her!

même (adj.) same (before the noun) e.g. la même chose
the same thing
(adj.) very (after the noun) e.g. le passage même
the very passage
(adj.) -self (after the disjunctive pronoun for emphasis)
e.g. le prêtre lui-même
the priest himself
or les prêtres eux-mêmes
the priests themselves

de même que (conj.) in the same way as

propre (adj.) own (before the noun) e.g. ma propre maison
my own house
propre (adj.) clean (after the noun) e.g. ma maison propre
my clean house
propre à (adj.) suitable to, appropriate to *or* for

propre (n.m.) distinctive characteristic

92. Special Case: *tel* and Variants

Tel (m.), *telle* (f.) is an adjective meaning "such" which reflects both the number and gender of the noun it modifies. It combines most commonly with the indefinite article as in English ("such a"), but in reverse order in the singular.

Examples

1. une telle personne
    such a person

2. de tels problèmes
    (some) such problems

Other usages include:

tel que   such as
tel quel   some sort or other
tellement   so (= *si*) & adj.

Examples

3. Qui pourrait croire en **un tel** rapprochement?
    Who could believe in **such a** reconciliation?

4. Il faut maintenir cette paix **telle quelle**.
    We must keep this peace **such as it is.**

5. L'espoir peut s'introduire sur le plan de l'esprit **tel qu**'il règne dans l'ensemble de l'Église.
    Hope can be introduced on the spiritual level **such as** it reigns in the whole of the Church.

6. Ils ont été **tellement** touchés que leur coeur[11] s'embrasa d'un amour nouveau.
    They were so touched that their hearts were enflamed with a new love.

---

11.   Synecdoche (part for the whole): heart = hearts.

93. Special Case: *tout* and Variants

This protean word *tout* changes its meaning like a chameleon according to its grammatical context. As an adjective (*tout, toute, tous, toutes*), it means "all" (pl) or "whole" (sg) only when it precedes the definite article. When it precedes the noun directly, it means "every". When it precedes an adjective or adverb, it means "quite". Finally, the masculine singular form can be used as an invariable noun ("the whole"), or pronoun ("all" or "everything"). The adjective *tout* tends to be translated as "the whole" in the singular and as "all" in the plural. In the singular, a similar inversion of word order occurs as in *tel* above, but the plural forms require no adjustment to the word order.

Whole (adj.)

tout le livre:	the whole book
toute la maison:	the whole house

All (adj.)

tous nos efforts:	all our efforts
toutes les variations possibles:	all possible variations

NOTE that without the definite article (*le, la* or *les*), *tout* means "every" (not "each" which is **chaque**). It may also mean "all".

Every (adj. without article)

tout livre:	every book
toute maison:	every house

Quite (adv.)

tout autre:	quite otherwise
tout évident:	quite obvious

Everything/All (invar. pron.)

tout est possible:	everything is possible
malgré tout:	in spite of everything
tout ce qui:	all that (which)[12]

Whole/All (n.)

le tout:	the whole
pas du tout:	not at all

---

12.   *tout ce qui/que*: cf. Chapter Seven §68.

Idioms (invar.)

tout à fait:	completely
tout le monde:	everybody (the whole world)
tout à coup:	suddenly
tout de suite:	immediately
tout à l'heure:	right away, in a moment
	or just a moment ago

Examples

1. La Parole de Dieu peut habiter parmi vous dans toute sa richesse.
    The Word of God can live among you in all its richness.

2. Il continue jusqu'au point de rejeter tout sacrement, toute organisation d'église.
    He continues to the point of rejecting every sacrament, all church organization.

Exercise E[13]

1. À tout péché miséricorde.

2. Tous les hommes sont mortels.

3. Tous ceux qui le veulent peuvent partir.

4. Tout ce qui brille n'est pas or.

5. Toute musique n'est pas propre à louer Dieu (*La Bruyère*, XVI, 23).

6. Il refuse de participer à leur étude tout en annonçant son propre projet.

7. Il a lu tout le livre en une séance.

8. Le pape peut s'adresser à toutes ces Églises.

9. Les protestants mêmes l'écouteront.

---

13. Most of the literary examples in Exercise E are taken from *Le bon usage*, §615.

10. La paroisse doit être la maison ouverte à tous, et au service de tous.

11. Ma propre[FF] méthode suit le même chemin.

12. Il les a même destinés à être l'image de son Fils, pour faire de ce Fils l'aîné d'une multitude de frères (Rom.8:29).

13. C'est de cette même unité que parle Jésus en utilisant l'image de la vigne et des sarments.

14. Le rire est le propre de l'homme (Rabelais en citant Aristote).

15. La faiblesse de Dieu reste, malgré tout, sa force.

94. Readings: Pope Jean-Paul II and Simone Weil

Exercise F

The following extract is taken from Jean-Paul II, *Les fidèles laïcs: Exhortation apostolique post-synodale Christifideles laici*, présenté par Bernard Housset (Paris: Centurion, 1989), p.110.

> Le Concile Vatican II le proclame très haut: "Tout ce qui s'oppose à la vie elle-même, comme toute espèce d'homicide, le génocide, l'avortement, l'euthanasie et même le suicide délibéré; tout ce qui constitue une violation de l'intégrité de la personne humaine, comme les mutilations, la torture physique ou morale, les contraintes psychologiques; tout ce qui est offense à la dignité de l'homme, comme les conditions de vie sous-humaines, les emprisonnements arbitraires, les déportations, l'esclavage, la prostitution, le commerce des femmes et des jeunes; ou encore les conditions de travail dégradantes qui réduisent les travailleurs au rang de purs instruments de rapport, sans égard pour leur personnalité libre et responsable: toutes ces pratiques et d'autres analogues sont, en vérité, infâmes. Tandis qu'elles corrompent la civilisation, elles déshonorent ceux qui s'y livrent plus encore que[14] ceux qui les subissent et insultent gravement à l'honneur du Créateur."

---

14. *plus encore que*: yet more than (cf. Ch. 10 following).

Exercise G

The following extract is taken from Simone Weil, *Pensées sans ordre concernant l'amour de Dieu* (Paris: Gallimard, 1962), pp. 14-15. Born in Paris, France, in 1908 into an agnostic Jewish family and poor health, Simone Weil became a French philosopher, practising her philosophy in a passionate abandonment to social activism. By living an ascetic lifestyle, she developed a mystical detachment which had been practised, historically, by Catholics; yet she appears never to have been formally integrated into the Church through baptism. After a short career of teaching, writing and political activism, Weil died at Grosvenor Sanatorium in Ashford, Kent, on August 24, 1943. The coroner's inquest declared it "suicide by starvation", although her anorexia was complicated by tuberculosis and exhaustion after throwing herself into the war effort. She was 34 years old when she died.[15] Whatever her status within Catholicism, her religious work, *Attente de Dieu* (Waiting Upon God) has established her as a Christian mystic.

> La vie telle qu'elle est faite aux hommes n'est supportable que par le mensonge. Ceux qui refusent le mensonge et préfèrent savoir que la vie est intolérable, sans pourtant se révolter contre **le sort**, finissent par recevoir du dehors, d'un lieu situé hors du temps, quelque chose qui permet d'accepter la vie telle qu'elle est.
>
> Tout le monde sent le mal, en a horreur et voudrait **s'en délivrer**. Le mal n'est ni la souffrance ni le péché, c'est **l'un et l'autre**; car ils sont liés, le péché fait souffrir et la souffrance rend mauvais, et ce mélange indissoluble de souffrance et de péché est le mal où nous sommes malgré nous et où nous avons horreur de nous trouver.
>
> Le mal qui est en nous, nous en **transportons** une partie sur les objets de notre attention et de notre désir. Et ils nous le renvoient comme si ce mal venait d'eux. C'est **pour cela** que nous prenons en haine et en dégoût les lieux dans lesquels nous nous trouvons submergés par le mal. Il nous semble que ces lieux mêmes nous emprisonnent dans le mal. C'est ainsi que les malades prennent en haine leur chambre et **leur entourage**, même si cet entourage est fait d'êtres aimés, que les ouvriers prennent parfois en haine leur usine, et ainsi de suite.
>
> Mais si par l'attention et le désir nous **transportons** une partie de notre mal sur une chose parfaitement pure, elle ne peut pas en être souillée; elle reste pure; elle ne nous renvoie pas ce mal; ainsi nous en sommes délivrés.

---

15. John M. Dunaway, *Simone Weil* (New York: Twayne Publishers, 1984), p. 24.

144

Vocabulary

le sort (n.m.)	their lot (*lit*. fate)
l'un et l'autre (pron.)	both
leur entourage (n.m.)	their social milieu
pour cela	for that reason

Verbs

s'en délivrer (v.pron.)	to be delivered from it
transporter	to project (in this case)

95. BASIC VOCABULARY: Chapters 7-9

NOUNS

amélioration (f.)	improvement, betterment
avocat (m.)	lawyer
discours (m.)	speech, discourse
espoir (m.)	hope
jeunesse (f.)	youth
manque (m.)	lack
occasion (f.)	opportunity
paix (f.)	peace
point de vue (m.)	point of view
psaume (m.)	psalm
rapprochement (m.)	reconciliation
sagesse (f.)	wisdom
sens	meaning, sense; direction
vérité (f.)	truth
vers (m.)	line of a poem
verset (m.)	Bible verse esp. of a psalm
vie (f.)	life
vieillesse (f.)	old age
voie (f.)	way
voix (f.)	voice (> *vox*, Latin)

PREPOSITIONS

à l'encontre de	against
à travers	through, throughout
au cours de	in the course of
au sein de	at the heart (in the bosom) of
malgré	in spite of

CONJUNCTIONS

ainsi que	as well as
alors que	when; whereas
comme	like, as; (*occasionally*) as if
dans la mesure où	to the degree that, insofar as
où (adv. rel.)	where
(pron.rel.)	when (possibly placement in time)
si	if, whether (conj.);
	so (adv. before adj.)
tandis que (conj.)	whereas

ADVERBS

ainsi	thus, in this way
aussitôt	immediately
d'emblée	at once, right away
de nouveau	again
à neuf	anew, as new
même	even (adv.); very; same (cf. §91)
-même/s	-self /-selves
pour cela	for that reason
pourtant	yet
pour autant	for all that
tellement	so (= *si,* before an adj.)

PRONOUNS & RELATED ADJECTIVES

ce qui, ce que	that which **<** what
	(more rarely: which)
chacun/e	every one (pron. + *de*: of) *possibly* each
chaque (adj.)	each
plusieurs (pl., invar.)	several
soi-disant (adj. invar.)	so-called
tel/le	such (listed in §92).
tout/e	every, all, whole (Listed in §93).

PERSONAL & OBJECT PRONOUNS Summarized in §86 & §90.

CORRELATIVE CONJUNCTIONS Listed in §62.

NEGATIVE ALTERNATIVES Listed in §58.

COMMON VERBS FOLLOWED BY "À" Listed in §88.

COMMON VERBS FOLLOWED BY "DE" Listed in §67.

VERBS

arriver (2)	to arrive, to happen
se passer	to happen
arriver à	to succeed in
réussir à / parvenir à	to succeed in
considérer comme	consider (as; not normally used in Eng.)
être au courant de qch.	to be "up to date" on sth.
faire partie de	to belong to, be a member of
s'intéresser à	to be interested in
menacer (de)	to threaten (esp. passive + with)
triompher (de)	to triumph (over)
se trouver	to be (found)
venir de (followed by inf.)	to have just (infinitive < pp.)
falloir	to be necessary
il faut	it is necessary (Listed in §76)
il reste	there remain/s (cf. §76)

10

QUANTITIES:
COMPARATIVES AND SUPERLATIVES

Please note that a "Basic Vocabulary" list for the following three chapters is found at the end of Chapter Twelve.

96. Numbers and Expressions of Quantity

A. Numbers and Approximations

A short list of cardinal and ordinal numbers can be found in Appendix V. To make any cardinal number into an approximate estimation (usually by tens or a dozen), add *-aine* to the end and use the indefinite female article *une*. The *de* which follows is invariable, as it is in the majority of the expressions of quantity below.

Examples

une dizaine (de)	about ten
une vingtaine (de)	about twenty
une douzaine de	a dozen of, etc.

B. Invariable Expressions of Quantity

The following expressions are sufficient in themselves to express plurality. The **de** which necessarily accompanies these terms never becomes plural: i.e. **des**, although it may drop its **e** before a vowel: e.g. **beaucoup d'énergie** (a lot of energy).

assez de	enough
beaucoup de	many, much, a lot of
moins de	less, fewer
peu de	very few, very little
un peu de	a few, a little
plus de	more

la plupart de	the majority of, most (of)
rien de	nothing, no
tant de	so much, so many
trop de	too much, too many
quantité de	a great many, a large number of
une boîte de	a box of
une bouteille de	a bottle of
un kilo de	a kilo of
deux litres de	two litres of
trois livres de	three pounds of, etc.
une tasse de	a cup of
un verre de	a glass of
un recueil de	a collection (anthology, compendium) of

The following two expressions are invariable because they are always plural and do not express the feminine gender. For example, *plusieurs* is never written *plusieures* even before feminine plural nouns.

quelques	a few, some
plusieurs	several (not "many")

C. Variable Expressions of Quantity

There is only one variable expression which acts as a synomym for *beaucoup de* (invar):

bien **de + le**	many, much, a lot of
e.g. bien **du** mal	much trouble, a great deal of trouble
bien **des** fois	many times

D. Peu when not used for Quantity

When used before an adjective without *de, peu* turns the adjective into its opposite. For example:

1. un détail précis < un détail peu précis
   a precise detail < an imprecise detail

2. une idée commune < une idée peu commune
   a common idea < an uncommon idea

3. l'eau profonde   < l'eau peu profonde
   deep water   < shallow water

Note that as soon as the indefinite article *un* is added, *peu* becomes a quantity again, even without *de*:

4.   Elle a l'air un peu triste.
     She seems a little sad.

Exercise A

Vocabulary: comprendre 1. comprise, include, cover, embrace } comprehend
                       2. understand (take in) } comprehend

1. Il nous reste un peu de vin.

2. Jean a bien des soucis.

3. Je suis convaincu qu'il nous arrive[FF] quantité d'événements qui paraissent n'avoir aucune raison d'être.

4. La plupart des gens est conservatrice.

5. Elle a lu beaucoup de romans historiques.

6. Ce roman comprend moins d'éléments caractéristiques.

7. Si nous avions eu assez de temps, nous aurions même lu le texte.

8. Un recueil d'inscriptions romaines (en latin) me dit peu.

9. Jésus a versé tant de sang sur la croix.

10. Trop de traductions montrent trop peu de sensibilité à la langue originale.

11. Peu de personnes ont assez d'expérience dans ce domaine.

12. Je voudrais accueillir plus de gens chez moi.

97. Comparative Adjectives and Adverbs: Regular Forms

Regular comparative forms of both adjectives and adverbs observe the following patterns, where *que* denotes either "than" or "as":

moins ..(adj., adv.).. **que**	less .... than (unequal comparison)
plus ..(adj., adv.).. **que**	more .... than
aussi ..(adj., adv.).. **que**	as .... as (comparison of equals)
même(s) ..(noun).. **que**	the same [noun].... as (comparison of equals)

Examples

Adjectives

Note that adjectives still usually follow their nouns.

1. C'est un problème **plus** difficile **que** l'autre.
   It's a **more** challenging problem **than** the other one.

2. C'est le **même** problème **que** nous avons vu hier.
   a. It is the **same** problem **as** we saw yesterday.
   b. That is the same problem that we saw yesterday [also possible in this case].

Adverbs

3. Ce cycliste va **plus** vite que l'autre.
   This cyclist is going fast**er than** the other.

4. Ce vélo-ci coûte **moins que** celui-là.
   The latter bike costs **less than** the former.

Equality of Both Adjectives and Adverbs

Adjective:

5. Les Canadiens sont **aussi** intelligents **que** les Américains!
   Canadians are **as** intelligent **as** Americans!

Adverb:

6. Je vais **aussi** lentement **que** lui.
   I am going **as** slowly **as** he (is).

98. Superlative Adjectives and Adverbs

The superlative builds upon the comparative forms by adding the definite article (m.,f. & pl.), just as English does. There is one difference between adjectives and adverbs, however. Whereas the definite article reflects gender and number in sympathy with the adjectives, for adverbs only *le* is used.

Examples

Adjectives

1. Celle-ci est une maison plus petite. C'est **la plus petite**.
    This one here is a smaller house. It is **the smallest**.

2. La réponse **la plus** précise était celle qu'il nous a donnée.
    The most precise answer was that which he gave us.

3. Elles étaient les réponses **les plus** précises **du** soir.
    They were **the most** precise answers **of the** evening.

Adverbs

4. Marie court **le plus** vite **des** trois.
    Mary runs **the** fast**est of the** three.

99. Irregular Forms

Just as in English, the adjectives and adverbs associated with "good" and "bad" have irregular forms, as short forms which are commonly used.

Adjectives	Comparative Forms	Superlatives
bon, bonne (good)	meilleur, meilleure	le meilleur (the best)
bons, bonnes	meilleurs, meilleures	la meilleure
	(better)	les meilleurs
		les meilleures
mauvais, mauvaise,	pire (invar)	le pire, la pire, les pires
(bad)	(worse)	(the worst)

Adverbs	Comparative Forms	Superlatives
bien (well)	mieux (better)	le mieux (the best)
mal (badly)	pire (worse)	le pire (the worst)

Examples

Adjectives

1. Il est **le meilleur** candidat **de** tous.
   He is **the best** candidate **of** all

2. Nos candidats sont **pires que** ceux de votre circonscription.
   Our candidates are **worse than** those of your constituency.

Adverbs

3. Il parle **bien**, il parle **mieux que** Jean.
   He speaks **well, better than** John.

4. Dans **les pires** circonstances, elle garde son calme.
   In **the worst** circumstances, she keeps her cool.

100. Comparisons of Quantities

A. Comparison of Quantities of Nouns

Instead of comparing adjectives or adverbs, this construction compares quantities of nouns.

autant de	... (nouns) ... que	as much, as many ...	as (equal)
moins de	... (nouns) ... que	fewer ... (nouns) ...	than (unequal)
plus de	... (nouns) ... que	more ... (nouns) ...	than

Examples

1. Hélène a lu **autant de** livres **que** moi.
   Helen has read **as many** books **as** I [have].

2. Pierre a examiné **moins de** livres **que** nous.
   Peter examined **fewer** books **than** we <did>.

B. A More Complicated Expression

d'autant mieux ... que	all the better... as
d'autant moins ... que	all the less .... as
d'autant plus ... que	all the more .... as

Example

Note that *que* (as) may connote "since".

1. La chaleur se conserve **d'autant mieux que** vous laissez les fenêtres fermées.
   The heat is kept in **all the better as/since** you are leaving the windows closed.

Exercise B

1. J'ai autant d'estime pour sa prose que pour sa poésie.

2. Dieu est la question *par excellence*, englobant et dépassant toutes les autres, présente aux esprits[FF] les plus modestes comme aux plus raffinés – quelquefois à leur insu.

3. Dieu constitue donc, du même coup, le plus complexe et le plus exigeant des défis posés à la pensée humaine.

4. Il est né autant de filles que de garçons.

5. La chose est d'autant plus frappante que le récit d'Emmaüs est organisé de manière identique à[1] deux autres récits lucaniens.

6. Ce récit se déroule plus vite que l'autre.

7. Notre décision est d'autant plus sûre qu'elle est prise après quelques semaines de délibérations.

8. La période pascale est la plus appropriée pour cette réconciliation qui réadmet le pénitent à la communion eucharistique.

9. Après la paix constantinienne, le système de pénitence antique devient de plus en plus impraticable, à tel point que certains évêques n'imposent la pénitence qu'à l'approche de la mort.

10. Il n'existe plus d'alternative exclusive entre le couple chair-sang et le couple esprit-vie parce que les deux aspects coïncident de manière la plus complète dans l'eucharistie (cf. Hans Urs von Balthasar, p.108).

---

1. For *de manière*, see Basic Vocabulary, Chapters 10-12. Although *identique* is an adjective which would normally be transferred in front of the noun *manière* for the English equivalent, it is better not to separate it from the following preposition which depends upon it; i.e. *identique à*: identical to.

101. Possessive Pronouns

To convert a possessive adjective into a pronoun which acts both as a noun (substantive) and an adjective (because it agrees in number and gender with the noun it stands for), one adds the definite articles and applies the conventional inflections.

Poss. Adj.	**English**	**Pronoun**	**English**
ma mon mes	my	la mienne le mien les miennes, les miens	mine
ta ton tes	your	la tienne le tien les tiennes, les tiens	yours
sa son ses		la sienne le sien les siennes, les siens	hers/his/its
notre (m.& f) nos	our	la nôtre, le nôtre les nôtres	ours
votre (m. & f) vos	your	la vôtre, le vôtre les vôtres	yours
leur (m. & f.) leurs	their	la leur, le leur les leurs	theirs

Examples

1. Nous avons fait notre **communion**; elle n'a pas fait **la sienne**.
   We have taken our **communion**; she has not taken **hers** (*lit.* made).

2. Ils feront **la leur** plus tard.
   They will take **theirs** later.

Note that *communion* is a feminine noun.

Exercise C

1. Plus on se hâte, moins on avance.

2. Il s'occupe de ses affaires et nous des nôtres.

3. Nous citerons la note de notre livre et toi celle du tien.

4. Ces passages et les nôtres sont très semblables.

5. Voici les livres qui viennent de paraître. Les leurs se trouvent sur le rayon le plus élevé; les siens sur celui le plus bas.

6. Ce sont les lettres que je viens d'écrire. Elles sont destinées au président parce qu'il est plus responsable des pauvres que le sous-président.

7. Tes lettres me semblent bonnes. Je n'ai pas encore écrit les miennes.

8. Notre premier ministre est le chef de notre gouvernement tandis qu'un président est le chef du vôtre.

9. Ma thèse et la tienne touchent au même sujet.

10. Ma foi et la sienne ne mènent pas dans le même sens.

102. Reading

Exercise D

The following passage is taken from: Lise Baroni, Yvonne Bergeron, Pierrette Daviau et Micheline Laguë, *Voix des femmes; voies de passage: pratiques pastorales et enjeux ecclésiaux* (Montréal: Paulines, 1995), pp. 112-13.

Certaines femmes ne tolèrent plus d'être marginalisées malgré leurs compétences et leurs expériences reconnues [...]: l'Église de ceux qui les maintiennent dans une condition de mineures, tout en prêchant l'égalité de nature des sexes et la justice pour « tous », ne peut **se réclamer de** l'Église de Jésus Christ. [...] Quelques-unes, plus exaspérées, attaquent même de front la loi et la théologie patriarcales et ne voient point d'avenir sans des transformations substantielles aux plans anthropologique, théologique et ecclésiologique. [...] Elles n'acceptent pas que les autorités remettent si peu en cause des traditions qui perpétuent l'inégalité entre les sexes. [...] Elles refusent **la fermeture hermétique** d'une loi dépassée mais toujours inébranlable. L'ampleur de cette rigidité institutionnelle ne leur échappe pas plus qu'elle n'**échappe à** des organismes de défense des droits humains. Ainsi, à titre d'exemple, le Conseil du statut de la femme du Québec, en **se référant à** cette autorité absolue de l'institution ecclésiale, n'hésite pas à parler de violence dans l'Eglise:

> ... [L]a subordination des femmes a été enracinée dans des mentalités et des institutions qui sont encore empreintes du sexisme séculaire qui les a caractérisées. La contribution de l'Église à l'infériorisation des femmes n'est plus à démontrer. Selon la version de la création la plus répandue, la femme a été tirée d'une côte de l'homme et lui était destinée. **D'après** saint Augustin, le corps de l'homme est à l'image de son âme, mais pas celui de la femme.

Et le texte ajoute à la page suivante:

> ... En théorie, plus l'inégalité est grande, plus le potentiel de violence est élevé. La violence contre les femmes, comme la violence raciale ou religieuse, est rendue possible par la conviction que « l'autre », la femme, le noir, le juif, vaut moins que soi, est moins intelligent, moins beau, moins utile à la société, moins proche de Dieu. La violence existe quand il y a mépris de l'autre et de ses désirs, quand il y a négation de son identité et de son égalité.[2]

---

2. *Pour que cesse l'inacceptable*, op. cit., pp. 25-29. C'est nous qui soulignons. Voir également certains passages des pages 28 et 29 de ce même texte.

VOCABULARY

VERBS

se réclamer de	to draw authority from; appeal to the authority of
échapper à	to escape from
se référer à	to refer to

OTHER

la fermeture hermétique (n.f.)	hermetic seal
D'après... (prep.)	According to... (syn. Selon...)

11

LITERARY PAST AND SYNTAX

103. The Literary Past (Past Definite): *passé défini ou simple*

The Literary Past is also known as the **past definite tense** or simple past (*passé défini* or *passé simple*). The term **simple past** signifies its opposition to the **compound past** (*passé composé*, see Chapter 3) which it is commonly said to replace. Therefore, the imperfect past tense is found alongside the literary past in the same way that it is used with the compound past.

In French, the written language is much more distinct from the oral language than in our twenty-first-century English. The compound past is used in oral expression and the simple past replaces it in literary texts, a function which accounts for the term **literary past**. The literary texts in which the reader may come across the literary past are specifically narrative, either in the form of a literary narration of past events or history. Whatever the events, they are objective, historical and detached, even quite remote, from the author's present. In comparison, the compound past is closer to the present, more immediate.

History and scholarly work may also be written in the **historic present**[1]. This tense suits texts which involve argumentation. An English translation may follow the same lead. However, if the translator prefers to transpose historic action into the past, he or she must be consistent from one end to the other of the translation. It requires both vigilance and proof reading to avoid slipping into error, since other related tenses will also have to be transposed: e.g. The future becomes conditional from a past perspective.

It is overly simplistic to assume that the literary past and the compound past can be used interchangeably. We may consider the literary past, following Roland Barthes, as artificial in nature; it is an artificial construct representing the fictitious time of myth or the novel (Cf. Barthes, *Le degré zéro de l'écriture*).

---

1. *Historic present*: the present tense even as it refers to the past. This is not the historic present in Greek.

104. Regular Forms of the Literary Past

Of the three regular verb forms ending in -er, -ir and -re, the endings of the first are related to the present tense of *avoir* in the singular, whereas the latter two are related to the present tense of -ir verbs. Irregular verbs may use either of the last two options, and often use their past participles as their roots: e.g. *eu* (past participle of *avoir*) < *eus* (had; literary past).

For this reason, the literary past is placed below the past participles in the verb chart.[2]

Subjects	**I. -er verbs**	**II. -ir -er verbs**		**III. Irregular**
	DONN/-er	**FIN/ -ir**	**PERD/-re**	**AVOIR/ eu (pp)**
je	donnai	finis	perdis	eus
tu	donnas	finis	perdis	eus
il, elle, on	donna	finit	perdit	eut
nous	donnâmes	finîmes	perdîmes	eûmes
vous	donnâtes	finîtes	perdîtes	eûtes
ils, elles	donnèrent	finirent	perdirent	eurent
Translation:	I gave...	I finished...	I lost...	I had...

Note that the English translation is the preterite in one word.

The only irregular verb associated with the first group is *aller* (to go): *j'allai, tu allas, elle alla, nous allâmes, vous allâtes, ils allèrent.*

Note also that the singular forms of the second -ir group are similar to, and may be confused with, the regular present tense of the same verbs. The confusion arises most often in the third person singular form of *dire* (to say, tell): e.g. ***Il dit***: He says *or* He said. Consider the tenses of the other surrounding verbs to determine the proper context and tense.

Irregular verbs in this group are *faire* (to do): *je fis, tu fis, etc.*, *voir* (to see): *je vis, tu vis....nous vîmes, etc.* The two verbs *mettre* (to put): *je mis...* and *prendre* (to take): *je pris... nous prîmes, etc.* conjugate the literary past upon the past participle.

105. Irregular Forms of the Literary Past

Irregular verbs in the third group which add the regular endings to irregular past participles ending in -u are *savoir* (to know): *sus, etc.* from the past participle *su*; *vouloir* (to wish): *voulus, etc.* from the past participle *voulu*; *pouvoir* (to be able): *pus, etc.* from *pu*; and *devoir* (must): *dus, etc.* from *dû*. The most irregular verb in this last group is *être*: *je fus, tu fus, elle fut, nous fûmes, vous fûtes, ils furent* (I was, etc.).

---

2. See Appendix II.

Two verbs which correspond to the second category, but with an added nasal *n* are *tenir* (to hold) and *venir* (to come):

Subjects	TENIR	English	VENIR	English
je	tins	I held	vins	I came
tu	tins	you held	vins	you came
il, elle, on	tint	he held	vint	she came
nous	tînmes	we held	vînmes	we came
vous	tîntes	you held	vîntes	you came
ils, elles	tinrent	they held	vinrent	they came

106. Summary of All Endings of the Literary Past

	I.	II. & III.	III. Irregular
Singular	-ai	-is	-us
	-as	-is	-us
	-a	-it	-ut
Plural	-âmes	-îmes	-ûmes
	-âtes	-îtes	-ûtes
	-èrent	-irent	-urent
Irregular Verbs	all- (aller)	fis (faire)*	fus (être)*
		appris (apprendre)	eus (avoir)
		dis (dire)	dus (devoir)
		mis (mettre)	pus (pouvoir)
		pris (prendre)	sus (savoir)
		vis (voir)*	voulus (vouloir)

* marks an irregular form of the Literary Past that is not built upon the past participle.

Exercise A

Translate the following passage from the Acts of the Apostles, noting the use of the literary past for past action, but the compound past in direct (oral) discourse referring to the past. This selection is taken from a mixture of two TOB editions (*Traduction Œcumémique de la Bible*), an ecumenical French Bible, translated in 1982 and 1988.

Ananias et Saphira

Mais un homme appelé Ananias, dont la femme se nommait Saphira, vendit, **d'accord avec** elle, un terrain qui leur appartenait. Il garda une partie de l'argent pour lui et alla remettre le reste aux apôtres. Sa femme le savait. Alors Pierre lui dit:

– Ananias, pourquoi Satan a-t-il pu **s'emparer de** ton coeur pour te faire mentir au Saint-Esprit et garder pour toi une partie de l'argent **rapporté** par ce terrain? Ne pouvais-tu pas le garder sans le vendre, ou, si tu le vendais, disposer du prix à ton gré? Comment donc as-tu pu décider en toi-même de commettre une telle action? Ce n'est pas aux hommes que tu as menti, mais à Dieu.

En entendant ces paroles, Ananias tomba et mourut. Et tous ceux qui l'apprirent furent **saisis d'**une grande crainte. Les jeunes gens vinrent envelopper le corps, puis ils l'**emportèrent** et l'enterrèrent.

Environ trois heures plus tard, la femme d'Ananias entra sans savoir ce qui s'était passé. Pierre lui demanda:

– Dis-moi, avez-vous vendu votre terrain pour cette somme-là?

Et elle répondit:

– Oui, pour cette somme-là.

Alors Pierre lui dit:

– Comment donc avez-vous pu décider ensemble de mettre à l'épreuve l'Esprit du Seigneur? Écoute, ceux qui ont enterré ton mari sont déjà à la porte et ils vont t'**emporter** toi aussi.

Au même instant, elle tomba aux pieds de l'apôtre et mourut. Les jeunes gens entrèrent et la trouvèrent morte; ils l'**emportèrent** et l'enterrèrent auprès de son mari. Toute l'Église et tous ceux qui apprirent ces faits furent **saisis d'**une grande crainte (*Actes des Apôtres* 5:1-11).

Vocabulary

d'accord avec	in agreement with
s'emparer (de)	to take hold of
porter	to carry (to wear)
apporter	to bring (*lat. ad* + *portare*: carry to)
emporter	to take away
rapporter	to yield (give back)
saisi de	seized by

107. Compound Adverbs and Adjectives

A. Adverbs

An adjective may be converted into an adverb by adding -ment to it: e.g. *vrai* (adj; true)
< *vraiment* (adv; truly)

    or a noun may be converted into an adverb by using it with *avec* or *à*: e.g.,

avec patience	patiently
avec soin	carefully
avec enthousiasme	enthusiastically
avec bruit	noisily
à contrecoeur	reluctantly
à regret	regretfully

Like any adverb, its position in the English sentence is likely to move either before the verb
or after the direct object. The French position after the verb is awkward in English.

B. Adjectival Attributes

Sometimes phrases introduced by the prepositions *à, de, en* describe the noun which they
follow. In these cases, the translation may be simplified in English to a single adjective:

bateau **à voiles**	sail boat
une lampe **à huile**	an oil lamp
une machine **à écrire**	a typewriter
un pain **au chocolat**	a chocolate pastry
une voix **de soprano**	a soprano voice
une salle **de réunion**	a meeting room
une galerie **de tableaux**	an art gallery
une montre **en or**	a gold watch

Exercise B

Translate the following passage from *Ozanam* by Madeleine des Rivières (pp. 102-3).
Frédéric Ozanam, the founder of the St. Vincent de Paul Society, was married to Amélie
when he taught modern languages at the Sorbonne in Paris.[3] See below for vocabulary.

    Note the use of the historic present tense in French, as usual.

---

3. See Chapter 8, §80, Ex. F, for further details concerning the life of Frédéric Ozanam.

Au mois de juillet, Amélie, à qui les médecins ont conseillé de nouveau un séjour au bord de la mer, quitte **à regret** un Frédéric bouleversé par la mort fortuite du professeur Fauriel dont il est le suppléant. Ozanam avait une grande estime pour cet homme brillant et sage qu'il considère comme un savant...

La chaire de Claude Fauriel se trouve donc vacante. On pourrait croire qu'elle revient **d'emblée** à Ozanam, mais Frédéric n'a que trente et un ans; ses titres sont minces, et ses publications restreintes. Le ministre a son mot à dire. On offre même le poste au professeur Jean-Jacques Ampère qui enseigne au Collège de France. Ce dernier le refuse **en faveur de** Frédéric. Ozanam est vivement touché du geste de son ami; la partie **toutefois** n'est pas gagnée **pour autant**. Il faut voir le ministre, puis ceux qui le conseillent, il faut écrire, demander[FF] audience, etc. Pour Frédéric, c'est recommencer les visites qu'il a faites quelques mois plus tôt **en faveur de** M. Soulacroix, c'est revoir les mêmes personnages influents en plaidant cette fois sa propre cause. Processus frustrant et pénible.

Ozanam s'échappe de temps à autre et court embrasser Amélie à Dieppe, mais revient aussitôt à Paris où l'attendent ses cours, ses obligations à la Sorbonne et un travail dont il veut hâter la parution: *l'histoire littéraire d'Allemagne*.

Frédéric demeure fidèle à ses lettres quotidiennes et décrit à sa bien-aimée combien l'éloignement lui est pénible:

« Cette maison où je rentre sans entendre ta douce voix qui m'appelait, ce salon où ta place est vide, ce piano silencieux, ces petits oiseaux sur le toit attendant inutilement ta jolie main qui leur jetait des miettes, tout m'attriste... »

Vocabulary

en faveur de (compound prep.)	for the benefit of
pour autant	for all that

Adverbs

à regret	cf. §107 above
d'emblée	cf. §95 above
toutefois	however, yet

166

108. Placement of Adjectives

The meaning of some adjectives depends upon their position with respect to the noun they modify. Since the adjective normally follows the noun, this placement usually denotes a literal meaning. The less usual placement before the noun lends it a more figurative meaning; e.g.,

Adjective	Before the Noun	After the Noun
ancien/ne	former	ancient, old
brave	fine, good	brave
certain/e	particular, certain	sure
cher/chère	dear	expensive
pauvre	unfortunate	poor
propre	own	clean[4]

Exercise C

1. Je suis ma propre personne.

2. Mon ancien professeur m'a donné un livre ancien.

3. Nous l'avons vue la semaine dernière.

4. Elle possédait une merveilleuse voix de soprano.

5. Il l'a fait avec soin.

6. Mon cher ami m'a acheté une bouteille de vin très chère.

7. La pauvre fille ne voulait plus vivre.

8. Une famille pauvre habitait une maison propre.

9. Il regarda avec soin sa montre en or.

10. Si nous considérons avec patience ce problème, nous le résoudrons.

---

4. The adjective *propre* was discussed in detail along with *même* in Chapter 9 §91.

109. Inverted Word Order

A. Remote noun subjects following subordinating conjunctions

In a subordinate clause (a sentence which depends upon another principal sentence) introduced by **que (qu')**, literary French will sometimes invert the word order by placing the subject of the subordinate clause after the verb. When translating, one must look for the noun or pronoun subject following **que** after the verb. The same phenomenon occurs when **ce que (ce qu')** is used, because it also involves a direct object pronoun, but **qui**, being itself a subject case, never triggers an inversion.

Example

1. Le protestantisme libéral a eu besoin du terrain **qu'**avait préparé **le dix-huitième siècle**.
    Liberal protestantism needed (had need of) the ground **which the eighteenth century** had prepared.

After **qu'** the subordinate clause is inverted: verb + subject, whereas the regular word order is subject + verb, as in English. The translator must therefore seek the subject (*le dix-huitième siècle*) after the verb (*avait préparé*).

A less literary possibility for the same sentence follows the normal word order:

2. Le protestantisme libéral a eu besoin du terrain **que** le dix-huitième siècle avait préparé.

Other subordinating conjunctions can cause inversions in the same way as *que*, with the exception of *qui* which is itself always the subject of the subordinating clause:

3. Il n' est pas d'atome de matière **où** ne résident **des forces** reliées[5] à la puissance universelle.
    There is not any atom of matter **in which forces** tied to the universal power do not reside.

---

5. **Note** that *reliées* is a past participle acting simultaneously as an adjective and as a verb. As an adjective, it agrees with the feminine gender and plural form of the noun *forces* (by the ending *-es*). As a verbal past participle, the phrase *à la puissance universelle* depends upon it. Because of this dependence, the adjective is not moved ahead of the noun in the English translation, but remains behind to maintain the direct connection with the dependent phrase. Cf. Chapter 3, §25.

B. Inverted Word Order at the Beginning of a Sentence
In theory, the subject demands first place in the sentence. If such adverbs as *peut-être* (perhaps) and *toujours* (always) or the conjunction *aussi* (therefore; instead of the commoner meaning "also") usurp the first-place position, the verb comes before the pronoun. The hyphen separates the inverted words as if they were forming a question, which they are not. If in doubt, the translator can always check the punctuation.

Examples

1. Aussi **chante-t-elle** le kyrie.
   Therefore she is singing the kyrie.

2. Peut-être **viendront-ils**.
   Perhaps they will come.

If explanatory verbs are preceded by part of a quotation in direct discourse, the same phenomenon occurs:

3. -Salut, **dit-il**, ça va?
   "Hello," he says, "how's it going?"

Note that French convention does not apply punctuation in the same way as English convention, especially concerning quotation marks.

C. Tips Concerning Word Order of Pronouns
When variations of *tout* or *moi-même* emphasize a subject, they follow the verb in French. This is not unlike the English Canadian pattern, when we prefer to say "You are *all* welcome" instead of "You *all* are welcome", as they might say in South Carolina. For the English speaker reading French, it is very important not to mistake these emphatic pronouns for direct objects of the verb.

Examples

1. Ils ont **tous** les cheveux noirs.
   They **all** have black hair.

2. Il faut prendre chaque livre de l'Écriture pour ce qu'il se donne **lui-même** (Jacques Ellul, *Politique de Dieu*).
   We must take each book of Scripture for what it **itself** presents itself <to be>.

Exercise D

Translate using a dictionary when necessary.

1. Nous savons que l'Évangile est une relecture de ce qu'a dit, fait et été Jésus.

2. Nous voudrions seulement mieux dire ce qu'ont été les objectifs et l'engagement d'un Calvin.

3. Dans leur majorité les néo-protestants préfèrent suivre la voie que leur ont toujours tracée leurs coreligionnaires genevois.

4. Voici le sujet qu'a présenté Michel Foucault dans son livre *Histoire de la folie à l'âge classique.*

5. Les symphonies qu'a composées Mozart sont d'un génie musical qu'on reconnaît facilement.

6. Aussi bien, Dieu commence-t-il par préserver et sauvegarder une part d'inconnaissable, et pour cela justement sans nom: "Je suis qui je suis" (Ex.3:14).

7. Le souci constant que manifeste l'auteur de démêler les doctrines erronées des doctrines légitimes, de chercher à savoir, par exemple, si l'influence d'Origène ...fut de transformer les pensées platoniciennes ou d'altérer la doctrine chrétienne..., l'amène parfois à juger des interactions entre le platonisme et le christianisme.

8. « Mais Dieu constitue le plus complexe et le plus exigeant des défis posés à la pensée humaine - à la manière, dans un autre ordre, de cette cime montagneuse ordinairement voilée par les nuages, » à laquelle Karl Popper aime comparer la « vérité objective ou absolue » dont l'existence ne se trouve pas plus affectée par notre ignorance, dit-il, que ne l'est[6] l'existence objective de la cime.

---

6. *ne l'est*: the *ne* is pleonastic (i.e. has no negative value). The direct object pronoun *l'* represents the proposition "l'existence ne se trouve pas [...] affectée par notre ignorance", without the comparative *plus*. For English speakers, the *l'* (it) would be considered redundant, if translated.

110. Readings: The Bible[7] and Chateaubriand

Exercise E

2 Chroniques 9: 1-7

La reine de Saba apprit la renommée de Salomon et vint à Jérusalem éprouver Salomon par des énigmes. Elle arriva avec de très grandes richesses, des chameaux chargés d'aromates, quantité d'or et de pierres précieuses. Quand elle fut arrivée, elle lui dit tout ce qu'elle avait médité. Salomon l'éclaira sur toutes ses questions et aucune ne fut pour lui un secret... **Lorsque** la reine de Saba vit la sagesse de Salomon..., le coeur lui **manqua** et elle dit au roi: « Ce que j'ai **entendu dire** dans mon pays sur toi et sur ta sagesse était donc vrai. Je n'ai pas voulu croire ce qu'on disait avant de venir et de voir de mes yeux, mais vraiment... tu surpasses la renommée dont j'avais eu l'écho. Bienheureux tes gens, bienheureux tes serviteurs que voici, qui **se tiennent** continuellement devant toi et qui entendent ta sagesse! »

Vocabulary

Lorsque (conj)	when

Verbs

manquer à qn.	to fail s.o. (*lit.* be lacking to)
entendre dire	to hear (= hear said)
se tenir... devant	to wait upon (*lit.* hold oneself ... before)

Exercise F

Chateaubriand is an important figure in the French romantic movement. His *Génie du christianisme* is especially significant for its contribution to the revival of Catholicism in France following the French Revolution.

---

7.   See also Exercise A above.

François-René Chateaubriand, *Le génie du christianisme*, 1802

L'Église, sous l'empereur Julien, fut exposé à une autre persécution du caractère le plus dangereux. On n'employa pas la violence contre les chrétiens, mais on leur prodigua le mépris. On commença par dépouiller les autels; on défendit[8] ensuite aux fidèles d'enseigner et d'étudier les lettres. Mais l'empereur, sentant l'avantage des institutions chrétiennes, voulut, en les abolissant, les imiter: il fonda des hôpitaux et des monastères; et, à l'instar du culte évangélique, il essaya d'unir la morale à la religion, en faisant prononcer des espèces de sermons dans les temples.

Les sophistes dont Julien était **environné** se déchaînèrent contre le christianisme; Julien même ne dédaigna pas de se mesurer avec les *Galiléens*. L'ouvrage qu'il écrivit contre eux ne nous est pas **parvenu**; mais saint Cyrille, patriarche d'Alexandrie, en cite des fragments dans la réfutation qu'il en a faite, et que nous avons encore[9]. Lorsque Julien est sérieux, saint Cyrille triomphe du philosophe; mais lorsque l'empereur a recours à l'ironie, le patriarche perd ses avantages. Le style de Julien est vif, animé, **spirituel**: saint Cyrille s'emporte, il est bizarre, obscur et **contourné**. Depuis Julien jusqu'à Luther, l'Église, dans toute sa force, n'eut plus besoin d'apologistes. Quand le schisme d'Occident se forma, avec les nouveaux ennemis parurent de nouveaux **défenseurs**. Il le faut avouer, les protestants eurent d'abord la supériorité sur les catholiques, du moins par les formes, comme le remarque[FF] Montesquieu. Érasme même fut faible contre Luther, et Théodore de Bèze eut une légèreté de style qui manqua trop souvent à ses adversaires.

Vocabulary

contourné (adj. < pp.)	contorted, convoluted
spirituel (adj.m.)	witty
défenseurs (n.pl.)	advocates, champions
environner (de)	to surround (with)
parvenir	to reach
parvenir à	to succeed in, to manage to

---

8. *défendit...aux...de*: see Chapter 12 §112, Example 3.

9. The Emperor Julian (332-63), named Julian the Apostate, wrote this work, *Adversus Christianos*, during his Persian campaign (after May, 362 AD). Almost the complete text can be recovered from Cyril of Alexandria's refutation of it, called an Apology. Cyril died in 444 A.D.

12

THE PASSIVE AND PRONOMINAL VERBS

111. The Passive

The authentic passive, insofar as it expresses an action in the process of being performed, is rare in French. This is because of a certain ambiguity between whether an action is being performed or has reached its end result. For example, one could translate *Il est fini* as either "It is being finished" or "It is finished". Therefore, the French tend to avoid using the passive whenever possible.

Even in English, the passive is considered awkward or convoluted, especially in academic discourse. It is used mainly when a certain ambiguity, as to who really was responsible for a certain action, is desirable. Politicians, for example, might want to make a vague promise without taking direct responsibility for the execution of it:

e.g. **This policy will be implemented immediately.**

The words **will be** indicate a future event, but the real action is expressed by the past participle **implemented**. No-one knows who will implement the policy (i.e. the agent), perhaps not even the politician!

A. The Formation of the Passive

The passive is composed, as in English, of the conjugated form of the verb *être* + a past participle. The auxiliary verb *être* determines the tense of the verb, without the past participle being taken into account. As in the English sentence, the agent of the action (the person, animal or object which actually performs the action) is expressed after the prepositions *par* ("by") or *de* ("with" <u>or</u> "by"). The past participle acts more like an adjective than a verb, since it agrees in number and gender with the subject of the sentence.

Note that verbs of transition and pronominal verbs also use *être* as an auxiliary in the compound past. These range of verbs conjugated with *être*, whose meaning is equal to the auxiliary *avoir* (has/have), must be memorized in order not to confuse them with the passive.

Examples

1. Active sentence
   Un chien mord l'enfant.
   A dog is biting the child.

2. Passive sentence
   L'enfant est mordu par un chien.
   The child is being bitten by a dog.

In the active sentence, the subject (*le chien*) performs the action which the child receives (or "suffers" in this case). The passive sentence expresses the same action in reverse. This time, the child is the subject, even if he or she is the recipient (or victim) of the action. We know that the dog performed the action because of the preposition *par* (by). The past participle (*mordu*) is singular because there is only one child, whose gender is masculine. Such an agreement between the subject and the past participle was discussed in Chapter 3 (§25), where the past participle was considered the subjective completion of the verb because of its adjectival function. In those cases, the verb *être* is simply a linking verb and does not form a passive construction. Nevertheless, an uneasy ambiguity remains which renders the passive an unattractive usage in French.

3. **La maison** a été vendue. / **La maison** fut vendue.
   The house has been sold <u>or</u> The house was sold.

4. La maison **était** vendue hier.
   The house **was** sold yesterday.

5. La maison **sera** vendue demain.
   The house **will be** sold tomorrow.

6. La maison **avait** déjà **été** vendue.
   The house **had** already **been** sold.

7. La maison **aura été** vendue avant la fin du mois.
   The house **will have been** sold before the end of the month.

In none of these cases, where the past participle reflects the feminine gender of the house (*la maison*), are we told who the agent was who actually sold or will sell the house.

B. The Agent

The preposition *par* is easier to recognize than *de*. The latter is often used before general nouns which are not accompanied by an article (i.e. *un, une, le, les, les, des*). It is also used to express emotion or a figurative, instead of a literal, meaning.

Examples

8.   Cet article sera certainement lu **par** tout le monde.
   a. This article will certainly be read **by** everyone.
   b. Surely everyone will read this article.

9.   La terre est couverte **de** neige.
   a. The land is being covered **with** snow (*or* **in** snow, **by** snow)
   b. The land is covered **with** snow....

In the first example (8b), an active sentence would even be preferred by the English speaker. **Note** the ambiguity between the two possible translations of the second example. This example also demonstrates the variety by which *de* may be translated, depending upon the context and the preference of the speaker. The translator, therefore, should not hesitate to allow freer translations of *de*, if the English warrants it. The same variety is possible even when *de* accompanies an active verb.

Exercise A

1. Dieu éternel, tu nous as nourris de ton aliment spirituel.

2. Il souffrit sa passion et fut mis au tombeau.

3. Le personnage de Marie de Magdala a été associé de tout temps à l'événement de Pâques (François Bovon).[1]

4. Le peu qu'on sait d'elle, c'est qu'elle fut exorcisée par Jésus.

5. Marie-Madeleine est reliée, du moins par son nom, à Magdala en Galilée, tandis que Marie, la soeur de Marthe, est installée à Béthanie en Judée.

---

1.   Sentences 3-6 were written by François Bovon, "Le privilège pascal de Marie-Madeleine, *New Testament Studies* 30 (1984) 50-62.

6. Marie est déclarée heureuse, bénie, pneumatique et pure.

7. L'identité de Jésus telle qu'elle est racontée par ceux qui ne l'ont pas fréquenté ne peut être retenue; celle des seuls commensaux de Jésus est considérée comme vraie.

8. On sait que Jésus n'était pas suivi d'un groupe de personnes qui notait ses paroles et ses gestes.

9. La conscience pure est actuellement[FF] considérée comme l'ultime essence de l'univers, y compris de l'univers physique.[2]

10. À cause du legs à un organisme[3] destiné à prouver scientifiquement l'existence de l'âme et la survie de la conscience individuelle après la mort, des représentations ont été faites par cent trente-trois organismes.

112. Avoidance of the Passive

There are two ways of avoiding the use of the passive in French:

1. When the agent of the action is unknown, one can still express it using the impersonal pronoun *on* with an active verb.

2. When there is a specified subject, a reflexive verb can be used.

Because both these conventions may be awkward in English, conversion of the French verb into the English passive is often the best option.

Examples

1. **On** nous demande de quitter la salle.
   a. They are asking us to leave the room.
   b. We are being asked to leave the room.

2. Ce livre **se vend** partout.
   This book is sold everywhere. [*Not:* This book sells itself everywhere.]

---

2. Lawrence H. Domash, *La conscience pure est-elle un état quantique macroscopique dans le cerveau?*, cited in <http://www.radio.canada.ca/par4/soc/scimyst.htm>.

3. *organisme*: organization; adapted from <http://www.radio.canada.ca/par4/soc/scimyst.htm>.

The *On* solution is particularly suited to certain verbs that regularly take indirect objects in French, when the corresponding English objects are direct. These verbs are constructed on the pattern of *demander*[FF] first presented in Chapter 1. For example, in English we ask someone (directly) to do something, whereas the English equivalent of the French would be:

3.   Nous demandons à quelqu'un de faire quelque chose.
  a. We are asking (to) someone (of _or_ from?) doing something.
  b. We are asking someone to do something.

Clearly, the two French prepositions (*à, de*) should not be translated. **Note** that without taking *de* into account, *faire* can be translated as a simple infinitive. Other verbs in this group are:

défendre à qn de faire qch	-	to forbid s.o. from doing sth.
dire à qn de faire qch	-	to ask s.o. to do sth.
interdire à qn de faire qch	-	to forbid s.o. from doing sth.
permettre à qn de faire qch	-	to permit s.o. to do sth.

Examples

4.   On **nous** interdit de fumer.
  a. They forbid us to smoke.
  b. We are forbidden to smoke.

5.   On a permis **à Suzanne** de passer le weekend chez les Grillet.
  a. They permitted Susan to spend the weekend at the Grillets' house.
  b. Susan was permitted to spend the weekend at the Grillets'.

In both cases, the passive translation works better in English, because "They" is vague and, furthermore, in the plural when the singular may be intended.

113. Pronominal Verbs

Pronominal verbs are verbs commonly accompanied by reflexive pronouns, but whose meaning is not necessarily reflexive. There is no English equivalent to them. Instead of a reflexive meaning, these verbs often connote a change of state, or a gradual transformation of some kind which may be expressed in English by "get" or "become":
e.g. s'habituer à = to become/get accustomed to (sth. *or* vb).

Note that pronominal verbs are conjugated with *être* in the compound tenses.

Reflexive Pronouns	**Present**		**Compound Past**
me	Je m'habitue	(à)	je me suis habitué(e)
te	Tu t'habitues		tu t'es habitué(e)
se	Il s'habitue		il s'est habitué
nous	Nous nous habituons		nous nous sommes habitués (m.)
vous	Vous vous habituez		vous vous êtes habitués
se	Elles s'habituent		elles se sont habituées
English	They are getting used	(to)	they got used (to)

Pluperfect	**English**
je m'étais habitué(e)	I had become accustomed
tu t'étais habitué(e)	you had become accustomed
il s'était habitué	he had become accustomed
elle s'était habituée	she had become accustomed
on s'était habitué	we had become accustomed
nous nous étions habitués (m.)	we had become accustomed
vous vous étiez habitués	you had become accustomed
ils s'étaient habitués	they had become " (m.)
elles s'étaient habituées	they had become " (f.)

Note that confusion can arise between the form *j'étais habitué* (I was accustomed), which excludes the reflexive pronoun, and the pluperfect conjugation *je m'étais habitué* (I had become accustomed), which implies a completed change of state. The only difference between the two forms is the presence or absence of the reflexive pronoun.

114. Common Pronominal Verbs & Prepositions

The reflexive pronouns in pronominal verbs are not usually translated.[4] Here are some other verbs in this group, of which the most helpful for readers are marked with an asterisk:

s'apprêter à	to get ready to
s'approcher de	to get closer to, to approach
se coucher	to go down (sun), to go to sleep
*se décider à	to come to a decision to, to make up one's mind to
se dépêcher	to hurry up
s'endormir	to fall asleep
*s'ennuyer	to become/get bored
s'habituer à	to become, get accustomed to
*s'installer, se fixer	to become established, to settle in/down
se lever	to get up (sun or person in the morning)
*se rendre compte de	to become aware of, to realize
*se taire	to fall silent, to become quiet
se mettre en colère	to become angry

Other pertinent pronominal verbs are:

*s'agir de	to be a question of, to be a matter of
*s'attendre à	to expect
*se demander	to wonder (to ask oneself)
*se douter de/que	to suspect (*de* + inf./ *que* = that)
s'en aller	to go away
*se fier à	to trust (to entrust oneself to)
*se méfier de	to distrust
*se mettre à	to begin
se moquer de	to make fun of
s'occuper de	to be busy with
se passer	to happen, take place (= 2. arriver)
se passer de	to go without
se plaindre de	to complain of
se préoccuper de	to worry about
*se servir de	to make use of, to use
se soucier de	to be concerned about
*se souvenir de	to remember

---

4. Reflexive (or pronominal) pronouns are also called conjunctive pronouns; for the forms and fuller range of usage, cf. Chapter 9, §85.

A bit like deponent verbs in Latin (passive in form, but translated into an active meaning in English), pronominal verbs are reflexive in form, but translated as active English verbs.

Examples

1. Il s'agit d'une erreur qu'ils ont faite hier.
    It concerns an error which they made yesterday
<u>or</u> It is a question of \ It is a matter of....

2. Nous nous sommes passés de la seconde lecture.
    We dispensed with the second reading.

3. Je me souviens de lui auprès de l'arbre.
    I remember him beside the tree.

4. Je me suis servi de ce dictionnaire.
    I used this dictionary.

115. Idiomatic Usages With *en* and *y*.

A. *en*

en avoir assez	to have had enough
en avoir marre	to be fed up.
en être	to be at a certain point.
s'en aller	to go away
ne pas s'en faire	not to worry
s'en ficher	not to give a damn
s' en prendre à qn.	to blame; to take it out on s.o.
en vouloir à qn.	to bear a grudge against s.o.

1. J' **en** ai assez de cette situation.
    I have had enough of this situation (Fr. = present tense)

2. J'**en** ai marre de tes plaintes.
    I am fed up with your complaints.

3. Où **en** sommes-nous?
    Where are we?

4. Va-t-**en**!
   Go away!

5. Elle ne s'**en** fait pas.
   She doesn't make a fuss over it.

6. Elle s'**en** fiche.
   She couldn't care less.

7. J'**en** veux à mon professeur.
   I have it in for my teacher.

B. *y*

aller y	go on
s'y connaître	to be an expert in sth.
s'y faire	to get used to sth.
s'y prendre	to get down to it

1. Vas-**y**! Allons-**y**!
   Go on! Let's go!

2. Nous nous **y** connaissons.
   We know all about it.

3. Ça va, je m'**y** fais.
   It is okay, I am getting used to it.

4. Il sait s'**y** prendre.
   He knows how to get down to it.

116. Passive, Pronominal, Reciprocal, Reflexive

Apart from the pronominal verbs (listed above) which are translated in the active, non-reflexive English voice, reflexive verbs in French may be translated in three ways:

1. as a true reflexive
2. as a passive
3. with reciprocity (only in the plural forms of verbs)

Examples

1. Je **me** lave.
   I wash **myself** (direct object).

2. Je **me** demande.
   a. I ask **myself** (indirect object: demander à qn).
   b. I wonder (pronominal verb having developed its own meaning).

3. Cela ne **se dit** pas.
   That **is** not **said** (passive).

4. Ils **se sont vus**, mais ils ne **se sont** pas **parlé** (reciprocal).
   They saw **each other**, but they did not speak **to each other**.

Remember that the reflexive pronoun can be either a direct or indirect object. In the fourth sentence, *vus* is inflected with the plural *s* because *se* is the direct object, but *parlé* is not inflected because *se* represents an indirect object. Note that there is some ambiguity in the meaning of the plural reflexive pronouns; e.g. *ils se parlent* could mean either "speak to themselves" or "speak to each other". To resolve this ambiguity, pronominal phrases are added.

A. Reflexive

To insist upon the reflexive meaning, the following clarifications may be added:

1. à nous-mêmes (1p.pl. - nous): to ourselves
2. à vous-mêmes (2p.pl. - vous): to yourselves
3. à eux-mêmes (m.pl. - se): to themselves
4. à elles-mêmes (f.pl. - se): to themselves

B. Reciprocity

To insist upon the reciprocal meaning, the following reinforcements may be added:

1. entre nous, vous, eux, elles: among ourselves, yourselves, themselves; between us, etc.
2. les un(e)s les autres, les un(e)s aux autres, l'un(e) à l'autre: one another; each other, etc.

Exercise B

1. Voilà! Les deux solitudes canadiennes viennent de se serrer la main.

2. Nous nous demandions ce qui se passait dans la rue.

3. Il se plaint du bruit que font les voisins.

4. Elle se doutait qu'elle avait perdu son livre.

5. Ils se regardaient sans rien dire.

6. Il voudrait bien se passer de fumer.

7. Je me suis promis de cesser de fumer.

8. Aimez-vous les uns les autres.

9. Nous nous sommes promis l'un à l'autre de nous revoir.

10. Cela ne se fait pas.

11. Il n'arrive[FF] pas à se passer de vin.

12. Ils se parlent à eux-mêmes.

13. Les journaux[FF] se vendent là-bas.

14. Tu ne dois t'en prendre qu'à toi-même.

15. Cela s'explique facilement.

16. Les partis politiques se battent entre eux.

17. Vous ne vous nuisez que l'un à l'autre.

18. En Aggée 1:2 Yahwé s'en prend à son peuple au sujet de son inactivité face à la ré édification du temple de Jérusalem (John Kessler).

19. La puissance de Dieu se voit dans la nature.

20. Instruisez-vous et avertissez-vous les uns les autres avec pleine sagesse (Col.3:16).

117. Readings: Marie-Paul Dion & Paul Ricoeur

Exercise C

Extract from Marie-Paul Dion, "La recluse de Montréal, Jeanne Le Ber". *Église et Théologie* 22 (1991), 50-51.

Monsieur Olier et Jérôme Le Royer de la Dauversière s'étaient rencontrés et reconnus providentiellement – miraculeusement? – à Paris. Ils s'étaient communiqué leur désir réciproque de travailler au salut des âmes en Nouvelle-France en y fondant une colonie. Depuis leur première rencontre, ils avaient toujours agi de concert pour la réalisation de ce grand dessein...

Rien de très précis ne nous permet de connaître les noms des membres de la Société Notre-Dame de Montréal. L'impuissance des chercheurs à trouver les noms est peut-être un indice de la pureté des motifs qui les animaient. Ils prenaient soin de se cacher aux yeux des hommes: presque tous n'étaient connus que de Dieu seul, même s'il y avait[5] parmi eux des magistrats, des comtes, des ducs, des dames de haute qualité dont la plupart étaient connus et influents dans Paris. Les Associés, en tant qu'associés, voulaient laisser à Dieu seul la gloire de l'oeuvre que lui-même leur avait inspirée; c'est du moins l'opinion de l'historien Faillon.

---

5. *même s'il y avait*: originally "quoiqu'il y eût" involving the imperfect subjunctive which we only study in Chapter 15.

Exercise D

The following passage is an extract from Paul Ricoeur (1913-2005), *La métaphore vive* (Paris: Éditions du Seuil, 1975), p.14. The words highlighted in bold are defined either in the footnotes or in the following list of vocabulary.

A Protestant philosopher, Paul Ricoeur attempted among many things to marry theology to philosophy. Having studied philosophy at the Université de Rennes and then the Sorbonne (Paris IV), he passed the national exam (*l'agrégation*) in philosophy in 1935. For the four years before the war broke out, he taught philosophy in Colmar while learning German and writing his thesis. World War II, for him, meant that he was first drafted and then detained as a prisoner of war for five years, thus delaying the completion of his thesis until 1948. He then taught philosophy at the University of Strasbourg until returning to teach at the Sorbonne (1956-67). One of the highlights of his teaching career was a seminar in phenomenology which he conducted at the Sorbonne in collaboration with Jacques Derrida.

After the student unrest of 1968, which began at the Université de Nanterre (now Paris X), which Ricoeur had helped to found, Ricoeur retreated to the Catholic University of Louvain. In 1980, he retired from teaching, but not from publishing.[6]

> La rhétorique mourut lorsque le goût de classer **les figures** eut entièrement supplanté le sens philosophique qui animait le vaste empire rhétorique, **faisait tenir ensemble**[7] ses parties et rattachait le tout à **l'organon**[8] et à la philosophie première[9].
>
> Ce sentiment d'une perte irrémédiable s'accroît encore si l'on considère que le vaste programme aristotélicien représentait lui-même, sinon une réduction, du moins la rationalisation d'une discipline qui, en son lieu d'origine, à Syracuse[10], s'était proposée de régir tous les usages de la parole publique. Il y eut rhétorique, parce qu'il y eut éloquence, éloquence publique. La remarque[FF] va loin: d'abord la parole fut une arme destinée à influencer le peuple, devant le tribunal, dans l'assemblée publique, ou encore pour l'éloge et le panégyrique: une arme **appelée** à donner la victoire dans les luttes où le discours fait la décision. Nietzsche écrit: "L'éloquence

---

6. Paul Ricoeur, "Intellectual Autobiography," *The Philosophy of Paul Ricoeur* (The Library of Living Philosophers, 22). Chicago: Open Court, 1995.

7. *faisait tenir ensemble*: caused (dir.obj.) to hold together. Cf. Chapter Thirteen, §119, The Causative.

8. The *Organon* is Artistotle's treatise on logic.

9. In Aristotle's *Metaphysics*, the first philosophy is "being *qua* being" which includes the study of theology, since he understood the divine to be "being" *par excellence*.

10. Gorgias, known for his eloquence, was born in Syracuse, where he taught rhetoric until he went to Athens in 427 B.C.E.

est républicaine." La vieille définition reçue des Siciliens - "la rhétorique est ouvrière (ou maîtresse) de persuasion" - **rappelle** que la rhétorique s'est ajoutée comme une "technique" à l'éloquence naturelle, mais que cette technique plonge dans **une démiurgie**[11] spontanée; parmi tous les traités didactiques écrits en Sicile, puis en Grèce, lorsque Gorgias se fut fixé à Athènes[12], la rhétorique fut cette *technê* qui rendit le discours conscient de lui-même et fit de la persuasion un but distinct à atteindre par le moyen d'une stratégie spécifique.

Avant donc la taxinomie **des figures**, il y eut la grande rhétorique d'Aristote; mais avant celle-ci, il y eut l'usage **sauvage** de la parole et l'ambition de capter par le moyen d'une technique spéciale sa puissance dangereuse.

Vocabulary

les figures (n.f.pl.)	[rhetorical] figures of speech
appelée (pp.f.)	called < invoked
rappelle (v.tr.3 pres.)	recalls < reminds <us>
sauvage (adj.m.)	untamed < unschooled

118. BASIC VOCABULARLY: Chapters 10-12

NOUNS

âme (f.)	soul
apparition (f.)	(resurrection) appearance
chair (f.)	flesh
corps (m.)	body
défi (m.)	challenge
esprit (m.)	spirit; mind
langue (f.)	language; tongue
pain (m.)	bread
parole (f; de Dieu)	word (of God)
recueil (m.)	collection, anthology
récit (m.)	narrative, story, account

---

11. *démiurgie*: creativity. The Platonic name for the Creator was *demiurgos* in Greek. Gnosticism placed the demiurge below the Supreme Being.

12. Gorgias (485-380 B.C.E.) was a Greek orator, Sophist and nihilist. He posited that nothing exists, but that if anything does exist, it cannot be known, and that even if it can be known, it cannot be communicated. Plato attacks Sophist rhetoric in his dialogue named after Gorgias. Cf. n.9 above.

sang (m.)	blood
sens (m.)	meaning, sense; direction
souci (m.)	worry, concern
survie (f.)	survival
vin (m.)	wine

COMPARATIVE & SUPERLATIVE FORMS   Listed in §97-99.

POSSESSIVE PRONOUNS   Listed in §101.

COMPOUND ADVERBS AND ADJECTIVES   Listed in §107.

CONJUNCTIONS

en même temps (que)	at the same time (as)
lorsque	when
quand	when
parce que	because
puisque	since

COMPOUND PREPOSITIONS

à cause de	because of
à la manière de (+ n.)	in the manner of, like
au lieu de	instead of
du moins (= au moins + quantity)	at least
en tant que	as (in the capacity of)
face à	in the face of, facing
sinon...	if not...; except
y compris qch.	including sth.

PREPOSITIONAL PHRASES AND IDIOMS

à mon gré, à ton gré, etc.	to my/your liking, etc.
à mon insu, à ton insu, etc.	without me/you knowing, etc.
	(*lit.* to my unknown, etc.)
d'accord	in agreement
de façon / de manière (+ adj.)	in a (adj.) way
de plus en plus (+ adj., adv.)	more and more/ ever more
destiné à	intended for, aimed at
rien à voir avec	nothing to do with

EXPRESSIONS OF QUANTITY   Listed in §96.

ESSENTIAL PRONOMINAL VERBS   Listed in §114.

VERBS

il s'agit de	it is a question of, it concerns
apporter	to bring
emporter	to carry away
l'emporter (sur)	to prevail (over), gain the upper hand
englober	to include, embody
comprendre*	to include[FF]; understand (comprehend)
défendre à *qn* de *inf.*(= interdire)	to forbid s.o. to do sth.
permettre à *qn* de *vb. inf.*	to permit s.o. to do sth.
dépasser	to surpass
dérouler (se)	to develop, unfold
enterrer	to bury
paraître	to appear, seem; be published
retenir	to accept; hold back; remember
sembler	to seem

13

THE CAUSATIVE AND DEVOIR

Please note that a "Basic Vocabulary" list for the final three chapters is found at the end of Chapter Fifteen.

119. The Causative

The verb *faire* used as an auxiliary (helper) before another verb in the infinitive **causes** something to be done by someone other than the subject of the sentence. In this case, *faire* is called a **causative verb**, as introduced in Chapter 5, §42.

A. Translation System

A suggested system of translation is the following:

1. Read *faire* as a form of "to cause" (sth. to be done).
2. Skip the following infinitive.
3. Read and translate the direct object (noun + modifiers).
4. Return to read the infinitive as a passive infinitive: e.g. "to be" and the past participle of the verb.
5. Smooth out the rough translation, once you have the sense of it. You can use forms of "to have" or "to make" (instead of "to cause"), which do not require "to be" after the direct object.

Example

1.   Le professeur **fera traduire** le poème.
   a.   The teacher **will cause** the poem **to be translated**.
   b.   The teacher **will have** the poem **translated**.

Note that the smoother translation (b) respects the tense of "fera" just as "will cause" does, but reduces the passive infinitive to the past participle ("translated"). The infinitive "to be" is no longer necessary. Therefore, it is always simpler and smoother to use the second style of translation (b above and in the examples below using "make"/"have").

B. Direct and Indirect Objects

In French, unlike in English, direct or indirect objects cannot be positioned between *faire* and the following infinitive. The two French verbs work so closely together that they cannot be separated; i.e. no object can come between "fera traduire" (above).

Examples

1. Nous **faisons faire** la vaisselle <u>à nos enfants</u>.
   We **have (make)** <u>our children</u> **do** the dishes.

2. Nous <u>leur</u> **faisons faire** la vaisselle.
   We **have** <u>them</u> **do** the dishes.

Note that in English the objects ("our children" *or* "them") of the first verb ("have") become the agents of the second verb ("do"). The English syntax allows this simple progression, whereas the French requires that the causative verb remain directly contiguous to the infinitive which it influences. In this case, the second verb is active.

120. Agents in the Causative Construction

An agent is introduced by *à, par* or *de* following the same patterns established by the passive (Chapter 12).

Examples

1. Je <u>me</u> **suis fait inviter** par un ami.
   I **had** <u>myself</u> **invited** by a friend.

2. Elle <u>s</u>'est fait[1] aimer <u>de lui</u>.
   a. She **made** <u>herself</u> **loved** <u>by him</u>.
   b. She **made** <u>him</u> love <u>her</u>.

3. Il **fait lire** des journaux <u>à son fils.</u>
   He **has** <u>his son</u> **read** newspapers.

---

1. One might expect *Elle s'est faite* here since the subject is feminine, before the auxiliary *être*. However, when such a construction is followed by an infinitive (e.g. *aimer*), implying the causative construction, the compound past tense (*passé composé*) is always invariable (*Le bon usage*, §915, p.1376).

Note that in the first example, "<u>myself</u>" is the direct object (reflexive pronoun), which slips in between "had" and "invited". The reflexive "herself" slips likewise in between "made" and "loved" unless one converts the passive into an active voice where the object pronouns are reversed. In the last example, the phrase *à son fils* is slightly ambiguous since it could be confused with an indirect object: i.e. He has newspapers read to his son. To avoid such ambiguity, one could substitute *par* for *à* (*Il fait lire des journaux **par son fils***), thus specifying that the son is the agent of the main action (reading).

121. Common Combinations

faire intervenir	to have s.o. intervene
faire remarquer	to point out
faire ressortir	to emphasize, to accentuate, to bring out
faire savoir	to inform, to make known
faire venir	to summon
faire valoir	to promote, assert

Examples

1. Le premier ministre **fait venir** le philosophe.
   a. The prime minister **has** the philosopher **come**.
   b. The prime minister **summons** the philosopher.

2. La toile mystique? Elle la leur **fera voir**.
   The mystical oil painting? She **will have** it **shown** to them.

122. *Ne faire que* [+verb]

"To do nothing but" [one action] <u>or</u> "to [verb] continually" can be expressed using *faire* with *ne...que*. This usage must be distinguished from that of the causative. **Note** that this construction allows *que* to separate *faire* from the main verb.

Example

1. Tu **ne** fais **que** parler!
   a. You do nothing except talk!
   b. All you do is talk!
   c. You talk continuously!

Exercise A

1. Il a fait ressortir le sens du texte.

2. Le philosophe nous fera savoir son sujet demain.

3. Elle s'est fait gronder par l'éditeur.[FF]

4. Il fait faire ses costumes à Paris.

5. Personne au monde ne le fera changer d'avis. (Cocteau, *Bacchus*, III,7)[2].

6. Il a réussi à se faire comprendre.

7. Ce jeune couple s'est fait construire une maison neuve.

8. Ils font faire du sport à leurs enfants.

9. On nous a fait attendre.

10. Elle fait lire ses enfants.

11. Devant les croyants, Nietzsche est plus réservé, comme s'il craignait de les faire souffrir en se faisant trop bien entendre (Henri de Lubac).

12. S'il l'avait voulu, il aurait pu faire envoyer une lettre par sa femme.

13. Le pouvoir royal utilisera les privilèges comme outils pour faire adhérer les universitaires à ses idées, selon les opportunités ou nécessités politiques (Lyse Roy).

14. Il fut ainsi plus difficile pour les universitaires de faire valoir leurs droits auprès du souverain (Lyse Roy).

15. Vous ne faites que vous plaindre.

---

2. *Le bon usage*, §791*e*.

123. *Devoir*

There are many possible translations for the auxiliary or modal verb *devoir* (which acts as an aid to another main verb). The semantic range includes *must, have to, be to, be obliged to, intend to, ought* and *should*.

A. Present Tense

The simplest translations for the present tense are "must" and "have to". The translations "should" or "ought to" are better suited to the context of a general precept or maxim.

Examples

1. Ça **doit** l'être.
    That **must** be it.

2. On doit tenir sa parole.
    One **must** (has to, ought to) keep one's word.

3. On doit honorer ses parents (general precept).
    One **ought to** (should) honour one's parents.

Note that *l'* divides the auxiliary verb (doit) from the infinitive (être). Direct objects (*le, la, les*) may divide modal or auxiliary verbs from the main verb they are helping, unlike the exceptional case of the causative *faire*.

B. Imperfect Tense

The imperfect tense expresses an action that was supposed to happen. The best translations are "was/were obliged/supposed to" or simply **"was to"** where neither "obliged" nor "supposed" are essential, but optional. The equally short "had to" may also work, implying that it was indeed done.

Examples

1. Elle **devait** voir le directeur, mais il était malade.
    a. She **was to** see the director, but he was ill.
    b. She **was supposed to** see the director, but he was ill.

2. Il **devait** le faire.
    a. He **was to** do it.
    b. He **was obliged to** do it [= had to do it].

C. Compound Past

The translation of compound past tenses involves an inversion of the word order: i.e. *a dû* is translated word-by-word as "has must", but the meaning is better expressed as "must have" (as in a chiasmas or mirror image). Unlike the tenses exemplified above, the main verb can no longer be expressed as a simple infinitive, but becomes a past participle.

Examples

3. Elles **ont dû manquer** le train.
They **must have missed** the train.

4. Il **a dû** le **faire**.
He **must have done** it.

Note that this compound form of *devoir* is practically invariable: i.e. *must have* is the correct translation for both singular and plural verbs.

Compound forms in the pluperfect and future perfect use "had had" and "will have had" respectively. In English again, neither of these vary according to number (or gender of course).

Examples

5. Ils **avaient dû** le faire.
They **had had** to do it.

6. Elle **aura dû** le faire.
She **will have had** to do it.

D. The Conditional

Always translate *devoir* in the conditional tense as **should**, even if it is in the past when the auxiliary verb *avoir* marks the past conditional tense. When *avoir* is in the past conditional, the translation is "should have".

Examples

7. Nous **devrions** le lire ce soir.
We **should** read it this evening.

8. On **aurait dû** partir avant minuit.
We **should have** left before midnight (OR they should have; lit. One should have...)

Note that *aurait dû* is reversed in English as "should have", and that the real verb is *partir*.

Exercice B

1. Il doit être en retard à cause du mauvais temps.

2. Ça doit l'être!

3. Elle devait lire tout le chapitre ce soir.

4. Il devrait travailler!

5. Il aurait dû travailler!!

6. Tu devrais partager tes connaissances avec tes amis.

7. Ils devaient rentrer plus tôt.

8. Nous devions nous arrêter.

9. Nous devrons les voir ce soir.

10. On doit aimer ses voisins.

124. Readings: Lyse Roy and Henri de Lubac[3]

Exercise C

Translate the following excerpt from Lyse Roy, "Espace urbain et système de représentations. Les entrées du Dauphin et de François Ier à Caen en 1532", *Memini. Travaux et documents publiés par la Sociétés des études médiévales du Québec* 5 (2001), 51-52. Lyse Roy specializes in the University of Caen of the fifteenth and sixteenth centuries, and is professor of history at the Université du Québec à Montréal.

**Espace urbain et système de représentations.
Les entrées du Dauphin et de François Ier à Caen en 1532**

L'entrée amène le roi à transgresser une limite et à la réinscrire en s'emparant de la ville et en reconnaissant la loyauté de ses sujets. Elle fait ainsi de l'ensemble spatial limité une partie d'une totalité (une ville parmi d'autres dans le royaume) et cette totalité est résumée et condensée dans une partie (tout le royaume dans cette ville). L'événement de l'entrée constitue également un moment privilégié de définition par la confrontation des identités de ceux qui reçoivent et de celui qui est reçu. Il structure la rencontre d'une identité urbaine et d'une identité princière. La communauté urbaine comme le pouvoir princier ou royal se définissent et se représentent dans un rituel dont les motifs s'inscrivent à la fois dans le temps court de l'événement et dans le temps long de l'histoire. **La structurelle** cérémonielle, découpée en séquences pratiquement invariantes, imposée et contrôlée par le pouvoir étatique et les programmes symboliques, festifs et décoratifs variés, imaginés par la ville, sont investis d'une fonction **identitaire** exprimant l'existence sociale et la reconnaissance d'une communauté et d'un pouvoir... Dans cette perspective sociologique, les luttes d'identité ont pour objectif le monopole du pouvoir symbolique (faire voir et faire croire, faire connaître et faire reconnaître) et la volonté d'imposer la définition légitime des divisions du monde social et la vision du monde social qui donne sens au groupe. L'analyse de **la mise en représentation** du champ politique fait dire à Pierre Bourdieu que la cérémonie est un acte de théâtralisation des groupes sociaux qui se donnent d'abord en spectacle à eux-mêmes, puis au monde.

---

3. See Appendix I.A for a supplementary passage from a literary source that offers further practice with the causative.

Vocabulary

structurelle (n.f)	structure
identitaire (adj)	identifying
mise en représentation (n.f)	performance

Exercise D

The following extract is taken from Henri de Lubac, "Nietzsche et la «mort de Dieu»" in *Le Drame de l'humanisme athée*, pp. 46-48. **Note** that the French style of quotation marks («...») and placement of footnotes (before punctuation) have been maintained to give the student an idea of the minor differences. An English translation must convert these conventions to English equivalents. For this exercise, please translate the footnotes as well.

> ...[L]e sens que Nietzsche attache à cette expression de la « mort de Dieu » est nouveau. Elle n'est pas dans sa bouche un simple **constat**. Elle n'est pas non plus une lamentation ni un sarcasme. Elle **traduit** une option. « Maintenant, dit Nietzsche, c'est notre goût qui décide contre le christianisme, ce ne sont pas des arguments[4]. » Elle est un acte. Acte aussi net, aussi brutal que l'est celui d'un meurtrier. « La mort de Dieu n'est pas seulement pour lui un fait terrible, elle est **voulue** par lui[5]. » Si Dieu est mort, ajoute-t-il en effet, « c'est nous qui l'avons tué ». « Nous sommes les assassins de Dieu[6]. »
>
> Beaucoup parmi les hommes, la grande masse, ne s'en aperçoivent pas. Ils prennent pour un fou celui qui vient leur en annoncer la nouvelle. Ce sont les deux vastes catégories des croyants et des athées vulgaires. Les premiers, ne comprenant rien à ses dires, n'en sont même pas troublés. Ils continuent leur rêve au milieu d'un monde qui s'éveille. Leur foi les rend pour ainsi dire aveugles et sourds. Les seconds, qui n'ont jamais cru à rien, l'accueillent avec un grand rire. Jamais ils n'ont soupçonné rien de vivant au delà de la vie **sensible**. Nietzsche voudrait arracher ceux-ci à leur insouciance, il voudrait leur faire apercevoir le vide qui s'est creusé en eux, et il les **interpelle** avec violence. Devant les croyants, au contraire, s'il les sent sincères et simples, son attitude est réservée, comme s'il craignait de les faire souffrir en se faisant trop bien entendre... « J'arrive trop tôt, se dit-

---

4. *Le gai savoir*. Bauemler se trompe donc lorsqu'il écrit [que]... la phrase décisive, «Dieu est mort», a le sens d'une constatation historique. *Nietzsche, le philosophe et le politique* (1931), p.98. Nietzsche fait beaucoup plus que constater.

5. John Wahl, *Le Nietzsche de Jaspers*, dans les *Recherches philosophiques*, t.6, p.356...

6. *Le gai savoir*, n. 125, *L'insensé* (p.104-105).

il, mon temps n'est pas encore venu. » C'est que « les événements les plus importants sont aussi les plus lents à s'imposer. »

Vocabulary

constat (n.m.)	observation, statement
traduit (v.tr.3 pres.)	expresses _or_ conveys (not "translates")
voulue (pp.f.)	willed
en effet (adv.)	in fact, actually
sensible (adj.)	sensate
interpeller (vb.tr.inf.)	to heckle

14

THE SUBJUNCTIVE: PRESENT AND PAST

125. The Subjunctive Mood

The mood of the subjunctive is hypothetical. It expresses only a possibility which may or may not come to pass, or an emotion which desires or wills something to happen. It is used when there is a change of subject between the principle clause and the subordinate clause. For example, *Il faut partir* (It is necessary to leave) involves no change of subject, because the entire sentence is impersonal; we do not know **who** should be leaving since no subject is specified (see §126 below). Whenever a real subject is introduced in the secondary clause after verbs of desiring, emotion, subjective judgement or will, the subjunctive follows the subordinating conjunction *que*, generally translated as

1) "that" at the beginning of a subordinate clause, or
2) "May", "Let" or "Would that" (Lat. *utinam*) at the very beginning of a sentence.

After the above two usages of *que,* the French application of the subjunctive mood follows the systematic rules laid out in this chapter. Post-modern English has a tendency not to use the subjunctive mood at all. Consequently, many of the French verbs in the subjunctive can simply be translated into the English indicative, or quite freely as "may", "might", "would" or "were to".

Examples

1.   Je veux qu'il vienne.
   a.   I wish that he would come.
   b.   I wish him to come.

2.   Qu'il vienne. Qu'il parte maintenant!
     Let him come! Would that he would leave now! (archaic)

3.   Que ton nom soit sanctifié. Que ton règne vienne.[1]
     May your name be sanctified. May your kingdom come.

The first example demonstrates the greater flexibility between subjects and objects in English than in French. The French subjunctive is normally used when there is a change of subject: i.e. there are two subjects, one for each clause. English can just use a direct object pronoun and an infinitive for the second subject and its action (as in "1.b" above): "him to come", but French cannot. French can only use this form when the subject remains the same:

4.   Je veux venir demain.
     I want to come tomorrow.

In this case, there is only one person wishing to perform his or her own action.

The first example above also demonstrates the proximity between the subjunctive and the conditional. Since the English subjunctive is under-employed, we often prefer the conditional (as in "1.a" above): "would come." French must use the subjunctive, however. The second example is jussive (a command) or at least hortatory (urging). The third example is optative (expressing a wish). All these forms descend from Latin origins.

Since there is no subjunctive mood for the future tense, a present subjunctive is sometimes best translated with the future in English. See "Verbal Forms Introducing Doubt" below (§135).

5.   Je doute qu'il **vienne**.
     I doubt that he **will come**.

126. Impersonal Expressions with the Subjunctive

We have already learned some impersonal expressions. Not all of them introduce the subjunctive:

1.   Il nous reste deux chapitres à étudier.
   a.   It remains to us two chapters to study.
   b.   We still have two chapters to study.

---

1. See the Lord's Prayer at the end of Chapter 2.

"It" (or possibly "There" as in "There remain") is an impersonal subject (which refers to no-one in particular). In such cases, look for the real subject following the impersonal verb and bring it up to replace the artificial subject ("There/It") as in #1b above where the real subject is "We" (> "to us").

Because *Il faut* expresses necessity (which still may not be accomplished, hypothetically), it introduces the subjunctive when there is a change of subject.

Examples

2. Il faut savoir la réponse.
   a. One must know the answer.
   b. The answer must be known.

3. Il faut que tu saches la réponse.
   a. It is necessary that you know the answer.
   b. It is necessary for you to know the answer.
   c. You have to know the answer.

In example #2, no real subject is ever expressed. We don't know who should know the answer (or why?), but we accept it as a general principle. In example #3, the general principle is applied to a specific case: *tu* (you). The second translation in each case (b) is less clumsy, because it dispenses with the circumlocution which *Il faut* (it is necessary) requires and replaces it with a simple auxiliary verb (either "have to" or "must"). *Il faut* is therefore almost a synonym for *devoir*, but used when a more impersonal, "arm's-length" distance is desirable. It suggests some higher authority or principle than the personal one of *devoir*; e.g. *je dois savoir...* (I ought to know...) by my own reckoning or conscience.

127. Formation of the Present Subjunctive

The subjunctive endings in the present tense are very similar to those of regular first conjugation verbs in the present indicative. However, the root requires a consonant which sounds. To produce the sound, the final consonant of the root (especially *l, n* or *s*) is doubled before the endings are added, if it is not already doubled in the present tense.

Regular Verbs

	I. -er verbs **donner** (to give)	II. -ir verbs **finir** (to finish)	III. -re verbs **perdre** (to lose)
que je	donne	finisse	perde
que tu	donnes	finisses	perdes
qu'elle	donne	finisse	perde
que nous	donnions	finissions	perdions
que vous	donniez	finissiez	perdiez
qu'ils	donnent	finissent	perdent

The paradigm for the singular endings is the same as the present tense of the **-er** verbs, so that there is no difference between all of the subjunctive and present tense of *donner* apart from the first two plural inflections: *donnions, donniez*. For these two plural persons (we and you), the paradigm follows the imperfect endings with the added "i: in all three conjugations.

128. Irregular Verbs

	AVOIR	**ÊTRE**
que	j'aie	je sois
	tu aies	tu sois
qu'	il ait	elle soit
	nous ayons	nous soyons
	vous ayez	vous soyez
qu'	elles aient	ils soient

Note that "y" takes the place of "i" in the first and second plural persons. The second persons singular and plural and the first person plural also supply the **imperative** forms in these two cases (e.g., *aie, ayons, ayez; sois, soyons, soyez*), as with "savoir" below (e.g., *sache*, etc.)

Other irregular forms of the subjunctive are:

	SAVOIR	**DEVOIR**	**POUVOIR**	**VOULOIR**	**ALLER**
que je	sache	doive	puisse	veuille	aille
que tu	saches	doives	puisses	veuilles	ailles
qu'il	sache	doive	puisse	veuille	aille
que ns	sachions	devions	puissions	voulions	allions
que vs	sachiez	deviez	puissiez	vouliez	alliez
qu'ils	sachent	doivent	puissent	veuillent	aillent

	DIRE	**FAIRE**	**TENIR**	**VENIR**	**VOIR**
que je	dise	fasse	tienne	vienne	voie
que tu	dises	fasses	tiennes	viennes	voies
qu'il	dise	fasse	tienne	vienne	voie
que ns	disions	fassions	tenions	venions	voyions
que vs	disiez	fassiez	teniez	veniez	voyiez
qu'ils	disent	fassent	tiennent	viennent	voient

129. Usage of the Subjunctive

Apart from the "jussive" (imperatives) and "optative" (wishes) forms described above, the subjunctive occurs in subordinate clauses which are adjectival or which always follow certain conjunctions, verbs or impersonal verbs.

130. Noun Clauses

Noun clauses are introduced by certain indefinite pronouns which involve *que* meaning -ever; and *soit*, the subjunctive of être; e.g,. whatever, whoever, etc.

Examples

1. **Qui que soit** cet homme, engageons-le à travailler pour nous.
    Whoever this man **may be**, let's hire him to work for us.

2. **Qui que** ce **soit** qui **dise** une telle chose n'est pas très intelligent.
    Whoever (it may be who) **would say** such a thing is not very intelligent.

3. **Quoi qu'**il **veuille**, écoutons-le.
    Whatever he may want, let us listen to him.

4. **Quel que soit** le chien qu'il **achète**, le chat s'énervera!
    a. **Whichever** the dog **may be** that he **will buy**, the cat....
    b. **Whichever** dog he **may buy**, the cat will become irritated!

The pronoun *quiconque* (whoever) does not require the subjunctive but still retains the indefinite meaning:

5. **Quiconque** reconnaît ses erreurs est à la fois modeste et intelligent/e.
    Whoever recognizes his/her errors is at once humble and intelligent.

131. Adjectival Clauses

The next group all involve adjectives in the main clause followed by *que*. The English equivalents can be slightly modified between the synonyms: e.g. However, For as (adj.) as, etc.

1. **Aussi** riche **que** vous **soyez**, vous n'avez pas le droit de venir.
   However rich you **may be**, you have no right to come.

2. **Si** célèbre   **qu'elle soit**, elle est restée très humble.
   As famous **as** she **may be**, she has remained very humble.

3. **Pour** triste **qu'elle nous apparaisse**, ce n'est pas le cas.
   For as sad **as** she **may appear** to us, it is not the case.

4. **Tout** vexé **qu'il** fasse semblant d'être, il ne l'est pas.
   As annoyed **as** he **may feign** to be, he is not [it].[2]
   As annoyed **as** he **seems**, he isn't <really>.

The final "it" in #4 above does not need to be translated literally into English. This is a fairly common occurrence.

Occasionally, adjectival clauses may create a similar effect without any use of *aussi, si* (variant of *aussi*), *pour, tout*, <u>or</u> even *que*, as in the following example.

5. L'interruption, **fût-elle momentanée**, introduit une pause significative.
   a. The interruption, **momentary as it may have been**, introduces a significant
         pause.
   b. The interruption, **no matter how momentary**, introduces....

Note that *fût* (3rd p.sg) is the imperfect subjunctive of *être*.[3]

The last group involves superlative adjectives in the main sentence, because the assertion of something superlative is considered a subjective judgement and therefore hypothetical.

6. Voici **le meilleur** livre **que j'aie** lu!
   Here is the best book that I have <ever> read!

Note that "ever" is implied and expected in English, even if it does not appear in the French.

---

2. The *l'* before *est* could be translated as "it", standing for "annoyed", but is redundant in English.
3. Cf. Chapter 15 for more details on the imperfect subjunctive.

132. Conjunctions, Pleonastic *ne, & sans que*

The following conjunctions always involve the introduction of a new subject and a verb in the subjunctive. If the conjunction is marked with an asterisk, there may be a **pleonastic** *ne* (superfluous; without meaning) before the subjunctive verb in the subordinate clause.

A. Concessive and Conditional Conjunctions

The following concessive and conditional (including restrictive conditional) conjunctions introduce subjunctive verbs which all express hypothetical statements.

i) Concessive Conjunctions

à supposer que	supposing that
bien que	although
encore que	even though
quoique	although

ii) Conditional Conjunctions

à condition que	on the condition that
à moins que*	unless
pourvu que	provided that
que[FF]	whether
sans que*	without (n.b. *que* is not translated)

The pleonastic *ne* is a stylistic feature of literary French. Without the *pas*, the French consider it an expletive (a word used to fill out the sentence) with no meaning. Its use in French is usually optional, but it is commonly found after a verb or conjunction which expresses fear (*craindre, avoir peur de, de peur que*), doubt (*douter*), negation (*nier*) or dependence (*dépendre de*), and, consequently, accompanied by the subjunctive, if, with the exception of fear, introduced by a question or negation. The conjunctions above marked by an asterisk which might be seen with the pleonastic *ne* are *à moins que, avant que, de peur que* and *sans que*. Its frequent use after comparative adjectives and adverbs does not involve the subjunctive.

Note that the pleonastic *ne* (without *pas*) must not be confused with the negative *ne* used by the COPS verbs which drop the *pas* through common usage. Cf. Chapter 7, §63.

Examples

1. Nous sortirons **à moins qu'il ne pleuve.**
   We will go out **unless** it **rains.**

2. Je **crains** qu'il **ne** vienne.
    I am afraid that he may come.

3. **Nierez-vous** que la Canadienne Emily Carr **ne** soit une grande artiste?
    Will you deny that the Canadian Emily Carr is a great artist?

The conjunction *sans que* differs from the preposition *sans* by the addition of *que* in French, but this *que* is not translated into English. The *que* is not translated precisely because it merely serves to mark the transition between two parts of speech, from preposition (*sans*) to conjunction (*sans que*). Among the other prepositions which make similar metamorphoses (*avant, jusqu'à, après*), *sans que* is the most difficult conjunction to translate. Sometimes, *que* alone might imply one of these conjunctions, depending upon the context.
In English, the subjunctive verb after *sans que* is best translated as a present participle (-ing) after the object pronoun of the subject (him = *il*).

4. Je voudrais sortir **sans qu'il sache** pourquoi.
    I would like to go out **without** <u>him</u> **knowing** why.

Que alone is the most problematic, since it is used so commonly in many diverse contexts. If it precedes two verbs in the subjunctive mood which are separated by "or", it means "whether":

5. L'homme est un pécheur **qu'il le sache** ou l'**ignore**.
    Man is a sinner **whether** he **knows** it or not.

It is quite difficult to avoid sexism with such generalizations in French. Even if one replaces "Man", it is awkward to say "he" or "she". If one switches the sentence into the plural, then the emphasis on individual responsibility will be lost. One could say "The Human"?

B. Temporal Conjunctions
These conjunctions express some doubt as to a future outcome.

avant que*	before
en attendant que	until, while waiting for
jusqu'à ce que	until

Note that *avant* and *jusqu'à* are prepositions without *que* (like *sans* above), but that the English translation does not change even with the addition of *que*. In French, the *que* in this context signifies a change in the function of the grammatical part of speech (from preposition to conjunction).

Examples

1. Nous rappelons ta mort, Seigneur, **avant que** tu **ne viennes**.
   We remember your death, Lord, **before** you **come** <again>.

Note that the English suggestion of the subjunctive (may) is unnecessary. The verb *viennes* is translated as an indicative.

2. Je siffle **en attendant qu'elle s'en aille.**
   a. I am whistling **while waiting for** her **to go away**.
   b. I am whistling **until** she **goes away**.

Note that the English suggestion of the subjunctive (may) is unnecessary.

C. Conjunctions Introducing Final Clauses

afin que	so that
pour que	"
de façon que	in such a way that
de sorte que	"
de manière que	"
de peur que*	for fear that

In many of the above conjunctions, the *que* is merely added to a preposition: i.e. *sans, avant, jusqu'à, pour, afin de*. Apart from the last two listed here, *pour que* (so that) and *afin que* (so that), which do include the *que* in the English translation, the others do not. In the other cases, the *que* merely signals a switch in function from preposition to conjunction. It has no meaning in itself.

Examples

1. Je pose mes questions **afin de** vous mieux **comprendre**.
   I am asking my questions **in order to understand** you better.

2. Je pose mes questions **afin qu'il comprenne** mieux.
   I am asking my questions **so that** he **may understand** better.

In the first case, there is no switch in subject from one clause to the next. "I" am asking questions so that "I" can understand; there is no need for a *que* and the preposition *afin de* is followed by the verb in the infinitive. In the second case, "I" am still asking questions, but not for my own benefit; "he" is the one who ought to understand. Because of this switch in subject, the *que* is required in #2 to introduce the second subject followed by the subjunctive.

Exercise A

For each sentence below, identify the verb in the subjunctive mood, if there is one, and explain why this mood is required.

1. Voici le meilleur restaurant que je connaisse dans cette ville.

2. Pendant longtemps De Gaulle a semblé être le seul homme à pouvoir sauver la France.

3. À votre avis, qui sont les premiers Européens à être arrivés en Amérique?

4. Le meilleur ami qu'un homme puisse avoir, c'est son chien.

5. Elle a attendu jusqu'à ce que les enfants reviennent.

6. Il a quitté le pays sans que les autorités le sachent.

7. Il n'est pas plus intelligent qu'elle n'est.

8. Quoique la situation soit difficile, vous ne devez pas vous décourager.

9. On a placé les plus belles statues de Rodin dans le musée afin qu'elles ne soient pas détériorées.

10. En vérité, en vérité, je te le dis, le coq ne chantera pas que[4] tu ne m'aies renié trois fois (Jean 13:38).

11. Dieu dit: "Que la lumière soit!" et la lumière fut (Gen.1:3).

12. Dieu veuille me pardonner! (Baudelaire)

13. Qu'ils reposent en paix.

14. Il ne se passe pas de semaine sans qu'un universitaire à la page[FF] ne parte en guerre contre la littérature antérieure à notre temps (P. Gaxotte, *Figaro*, 15-16 avril, 1972).

____

4. In sentences 10 and 16, *avant que* and *sans que* may be reduced to simply *que* without the implied meaning being lost.

15. [Selon le Talmud,] Dieu se demanda de quelle partie du corps de l'homme il formerait la femme. [Il se répondit:] "Je ne choisirai pas la tête à cet effet, afin qu'elle n'élève pas trop fièrement sa propre tête; ni l'oeil, pour qu'elle ne soit pas trop curieuse, ni l'oreille, pour qu'elle n'aille pas écouter aux portes, ni la bouche, pour qu'elle ne soit pas trop bavarde, ni la main, pour qu'elle ne se livre pas à la prodigalité, ni le pied, pour qu'elle ne sorte pas continuellement de chez elle: je vais la tirer d'une partie du corps qui reste cachée, afin de la rendre modeste." (Robert Aron, *Les années obscures*, pp.174-75)

16. Ton fils ne sortira pas sans qu'il ne t'ait demandé pardon.

17. ...[C]'est la détermination ferme et persévérante d'un engagement pour le bien commun, en d'autres termes pour le bien de tous et de chacun, afin que *tous nous soyons vraiment responsables de tous* (L'Encyclique, *Sollicitudo rei socialis* cité à la page 127 de Jean Paul II, *Les Fidèles Laïcs*, 1989)

18. Il craint qu'elle ne le trompe.

19. Doutez-vous que cela ne soit vrai?

20. N'y va pas sans que personne ne le sache!

133. Verbs Introducing the Subjunctive

The following verbs necessitate the subjunctive when *que* introduces a change of subject. All of them express emotion, judgement or necessity. Synonyms are grouped in rows.

demander	to ask	ordonner	to command
défendre	to forbid	interdire	to forbid
empêcher*	to prevent	éviter*	to prevent, avoid
vouloir (que)	*désirer*	souhaiter	to wish, desire
regretter	to regret		
préférer	to prefer	aimer mieux	to prefer
suggérer	to suggest	proposer	to offer
être content	to be happy	vouloir bien	to wish (politely)
accepter	to accept	admettre	to accept
avoir peur	to fear	craindre*	to fear
être fâché	to be angry	s'étonner	to be astonished
être surpris	to be surprised	douter*	to doubt
exiger	to demand	nier*	to deny
supposer	to assume		

Of these, the commonest to require a modified translation is *vouloir*. As with *sans que*, the secondary subject is best translated as an object, but the following verb must then be expressed in an infinitive form (passive below).

Examples

1. Nous ne **voulons** pas **que** vous vous **irritiez**.
    We do not **wish**　　　　　you **to be annoyed**.

2. Ceux qui veulent que l'engagement politique soit essentiel ont raison.
    Those who **wish** political commitment **to be** essential are right.

134. Impersonal Expressions and the Subjunctive

The following impersonal expressions introduce *que* and a verb in the subjunctive.[5]

il faut	il est indispensable
il est nécessaire	il est essentiel
il est bon	il est (in)utile
il est difficile	il est (im)possible
il est important	il importe
il semble	c'est bizarre
c'est naturel	c'est normal
c'est ridicule	c'est drôle
il est temps	il se peut
c'est étrange	il est curieux
c'est (in)juste	il vaut mieux (= It is preferable)

Example

1. **Il faudra que** nous lui **écrivions**.
    a. It will be necessary **that we write** to her
    b. It will be necessary **for us to write** to her.
    c. **We** will have **to write** to her.

2. **Il semble qu'il soit** angoissé
    It seems that he **may be** distressed (*lit.* in anguish).

---

5. Cf. the introduction to impersonal expressions without the subjunctive in Chapter 6, §55.

Note that once the indirect object is included in the impersonal expression *il me semble*, it is normally not followed by the subjunctive. The synonymous verb *paraître* works in the opposite way; i.e. *il paraît* (it seems, appears) must be followed by the indicative, whereas *il me paraît* is found with the subjunctive. In literary French, *il semble* can also be found with the indicative.[6]

135. Verbal Forms Introducing Doubt

Three verbs and three impersonal expressions do not introduce the subjunctive unless they are in the form of a question or a negative. The second verb in the subjunctive often works best in the future in English.

croire	to believe
penser	to think
espérer	to hope

il est sûr que...	it is sure that...
il est certain que...	it is certain that...
il est évident[FF] que...	it is obvious that...

Examples

1. Pensez-vous qu'il **vienne**?
   Do you think that he **will come**?

2. Il n'est pas sûr que le témoin **se révèle** enfin.
   It is not certain whether the witness **will reveal himself** in the end.

Exercise B

In each case below in which a verb in the subjunctive mood appears, be prepared to explain why.

1. Restez[FF] tranquilles!

2. Cela exige que les fidèles laïcs trouvent toujours plus d'élan spirituel grâce à une participation réelle à la vie de l'Eglise et qu'ils soient éclairés par sa doctrine sociale.

---

6. Cf. *Le bon usage*, §1073.

3. Le moyen et la manière pour réaliser une politique qui puisse viser un véritable développement humain, c'est la solidarité.

4. Qu'elle soit miséricordieuse!

5. Je voudrais que vous m'expliquiez ce passage.

6. Il semble douteux qu'il y ait des êtres sur les autres planètes.

7. Il faut que cet enfant vainque sa timidité.

8. Veuillez agréer, cher Monsieur, l'expression de mes sentiments distingués, Pierre Trudeau.

9. Je doute qu'il dise la vérité.

10. Je suis contente que vous soyez avec nous cet après-midi.

11. Il est possible que Jésus soit ressuscité![7]

12. Il faudrait que vous lisiez les oeuvres de Rousseau.

13. Je doute que l'on parvienne à retrouver le manuscrit.

14. Toute sa vie cette femme a cherché un homme qui soit parfait. C'est pourquoi elle ne s'est jamais mariée.

15. D'après la pensée juive biblique, l'univers est sacré. Pas de distinction d'aucune sorte entre profane et sacré. Il n'est pas d'atome de matière, où ne résident des forces reliées à la puissance universelle: il n'est pas de geste ou d'acte, en apparence indifférent, qui ne soit en fait rattaché à la destinée cosmique, et qui ne puisse influer sur son déroulement. (Robert Aron, 223).

---

7. *Ressusciter* belongs to a specialized group of verbs conjugated either with *avoir* or *être* like *passer* and *retourner*. If the verb is transitive, it is conjugated with *avoir*, if intransitive, with *être*. See Chapter 3 §24. For a complete list of such specialized verbs, see Goosse, *Le bon usage* §783, p.1220.

136. Reading: Hans Urs von Balthasar

Exercise C

The following passage is taken from Hans Urs von Balthasar, *Pâques, le mystère*, p.265. This Swiss intellectual and Catholic theologian (1905-88) wrote over 1,000 books and articles in German. His reputation in France has been great enough for Henri de Lubac to consider him one of the most cultured men of his time.

The vocabulary for the highlighted words is given below. Note that ***bénéficient d'une apparition***, the verb and its object, are split up by a number of interposed words, mainly adverbial. In such cases, the English translation will be clearer if the verb and its object are brought back together by re-arranging the syntax of the interposed material. Adverbs or adverbial phrases can often be thrown back to the beginning or down to the end of the sentence.

La question qui se pose maintenant est la suivante: pouvons-nous, dans les textes qui sont à notre disposition, reconnaître le travail de composition, et dans quelle mesure? On constate incontestablement de nombreux textes **de suture.** "Lorsque les disciples d'Emmaüs viennent **faire part de** leur expérience de la Résurrection, les Onze qui les accueillent joyeusement en leur apprenant la vision de Pierre, s'accordent mal avec les disciples qui, dans la péricope suivante, s'effraient lorsque Jésus apparaît, et qui ne sont convaincus que par de nombreuses preuves tangibles" (Luc 24, 33-42). Le fait que les anges, chez Matthieu, ordonnent aux femmes de dire aux disciples d'aller en Galilée où ils verront le Seigneur, s'accorde mal avec cet autre fait que les femmes **bénéficient** elles-mêmes en chemin, à Jérusalem par conséquent, **d'**une apparition du Ressuscité. En outre, il est invraisemblable que Jésus leur répète simplement les paroles qu'elles ont déjà entendues des anges (28, 7-10). Il est difficile d'admettre que, chez Jean, Marie de Magdala s'attarde deux fois près du tombeau: qu'elle le trouve, la première fois, vide et sans qu'il y ait d'ange pour interpréter l'événement, qu'apparaissent la seconde fois les mêmes anges interprètes que dans les synoptiques, mais sans qu'ils aient rien à lui annoncer, et finalement qu'elle **vive** une rencontre avec Jésus.

Vocabulary

bénéficier de	(v.t.)	to enjoy (benefit or profit from)
faire part de	(v.t.)	to share, impart
vivre	(v.i.)	to experience (vive = subjunctive)
de suture	(adjectival)	stitched together

15

THE SUBJUNCTIVE (CONT.): PAST, PERFECT AND PLUPERFECT

There are only two subjunctive tenses in spoken French: the present and imperfect subjunctives. The present subjunctive includes the future, and the compound past. The imperfect subjunctive is a strictly literary mood which is slowly falling out of use, even in written French. Consequently, the same range of options for translation into English holds true for the imperfect subjunctive as for the present, but the imperfect overlaps much more with the conditional; i.e. "would" or "would have". The expression of time in the subjunctive clause is always relative to the time in the main clause.

137. The Past Indefinite Subjunctive

The Past Indefinite is the Compound Past (passe composé). The subjunctive forms of it merely apply to the auxiliary verbs which place the main verbs (past participles) in the past.

Examples

1. Je **ne crois pas qu**'il le lui **ait** donné.
    I do not think that he gave it to her <u>or</u> may have given...

2. Il **a peur qu**'elle **soit** venue.
    He is afraid that she may have come.

138. The Imperfect Subjunctive

The imperfect subjunctive is built upon the third person singular of the literary past. The circumflex over the vowel marks the most commonly used third person of the *passé simple* converted into the imperfect subjunctive. The following list of regular and irregular verbs in the infinitive, past participle and the third person singular demonstrates that the same rule applies across the board.

Literary Past/

Infinitive	**Past Participle**	**Past Definite**	**Imperf. Subj.**
donner	donné	donna	qu'il donnât
finir	fini	finit	qu'il finît
connaître	connu	connut	qu'il connût
être	été	fut	qu'il fût
avoir	eu	eut	qu'il eût

The other persons are built upon the same root without the circumflex and "t", but with "ss":

A. THE THREE REGULAR CONJUGATIONS

I	**II**	**III**
que je donnasse	que je finisse	que je connusse
que tu donnasses	que tu finisses	que tu connusses
qu'elle donnât	qu'elle finît	qu'elle connût
que ns donnassions	que ns finissions	que ns connussions
que vs donnassiez	que vs finissiez	que vs connussiez
qu'ils donnassent	qu'ils finissent	qu'ils connussent

NOTE that regular II conjugation verbs which already double the *s* share forms with the imperfect indicative (finissions, finissiez) and the present indicative (finissent). **Note** also that the literary past determines the imperfect subjunctive more than the past participle: for example

perdre (to lose)   < **perdu** (past participle), but the literary past
il perdit (he lost) < **il perdît** (imperfect subjunctive).

B. AUXILIARY VERBS

Imperfect of	**ÊTRE**	**AVOIR**
que je	fusse	eusse
que tu	fusses	eusses
qu'il/elle/on	fût	eût
que nous	fussions	eussions
que vous	fussiez	eussiez
qu'ils/elles	fussent	eussent

139. Usage of the Imperfect and Pluperfect Subjunctive

The imperfect and pluperfect subjunctive are falling out of use, even in literary French. But students using nineteenth-century material in their research certainly need to recognize both these forms. They are still found infrequently in modern authors, but the usage of the imperfect and pluperfect subjunctives is rarely oral. In literary texts, the imperfect subjunctive follows a main verb in the imperfect indicative tense:

Present subjunctive
1.   Elle veut qu'il lise le second chapitre.
     She wants him to read the second chapter.

Imperfect subjunctive
2.   Elle voulait qu'il lût le second chapitre.
     a. She wished [that] he would have (_or_ had) read the second chapter.
     b. She wanted him to read the second chapter.

In English, 1 and 2b are the best options, using the infinitive. The imperfect subjunctive can also overlap with the conditional in English translation; i.e. using "would".

3.   Je doutais qu'il **vendît** sa maison.
     I doubted that he **would have sold** his house (<that he would sell ...)

140. Translation of the Pluperfect Subjunctive

Just like the regular, indicative pluperfect, one uses the imperfect subjunctive form of the auxiliary verb. The translation resembles the imperfect subjunctive insofar as it may be expressed with an infinitive, with the regular pluperfect tense or with "would have":

1.   J'aurais bien aimé qu'il vînt ce soir.
     I really would have liked him to come this evening.

2.   Je n'aurais pas cru qu'ils fussent partis.
     I would not have believed that they would have left.

Finally, conditional sentences in the pluperfect and past conditional might be expressed using the pluperfect subjunctive:

3.   Si elle avait vu le film, elle aurait été moins tranquille.
     If she had seen the film, she would have been less peaceful.

4.   Si elle eût vu le film, elle eût été moins tranquille.
     (same as above)

Exercise A

Always be prepared to explain why a verb may appear in the subjunctive mood.

1. Il n'est pas venu autant que je sache.

2. Nous doutions qu'il écrivît son histoire du Canada.

3. Supposons qu'il se passe un événement surnaturel.

4. Arthur Rimbaud, poète symboliste par excellence, écrivit de la poésie exquise jusqu'à ce qu'il quitte la France à l'âge de dix-neuf ans pour mener une vie d'aventurier en Éthiopie (Stack).

5. J'aurais bien aimé qu'il finisse ses études.

6. Les poèmes de E.J. Pratt comptent parmi les poèmes canadiens les plus longs que j'aie jamais lus.

7. Nous regrettons vivement que cet auteur veuille quitter le Canada; nous doutons qu'il revienne de New York.

8. Ces journaux sont les meilleurs que l'on puisse trouver ici.

9. Je craignis que ma thèse ne fût inacceptable.

10. Rousseau doute que les enfants comprennent ce qu'ils étudient.

11. Rousseau se doutait que les précédentes méthodes d'enseignement n'étaient pas efficaces.

12. Elle voulait qu'il finît ses études.

13. Peu de jours se passaient sans que Paris, épouvanté, n'apprît quelque meurtre mystérieux (A. France, *Révolte des anges*).

14. De pareilles choses arrivaient tous les jours, sans que personne ne songeât à s'en scandaliser.

15. On s'est prononcé sur sa culpabilité, avant qu'il n'ouvre la bouche.

Exercise B

The following sentences all contain examples of the imperfect subjunctive. All but the last are drawn from one nineteenth-century author, Ernest Boysse (*Le Théâtre des Jésuites*, pp.6-7, 21, 23-24, 28-29).

When considering tragedy apart from comedy or farce, it is helpful to know that, in sixteenth-century France, classical tragedy was thought to be divided into five acts. Along with this requirement, the Jesuits codified their pedagogical principles in the *Ratio studiorum* of 1583. There they laid down other equally rigid stipulations for the tragic form. Since the school boys performed such plays to improve their elocution, their oratorical skills and their Latin, the tragedies had to be composed entirely in Latin on sacred subjects and exclude all feminine characters. The latter requirement avoided the necessity for males to act in female parts. Fifty years later, these rules were considerably relaxed to allow for French interludes and female roles. At this later time, three-act plays became acceptable, as justified below (#7).

1. Il n'est pas douteux que les farces et pièces satiriques ne jouassent un grand rôle dans ces 'réjouissances folles'.

2. Ils furent permis à l'Épiphanie, mais sous certaines conditions. Ils ne devaient commencer que la veille au soir, ou, le jour même, seulement après vêpres, pour que l'office divin ne fût pas interrompu.

3. Quant aux comédies, elles n'étaient pas défendues[FF]; mais elles devaient être examinées par le principal, "afin qu'il n'y restât ni trait mordant ni satirique, ni rien déshonnête qui pût offenser un homme de bien."

4. C'est en 1683 et non en 1674 que l'inscription a été placée sur la porte. Le père de La Chaise[1] n'aurait pas signalé cette circonstance dans les termes qu'on vient de lire, si elle eût été un fait accompli depuis neuf ans.

5. L'oeuvre tragique des Pères Jésuites est considérable... Il fallait qu'une production incessante vînt répondre à cette exigence annuelle.

6. Bien que les Pères, qui avaient mission d'alimenter les théâtres des collèges, connussent mieux que personne les modèles anciens, cependant ils n'ont pas laissé tout d'abord de s'en éloigner sensiblement.

7. [L]a tragédie..., selon Aristote, se compose de trois parties, le commencement, le milieu et la fin. Si ces trois parties peuvent être comprises en trois actes, sans que l'action en souffre, qui donc aurait le droit de s'en plaindre?

8. L'interruption, fût-elle momentanée, du lien qui unit le Christ à son Père et à la vie, introduit dans la représentation mythique du Sujet une discontinuité fondamentale et psychiquement nécessaire (Kristeva, p.143).

141. Summary of Translation Hints

A. French word order is not much different than English, with the following major exceptions:

1) French adjectives commonly follow nouns; move them up!

2) French adverbs commonly follow verbs; their English equivalents usually sound better when moved up before the verb. An adjustment in the placement of an awkward adverb, adverbial compound or adverbial phrase is even more important when it blocks the direct line between the verb and its direct object. For example, notice the removal of the adverbial phrase in a clause written by Camus, as given in Appendix I (II.A):

> [I]l y avait <u>dans son cabinet</u> de grosses mouches.
> There were some big flies <u>in his office.</u>

---

1 Father La Chaise (d. 1709), the Jesuit after whom a cemetery in Paris is named, was the confessor of Louis XIV.

3) Always be prepared for the subject-verb inversion in subordinate clauses after *que* or, occasionally, other subordinating conjunctions like *où*. If one finds a verb directly after a *que* meaning "that" or "which", look for the subject with its modifiers first, before translating the verb. Such a subject-verb inversion away from the normative English order does not occur in French after *qui*, because *qui* already represents the subject in the subordinate clause. The verb will naturally follow *qui*, unless there is some other parenthetical expression interposed for suspense.

4) French syntax must be adjusted when it comes to object pronouns or adverbial pronouns as well. Pronouns placed between the subject and the verb must be skipped over in translation until the verb has been translated and possibly a direct object if it is not a pronoun:

Nous **en** avons compris le sens.
We understood the meaning **of it**.

Nevertheless, if *en* precedes a verb which ends in -*ant*, it cannot be jumped:

en lisant le *passage*
in/while/by reading the passage

B. Because nouns, verbs and adjectives are inflected in French to agree with each other in number and gender, one should always be able to explain why a certain inflection occurs.

1) Agreements in verbs are especially complicated, since any verb conjugated with *être* in the passive or a compound form (verbs of transition) agree with the subject of the sentence. Conversely, verbs conjugated with *avoir* in a compound form agree with the direct object of the verb, only when it is placed before the past participle, usually in the form of a direct object pronoun or the relative pronoun *que*. Pronominal verbs, conjugated with *être* in compound tenses, likewise agree with their direct object, represented by the reflexive pronoun.

2) Be conscious of the antecedent of every pronoun and be certain that the pronoun agrees with its antecedent in number and gender. Watch combinations like *mon entreprise* (my company) which appear to involve a masculine noun, but are really feminine. The final "n" in *mon* here is needed to prevent a contraction before a noun beginning with a vowel. If *elle* were to represent this same noun in the next sentence, it might appear to signify "she", but must be translated as "it" because its referent is inanimate.

3) Agreements between adjectives and nouns are easier to spot.

142. READING: Adolphe Gesché

Exercise C

Read the passage below, taken from an article by Adolphe Gesché in the *Revue théologique de Louvain* 29 (1998), pp.3-4.

"L'IDENTITÉ DE L'HOMME DEVANT DIEU"

Quand Moïse interroge[FF] le Dieu dont il vient d'avoir l'éblouissement et lui dit: « Si les fils d'Israël me demandent quel est ton nom, que leur répondrai-je? » (Ex 3, 13), il pose la vraie question. Une question d'identité, qui seule importe vraiment, **en définitive**. Quel cst ton nom, pour que je sache qui tu es, pour qu'ils sachent qui tu es, pour que nous sachions à quel Dieu nous nous donnons. L'homme, ce faisant, s'interroge autant sur Dieu que sur l'avenir de sa propre identité. Car il n'est pas **indifférent** à l'homme de savoir à qui il va donner sa foi. Que suis-je, que deviendrai-je lorsque j'aurai Dieu comme vis-à-vis? Comme en toute relation, mon identité est en jeu quand l'autre apparaît. Il importe de savoir qui il est, si je veux savoir ce qu'il m'en adviendra.

Certes, toute la question ne se décide pas **là-dessus**. **Aussi bien**, Dieu commence-t-il par préserver et sauvegarder une part d'inconnaissable, et pour cela justement sans nom: « Je suis qui je suis » (Ex 3, 14). En cela, d'ailleurs, rien qui doive nous heurter. Il importe pour l'homme que Dieu soit ce qu'il est, et non point une idole que j'aurais façonné au gré de mes besoins et en laquelle je ne ferais que me retrouver et me servir moi-même. C'est bien en étant d'abord ce qu'il est, et non point ce que je veux qu'il soit, que Dieu sera alors pour moi ce face à face dont l'identité, dont le nom **m'intéresse** pour me comprendre...

Aujourd'hui encore, c'est cette question de Moïse que pose l'homme. Non plus simplement, en effet, celle de l'existence en soi de Dieu, mais bien plutôt celle, plus déterminante en un sens, qui porte sur le rapport entre l'homme et Dieu: ce rapport est-il constitutif de mon être ou destructeur? Vais-je être abîmé dans cette relation ou en sortir grandi?

Vocabulary

en définitive (adv.)	eventually, when all is said and done
indifférent (adj.)	immaterial
là-dessus (adv.)	thereupon
Aussi bien (adv.)	As well, moreover
m'intéresse (v.tr.3 pr.)	affects or concerns me

143. BASIC VOCABULARY: Chapters 13-15

NOUNS

avenir (m.)	future
bouc émissaire (m.)	scapegoat
chemin (m.)	path, way
croyants (m.pl.)	believers
décennie (f.)	decade
élan (m.)	momentum; surge, boost, burst
enfer (m.)	hell (& in pl. *aux enfers*: to/in hell)
monde (m.)	world
prédication (f.)	sermon; preaching
siècle (m.)	century
témoin (oculaire; m.)	(eye-) witness
temps (m.)	time; season; weather
terre (f.)	earth
quiconque (rel. pron.)	whoever, whosoever

ADVERBS

ailleurs	elsewhere
d'ailleurs	moreover
par ailleurs	otherwise
car	for
d'habitude	usually
encore	still, yet
encore une fois	again (*lit.* once again)
bien (adv.; before adj.)	very well; certainly, really
fort (adv.)	loudly
fort (before adj.)	very
plus haut (= ci-dessus)	above (in a text; here above)
plus bas (= ci-dessous)	below (in a text; here below)

CONJUNCTIONS FOLLOWED BY THE SUBJUNCTIVE   Listed in §132

PREPOSITIONS

à la différence de	unlike
à l'égard de	concerning, with respect to, in comparison with
à l'instar de	on the model/following the example of
à part	apart from, except for
à partir de	beginning with, from
à plusieurs reprises	several times (from f.pp. of *reprendre*)
à propos de	concerning
en ce qui concerne	concerning
auprès de	to, with (*lit.* next to)
grâce à	thanks to
quant à	as for
selon (l'évangile de x)	according to (the Gospel of x)
vis à vis de	concerning, facing (in the face of)
à titre de	by way of; as
par l'intermédiaire de	through (the intercession of)
par le moyen de	by means of

IDIOMS or EXPRESSIONS

à savoir	namely, that is to say
c'est à dire	that is to say
dans les années 60	in the sixties (decade)
pour ainsi dire	so to speak
pour cela	for that reason
vaille que vaille	for what it is worth

VERBS FOLLOWED BY THE SUBJUNCTIVE   Listed in §133

IMPERSONAL EXPRESSIONS FOLLOWED BY THE SUBJUNCTIVE
Listed in §134

VERBS

avoir lieu	to take place
bénir	to bless
changer d'avis	to change one's mind
craindre	to fear, to be afraid
faire ressortir	to emphasize (*lit.* to cause to stand out)
faire valoir	to promote (*lit.* to cause to be valued)
faire semblant d'être	to feign (*lit.* to make a semblance of being)
ne laisser pas de	not fail to
mettre au point	to perfect, to refine
se mettre à	to begin, set oneself to (do sth.)
mettre en cause/question	to call into question
porter sur	to concern (bear upon)
servir à	serves to, to be useful for
se servir de qch.	to use (sth.), to make use of
témoigner (de)	to bear witness (to)
véhiculer	to convey
vouloir dire	to mean (to wish to say)
ça veut dire	that means (= that is to say)

APPENDIX I

Supplementary Readings – Literature

1. Supplement to Chapter 13 on the Causative

Alphonse Daudet developed the short story, from which an extract has been drawn, between 1864 and 1869 when his *Lettres de mon moulin* was published. It is still considered a classic in French literature. When translating this passage, watch for structures which we call "sentence fragments" in English, and try to modify them to satisfy the English demand for full sentences. Capital letters do not have accents, even when required, in this older style.

"Le secret de Maître Cornille"

Tout cela sentait le mystère et faisait beaucoup jaser le monde. Chacun expliquait à sa façon le secret de maître Cornille, mais le bruit général était qu'il y avait dans ce moulin-là encore plus de sacs d'**écus** que de sacs de farine.

A la longue pourtant tout se découvrit; voici comment:

En faisant danser la jeunesse avec mon fifre, je m'aperçus un beau jour que l'aîné de mes garçons et la petite Vivette s'étaient rendus amoureux l'un de l'autre. Au fond je n'en fus pas fâché, parce qu'après tout le nom de Cornille était en honneur chez nous, et puis ce joli petit **passereau** de Vivette m'aurait fait plaisir à voir trotter dans ma maison. Seulement, comme nos amoureux avaient souvent occasion d'être ensemble, je voulus, de peur d'accidents, **régler** l'affaire tout de suite, et je montai jusqu'au moulin pour en toucher deux mots au grand-père... Ah! le vieux sorcier! il faut voir de quelle manière il me reçut! Impossible de lui faire ouvrir la porte. Je lui expliquai mes raisons **tant bien que mal**, à travers le trou de la serrure; et tout le temps que je parlais, il y avait ce coquin de chat maigre qui **soufflait** comme un diable au-dessus de ma tête.

Vocabulary

écu (n.m.)	crown, an ancient coin dating from 1336 when it was first minted with the arms of France upon it. Used in the plural, it can be translated as simply "money".
passereau (n.m.)	sparrow (metaphor for the young girl)
régler (v.tr.)	to settle
tant bien que mal (adv.)	as well as can be expected <u>or</u> with great difficulty
souffler (v.intr.)	to hiss

2. Further Advanced Readings

The following selections are drawn from well-known French authors. They should only be read when all the grammar of the fifteen previous chapters has been digested.

The selections from Camus and Proust have been chosen to reveal, in a striking way, the influence of philosophy (or religious beliefs) upon style. An existentialist who adopted nihilism, Camus avoids all embellishment of the French language. The broken state of his beliefs is reflected in the brevity of his fractured sentences. Today, the literary style of the *roman fracturé* has developed out of this tradition.

At the opposite end of the spectrum, Proust affirms the Platonic beauty of material life as a reflection of a higher reality, even if it is not a particularly Christian one. His florid style and practice of *emboîtement* (couching subordinate sentences within others like the Russian *matryoshki*, those wooden dolls that open into a whole series of similar figures, the smaller ones hiding in the wombs of the bigger) is famous. Neither author, however, dispenses with Christian symbolism.

A. From Albert Camus, *L'Étranger* (Paris: Librairie Gallimard, 1957), pp.7-8, 100-101.

When the protagonist is put on trial for having killed an Algerian with five gunshots, he is sentenced, not for the murder, but for having failed to grieve at his mother's funeral.

> Aujourd'hui, maman est morte. Ou peut-être hier, je ne sais pas. J'ai reçu un télégramme de l'asile: "Mère décédée. Enterrement demain. Sentiments distingués." Cela ne veut rien dire. C'était peut-être hier...
>
> J'ai pris l'autobus à deux heures. Il faisait très chaud. J'ai mangé au restaurant chez Céleste, comme d'habitude. Ils avaient tous beaucoup de peine pour moi et Céleste m'a dit:" On n'a qu'une mère." J'étais un peu étourdi parce qu'il a fallu que je monte chez Emmanuel pour lui emprunter une cravate noire et **un brassard**. Il a perdu son oncle, il y a quelques mois...

[Le procès sur le meurtre de l'Algérien]

"Pourquoi avez-vous attendu entre le premier et le second **coup**?" dit-il alors. Une fois de plus, j'ai revu la plage rouge et j'ai senti sur mon front la brûlure du soleil. Mais cette fois, je n'ai rien répondu. Pendant tout le silence qui a suivi le juge **a eu l'air de** s'agiter. Il... a passé ses mains sur son front et a répété sa question d'une voix un peu altérée: "Pourquoi? Il faut que vous me le disiez. Pourquoi?" Je me taisais toujours.

Brusquement, il s'est levé, a marché à grand pas vers une extrémité de son bureau et a ouvert un tiroir dans **un classeur**. Il en a tiré un crucifix d'argent qu'il a brandi en revenant vers moi. Et d'une voix toute changée, presque tremblante, il s'est écrié: "Est-ce que vous le connaissez, celui-là?" J'ai dit: "Oui, naturellement." Alors il m'a dit très vite et d'une façon passionnée que lui croyait en Dieu, que sa conviction était qu'aucun homme n'était assez coupable pour que Dieu ne lui pardonnât pas, mais qu'il fallait pour cela que l'homme par son repentir devînt comme un enfant dont l'âme est vide et prête à tout accueillir. Il avait tout son corps penché sur la table. Il agitait son crucifix presque au-dessus de moi. A vrai dire, je l'avais très mal suivi dans son raisonnement, d'abord parce que j'avais chaud et qu'il y avait dans son cabinet de grosses mouches qui se posaient sur ma figure, et aussi parce qu'il me faisait un peu peur. Je reconnaissais en même temps que c'était ridicule parce que, après tout, c'était moi le criminel. Il a continué pourtant. J'ai à peu près compris qu'à son avis il n'y avait qu'un point d'obscur dans ma confession, le fait d'avoir attendu pour tirer mon second coup de revolver. Pour le reste, c'était très bien, mais cela, il ne le comprenait pas.

VOCABULARY

avoir l'air de	to seem
un brassard	a black armband that one placed on one's arm (*le bras*) to indicate mourning.
un classeur	a filing cabinet. The verb *classer* can mean to classify and/or to file.
un coup	a shot (from a gun) in this context.

B. Excerpts from Marcel Proust, *À la recherche du temps perdu: du côté de chez Swann* (Bournemouth, England: Parkstone Press, 1994) pp. 54 (A), 90-93 (B).

The vocabulary aids are given after both excerpts.

i. Le mystère de la mémoire

Je trouve très raisonnable la croyance celtique que les âmes de ceux que nous avons perdus sont captives dans quelque être inférieur, dans une bête, un végétal, une chose inanimée, perdues en effet pour nous jusqu'au jour, qui pour beaucoup, ne vient jamais, où nous nous trouvons passer près de l'arbre, entrer en possession de l'objet qui est leur prison. Alors elles tressaillent, nous appellent, et sitôt que nous les avons reconnues, l'enchantement est brisé. Délivrées par nous, elles ont vaincu la mort et reviennent vivre avec nous.

Il en est ainsi de notre passé. C'est **peine perdue** que nous cherchions à l'évoquer, tous les efforts de notre intelligence sont inutiles. Il est caché hors de son domaine et de sa portée, en quelque objet matériel (en la sensation que nous donnerait cet objet matériel), ... que nous ne soupçonnons pas. Cet objet, il dépend du hasard que nous le rencontrions avant de mourir, ou que nous ne le rencontrions pas.

ii. L'art et la symbolique

L'année où nous mangeâmes tant d'asperges, la fille de cuisine habituellement chargée de les "plumer" était une pauvre créature maladive, dans un état de grossesse déjà assez avancé quand nous arrivâmes à Pàques, et on s'étonnait même que Françoise lui laissât faire tant de courses et de besogne, car elle commençait à porter difficilement devant elle la mystérieuse corbeille, chaque jour plus remplie, dont on devinait sous ses amples sarraus la forme magnifique. Ceux-ci rappelaient **les houppelandes** qui revêtent certaines des figures symboliques de Giotto dont M. Swann m'avait donné des photographies. C'est lui-même qui nous l'avait fait remarquer et quand il nous demandait des nouvelles de la fille de cuisine il nous disait: "Comment va la Charité de Giotto?" D'ailleurs elle-même, la pauvre fille, engraissée par sa grossesse, jusqu'à la figure, jusqu'aux joues qui tombaient droites et carrées, ressemblait en effet assez à ces vierges, fortes et hommasses, matrones plutôt, dans lesquelles les vertus sont personnifiées **à l'Arena**. Et je me rends compte maintenant que ces Vertus et ces Vices de Padoue lui ressemblaient encore d'une autre manière. De même que l'image de cette fille était **accrue** par le symbole ajouté qu'elle portait devant son ventre, sans avoir l'air d'en comprendre le sens, sans que rien dans son visage en **traduisît** la beauté et l'esprit, comme un simple et pesant fardeau, de même c'est sans paraître s'en douter que la puissante ménagère qui est représentée **à l'Arena** au-dessous du nom "Caritas" et dont la reproduction était accrochée au mur de ma salle d'études, à Combray, incarne cette vertu, c'est sans qu'aucune pensée de charité semble avoir jamais pu être exprimée par son visage énergique et vulgaire. Par une belle invention du peintre elle foule aux pieds les trésors de la terre, mais absolument comme si elle **piétinait** des raisins pour en extraire le jus...

Il fallait que ces Vertus et ces Vices de Padoue eussent en eux bien de la réalité puisqu'ils m'apparaissaient comme aussi vivants que la servante enceinte, et qu'elle-même ne me semblait pas beaucoup moins allégorique. Et peut-être cette non-participation (du moins apparente) de l'âme d'un être à la vertu... a aussi en dehors de sa valeur esthétique une réalité sinon psychologique, au moins, comme on dit, physiognomonique. Quand, plus tard, j'ai eu l'occasion de rencontrer, au cours de ma vie, dans des couvents par exemple, des incarnations vraiment saintes de la charité active, elles avaient généralement un air allègre, positif, indifférent et brusque de chirurgien pressé, ce visage où ne se lit aucune commisération, aucun attendrissement devant la souffrance humaine, aucune crainte de la heurter, et qui est le visage sans douceur, le visage antipathique et sublime de la vraie bonté.

Vocabulary

végétal (nm.)	plant (vegetable)
peine perdue (nf.)	a waste of time
houppelande (nf.)	cloak
à l'Arena	in the Arena Chapel in Padua
accrue	heightened (pp.f. of accroître)
traduire (v.t.)	to convey, express
piétiner	to stamp upon

APPENDIX II

Verb Chart

The following chart has been established as a mnemonic device for remembering one's verb endings in all of the tenses. The layout is significant because it juxtaposes the roots of verbs with those tenses which are built upon them.

The future, for example, is mainly built upon the infinitive as its root. This means that at least one *r* serves as a sign of the future root, two *r*s for some irregular verbs.

Other juxtapositions are equally significant. The conditional, for example, borrows its root from the future tense to its left, but its endings from the imperfect tense above.

The present participle, which itself uses the root of the first person plural of the present tense, serves in turn as the root of the imperfect tense. If one removes *-ant* (=-ing), the endings *ais, ais, ait...* merely replace it.

Skipping two boxes to the right on the top column, the past participle regularly supplies the root of the passé simple (simple past, literary past) below. For example, *eu* is the past participle of *avoir*, so that *eus* is the first and second singular person of the same verb (*j'eus:* I had). The rest of the paradigm follows along on the same root. Finally, the imperfect subjunctive tends to grow out of the passé simple by doubling final consonants: e.g. *j'eusse* (I would have). The rest is memorization, which is rather essential for comprehension in any language.

Practice Table for French Verbs

Eng. Inf._____________	Present Participle	Imperfect	Past Participle	Subjunctive (pr.)
je tu elle, il, on nous vous elles		je tu elle nous vous elles		je tu il nous vous ils
Infinitive	Future	Conditional	*Passé Simple*	Subjunctive (impf.)
	je tu il nous vous ils	je tu elle nous vous elles	je tu il nous vous ils	je tu elle nous vous elles

APPENDIX III

False Friends / Faux Amis

In the following list, some words have meanings that are cognates of the English, but other common meanings that are unrelated to English. They are listed here to warn you not to take the cognate immediately for granted.

à la page	up to date
actualités (f. pl.)	current affairs
actuel, actuelle (adj.)	current, present-day
actuellement (adv.)	currently (not actually)
effectivement (adv)	actually
assister (à)	to attend, to be present (at)
chair (f.)	flesh
chose (f.)	thing (not choice: *le choix*)
cloche (f.)	bell
conférence (f.)	lecture (possibly at a conference)
crayon (m.)	pencil
critique (f.)	criticism, review
curieux/ -ieuse (adj.)	careful; odd; curious
défendre (v.tr.) (à qn)	to forbid (s.o.); defend
demander (v.tr.)	to ask (to demand is too strong)
éditeur (mf.)	publisher (also applies to a woman)
rédacteur (mf.)	editor "
embarras (m.)	difficulty, trouble
errer (v.int.)	to wander
éventuel, éventuelle (adj.)	possible, potential
évidemment (adv.)	obviously
évident, évidente (adj.)	obvious
figure (f.)	face; figure
formation (f.)	training
front (m.)	forehead
ignorer (v.tr.)	to be unaware of, not to know

234

inconvénient (m.)	disadvantage
interroger (v.tr.)	to question (not interrogate)
journal (m.)	newspaper; but journal as "diary"
journée (f.)	day (considered qualitatively)
large (adj.)	wide
lecteur (nm.) / lectrice (nf.)	reader (teacher in European universities)
lecture (nf.)	reading (not a lecture)
librairie (nf.)	bookstore
bibliothèque (nf.)	library
magasin (nm.)	store
misère (nf.)	poverty
misères (nf pl.)	woes, miseries
occasion (f.)	opportunity; occasion
parent (m.)	relative
relation (f.)	relationship
personnage (m.)	character (in a play, etc)
phrase (nf.)	sentence (more often than phrase)
pièce (f.)	room; coin; play; & in idioms
prétendre (v.tr.)	to claim
propre (adj.)	own (before the n.); clean (after)
recherche de (nf.)	search of/for (not research)
régime (nm.)	system of government, system; diet
regretter (v.tr.)	to miss, long for
remarquer (v.tr.)	notice, observe
répétition (f.)	rehearsal
rester (v.i.)	to remain
résumer (v.tr.)	to summarize
revue (nf.)	academic journal as "review"
roman (m.)	novel
sensible (adj.)	sensitive
sensibilité (nf.)	sensitivity
sensibiliser (v.tr.)	to make sensitive
sentence (nf.)	maxim < *sententia* (Lat.)
sort (m.)	fate
supporter (v.tr.)	to endure, bear
sympathique (adj.)	likeable
travailler (v.i.)	to work (i.e. travail)
voyager (v.i.)	to travel
wagon (m.)	car (on a train or subway)

APPENDIX IV

Verbs Taking Prepositions Before Infinitives

1. Verbs that use *à* before the infinitive or an object:

s'amuser à	to have fun (doing)
apprendre à	to learn, to teach to (do)
arriver à	to succeed in (doing)
assister à qch.	to be present at sth.
avoir à	to have to (do)
céder le pas à qn	to yield to s.o.
chercher à	to seek to (do)
commencer à	to begin to
conclure à	to decide on/ in favour of (doing)
confier à qn	to entrust to s.o.
consentir à	to consent to (do)
continuer à	to continue to
se décider à	to come to the decision to
échapper à	to escape from (sth., s.o.)
enseigner à	to teach to (do)
s'habituer à	to become accustomed to
hésiter à	to hesitate to
se heurter à qch.	to come up against, collide with sth.
s'intéresser à	to be _or_ become interested in (sth., doing)
se mettre à	to begin to (do)
participer à	to participate in
parvenir à	to succeed in (doing)
prendre part à qch.	to take part in (sth.)
se préparer à	to prepare to (do)
recourir à qch., qn	to have recourse to sth./s.o.
renoncer à qch.	to renounce (doing, sth.)
se résoudre à	to resolve to (do)
réussir à	to succeed in (doing)
servir à	to serve to (do) _or_ to be useful for (doing)
tarder à	to delay in (doing)
tenir à	to be anxious to (do)

2. Verbs that use *de* before the infinitive or an object:

achever de	to finish (doing)
s'apercevoir de qch.	to perceive sth.
s'arrêter de	to stop (doing)
avertir de	to warn to (do) <u>or</u> warn against (doing)
cesser de	to cease (doing)
se charger de	to assume the task/burden of (doing)
choisir de	to choose to (do)
commander à qn de	to order s.o. to
conseiller à qn de	to advise s.o. to
se contenter de	to be happy to
convaincre à qn de	to convince s.o. to
craindre de	to fear (doing)
décider de	to decide to (do)
défendre à qn de	to forbid s.o. to
demander à qn de	to ask s.o. to
se dépêcher de	to hurry to
empêcher à qn de	to prevent s.o. from (doing)
essayer de	to try to (do)
éviter de	to avoid (doing)
s'excuser de	to excuse oneself from (doing)
finir de	to finish (doing)
interdire à qn de	to forbid s.o. to (do)
jurer de	to swear to
manquer de	to fail to
se méfier de qn	to distrust s.o.
menacer de	to threaten to
offrir de	to offer to
ordonner à qn de	to order s.o. to
oublier de	to forget to
pardonner à qn de	to forgive s.o. for (doing)
parler de	to talk about (doing)
permettre à qn de	to permit s.o. to do
persuader à qn de	to persuade s.o. to
prendre garde de	to be careful to
prendre soin de	to be careful to
se préoccuper de	to be worried about (doing)
prier qn de	to pray to s.o. to (do)
promettre à qn de	to promise s.o. to

proposer de	to propose to
se rappeler de	to remember
refuser de	to refuse to
regretter de	to regret to
remercier de	to thank for (doing)
reprocher de	to reproach for (doing)
risquer de	to run the risk of (doing)
soupçonner qn de	to suspect s.o. of (doing)
se souvenir de	to remember to
tâcher de	to attempt to
témoigner de qch.	to witness to sth.
triompher de qch.	to triumph over sth.

3. Verbs used with *par* before an infinitive

commencer par	to begin by (doing)
finir par	to finish by, to end up (doing)

APPENDIX V

Cardinal and Ordinal Numbers

CARDINAL

ORDINAL (add *-ième*)

un, une	one	premier, première	first
deux	two	second/e, deuxième	second
trois	three	troisième	third
quatre	four	quatrième	fourth
cinq	five	cinquième	fifth
six	six	sixième	sixth
sept	seven	septième	seventh
huit	eight	huitième	eighth
neuf	nine	neuvième	ninth
dix	ten	dixième	tenth
vingt	twenty	vingtième	twentieth
cent	a hundred	centième	one-hundredth
mille	a thousand	millième	one-thousandth, etc.

OTHER CARDINAL NUMBERS

11	onze	15	quinze	19	dix-neuf
12	douze	16	seize	20	vingt
13	treize	17	dix-sept	21	vingt-et-un
14	quatorze	18	dix-huit	22	vingt-deux
30	trente	31-32	trente et un, trente-deux		
40	quarante	41-42	quarante et un, quarante-deux		
50	cinquante				
60	soixante				
70	soixante-dix	71-72	soixante et onze, soixante-douze		
80	quatre-vingts	81	quatre-vingt-un		
90	quatre-vingt-dix	91	quatre-vingt-onze		
100	cent	101	cent un		
a million	un million (de)				
a billion	un milliard (de)				

APPENDIX VI

A Summary of English Grammar

The French have quite a complex understanding of French grammar. They think, quite differently, in terms of complements of verbs, of noun subjects and noun objects, and in terms of agreements made by inflections. Conversely, English-speaking people (possibly because English is now the international language) have come to care so little for correct speech that our school system hardly teaches grammar at all. Recognizing the reality of such a lack in Canada, whether in the past or present, this summary attempts to fill the lacuna in the most simplified terms possible.

1. Parts of Speech

Noun (n.): the name of a person, place, thing, quality, action or idea. To test if a word is a noun, place "the" before it; if it sounds right, then it is probably a noun. If this fails, look in the dictionary. Nouns are called common nouns, unless they are formal names.

Proper nouns: the names of specific people and places, normally capitalized.

Articles: precede nouns in one of two ways.
> **Definite art.**: *the* is used for a "defined" object
> **Indefinite art.**: *a* is used before a noun which is general

Pronouns: a word that takes the place of a noun in a sentence.
> The noun which it replaces is called its **antecedent**.
> **Possessive pron.**: expresses ownership: e.g. its, my <u>or</u> mine.
> **Demonstrative pron.**: points out the noun it has replaced.
> > e.g. this, that, these, those
> **Interrogative pron.**: introduces a question. e.g. who, which, what...?
> **Reflexive pron.**: refers back to the subject of the sentence, using the addition of
> > *-self* (sg.), *-selves* (pl.).
> > e.g. myself (sg.), ourselves (pl.) as in *I wash myself.*
> **Indefinite pron.**: refers to a nonspecific person or thing.
> > e.g. all, any, anybody, anything, few, nobody, etc.

240

Adjectives: describe or modify nouns.

      e.g. a <u>beautiful</u> woman <u>or</u> the <u>wicked</u> stepfather.

   Comparative adjectives: add <u>more</u> or <u>less, or</u> -<u>er</u>.

      e.g. She is <u>more</u> beautiful than I am, but the other woman is pretti<u>er</u> than the actress.

   Superlative adjectives: add <u>the most, the least</u> or -<u>est</u>.

      e.g. She is <u>the most</u> beautiful, but not the <u>best</u> student.

Adverbs: describe or modify verbs, adjectives or other adverbs. They describe "where, when, how, why, under what circumstances, and to what extent" an action is performed. Comparative & superlative forms follow the same patterns as the adjective.

      e.g.   He spoke <u>softly</u>. She played the piano <u>well</u>.

              She spoke <u>more softly</u> (comparative).

              He then spoke <u>the most softly</u> (superlative).

Prepositions: small words which are none of the above and which occur in **phrases** before a noun which acts as the **object of the preposition (obj. of prep.)**.

      e.g.   The book fell **off** <u>the table</u>. The leaf **of** <u>the tree</u>.

Postpositions: words which are labelled "prepositions" when they take objects such as "<u>the table</u>" and "<u>the tree</u>" above. However, when they are placed after, and depend upon, verbs, the term postposition suits them very well. The prefix *post* is Latin for "after". The English postposition must be related to the separable prefix in German.

      e.g. I am <u>taking</u> **off** at 7:00 p.m. <u>Try</u> this dress **on**!

Conjunctions: join parts of sentences together in three different ways:

Coordinating conj. connects words, phrases and clauses of equal value.

Subordinating conj. joins two unequal **clauses** (sentences).

Correlative conj. two conj. which work together.

      e.g. either/or.

VERBS: express actions (*runs, hits, thinks*)

   or states of being (*is, becomes, seems*) = linking v.

Infinitive: the basic form of the verb before it is conjugated. In English, it is recognizable by the prep. <u>to</u> which precedes it; e.g. <u>to</u> run, <u>to</u> see, <u>to</u> pray, etc. In French verbs, the "to" is implied by the endings -*er*, -*ir* and -*re*, with no equivalent to "to" before the verb.

Conjugated verbs: verbs which perform because an agent does them at a certain time. There are 6 possible persons: first, second and third person singular and first, second and third person plural.

Simple Tenses: express time in the present, past and future.
Since French uses the present perfect for one completed action in the past (e.g. *je suis allé*), there is potential confusion when referring to the past tense. To clarify the English usage, we can refer to the simple past tense as the **preterite** form of the verb, which can be either **weak** and regular (e.g. **brok<u>en</u>, learn<u>ed</u>**) or **strong** (irregular) insofar as the root of the verb changes (**see < s<u>aw</u>**).

Perfect Tenses: use the **auxiliary verb** (helping v.) <u>to have</u> to describe actions which have completed in the past; e.g. present perfect, past perfect and future perfect. These are the French compound tenses (*passé composé*, etc.) because they are composed of the past participle of a verb and an auxiliary verb (either *avoir* or *être*).

Progressive Tenses: use the **aux. v.** <u>to be</u> to express an ongoing, recurring or habitual action. The main v. which follows the auxiliary verb is a present participle, which ends in *-ing*; e.g. am fish<u>ing</u>. The present tense in French can be translated as either progressive (e.g. I am finishing) or as a simple tense (e.g. I finish). The future is the same. The imperfect tense is the past progressive (*je finissais: I was finishing <u>or</u> I used to finish*).

SUMMARY OF TENSES

	REGULAR VERBS	**IRREGULAR**	**PROGRESSIVE**
PRESENT	I talk	I eat	I am talking I am eating
PAST	I talked	I ate	I was talking I was eating
FUTURE	I will talk	I will eat	I will be talking/eating

PERFECT TENSES

	REGULAR VERBS	**IRREGULAR**	**PROGRESSIVE**
PRESENT PERFECT	I have talked	I have eaten	I have been talking/eating
PAST PERF.	I had talked	I had eaten	I had been talking/eating
FUTURE PERFECT	I will have talked / eaten		I will have been talking/eating

Moods: verbs express an **indicative** mood (a normal statement), the **imperative** mood (a command or order) or a **subjunctive** mood (unreal conditions, conjectures)

> e.g. If I <u>were</u> you, I would ask for a tutor!
>
> Come what <u>may</u> *or* Far <u>be</u> it from me...

Voice: is **active** or **passive** depending upon whether the subject of the sentence acts or is acted upon.

> **Active**: I like clams (I am doing the liking).
> **Passive**: Clams are liked <u>by</u> hundreds of gourmands
> (the people who are doing the liking (the agent) follow after the prep. <u>by</u>.).

Transitive verb: has a direct object, unlike the **intransitive** one.

> To identify a transitive verb by its direct object, ask "what?" receives the action; e.g.

> The scholar is reading a poem.
> The scholar is reading **what?** <u>a poem</u> (direct object); therefore the verb "to read" is transitive.

Intransitive verb: has no direct object; e.g.

> The lawyer is arriving tomorrow.
> There is no word here which would answer the question "what?".
> The adverb <u>tomorrow</u> answers the question "when"?
> He is arriving **when?** Tomorrow!

Case: the form that nouns or pronouns take within a sentence which reveals how the noun or pronoun relates to the other words in the sentence.

> **Nominative** (or subjective case): functions as the <u>subject</u> of the sentence;
> e.g. The <u>snow</u> falls gently down from heaven.

> **Possessive**: expresses the noun's possession of another by an apostrophe;
> e.g. The musician's contract...; His contract expired!

> **Accusative** (or direct object): receives the action of the sentence;
> e.g. I raised my <u>arm</u>.

> **Dative**: (or indirect object): receives the action indirectly, after the direct object has received it.

> e.g. I gave the book <u>to him</u>.
> We showed <u>him</u> our budget
> (when the indefinite obj. "him" is first, "to" is dropped).

Subjective completion (predicate adj. or predicate n.):
The noun or adjective which follows the linking verb and is equated with the subject. In French, the adjective still agrees in number and gender with the noun it modifies, even if the linking verb separates the two.

e.g. The rose is <u>watered</u> (linking verb =<u>is</u>).

Linking verbs: The verb which regularly links two equal entities (subject with subjective completion) is **to be**. Other verbs which link two equal things express state of being, often using the senses

e.g. *look, smell, taste, sound, feel*; I <u>feel</u> tired.
Or they can express a sense of existing or becoming;
e.g. *appear, seem, become, get, grow, turn, remain...*
The food <u>stays</u> hot, if one keeps it covered.

Main clause: The sentence (subject and verb, and all related adj., adv., phrases) which carries the primary meaning when a subordinate clause is attached to it by a conj.

Subordinate clause: The subject and verb (and all related adj., adv. and phrases) which depend upon another main clause for its meaning. It cannot stand alone and still make sense.

Subordinating conjunctions (see "conjunctions" above): Linkages between the main and the subordinate clause may be made by these self-standing words (e.g. after, although, as, because, before, unless, etc.) which perform no other grammatical function within either of the two sentences. To this group also belongs one usage of "that": e.g.

I know **that** my brother is alive.

In these sorts of sentences, **that** links the main clause (I know) to the subordinate clause (my brother is alive) without being grammatically essential to either of the sentences. This usage is always represented by *que* in French.

Relative pronouns:
Another way of relating main clauses to subordinate ones makes use of relative pronouns, which actually fulfill a grammatical function in the subordinate clause. These relative pronouns in English are: **who, whom, which, that**, represented by only two in French: **qui, que.** Whereas the French use their relative pronouns according to case in the subordinate clause (**qui** = nominative; **que** = accusative), English distinguishes people from things and restrictive from non-restrictive clauses:

> 1. The president, **who** is currently a woman, will speak.
> 2. The president, **whom** you are discussing, will speak.

In both cases, **who** and **whom** refer to the president (their antecedent), but the first (who) acts as the subject of the subordinate clause, while the second (whom) acts as the object. In French, the first is *qui*, the second **que**.

> 3. The church **that** depends upon male celibacy is at risk.
> 4. The church, **which** depends upon male celibacy, is at risk.

The subordinate clause in #3 (after **that**) is restrictive in that it restricts the meaning of "church" to only that one which depends upon "male celibacy". There are other churches, but they are not at risk. The second one in #4 (after **which**) is non-restrictive because it adds information that is not essential to the meaning of the whole. The only church that the speaker is considering is the one at risk. Both **that** and **which** would be *qui* in French, because *qui* constitutes the subject of the subordinate clause.

In oral English, few people make the distinction between **that** and **which**. From a French perspective, **that** is an essential translation for indirect discourse where it has no grammatical function in the subordinate clause apart from joining the two sentences together; e.g.

> I think. Grammar is unnecessary.
> 1. I think **that** (*que*) grammar is unnecessary.
> 2. Let us omit grammar **which/that** (*qui*) is unnecessary.

In the first compound sentence, **that** would be *que* in French, since it links the first sentence to the second in the manner of indirect discourse without any other grammatical role. In this case, it is a **subordinating conjunction**. In the second sentence, **which** or **that** stands for "grammar" (like a pronoun) in the subordinate clause and functions as the subject of "is necessary". This **which** is a **relative pronoun** because, as a pronoun, it relates the subordinate clause to the principal one. The distinction "which" as non-restrictive, "that" as restrictive still holds. In this second case, we might say "Let us omit the grammar that is unnecessary", meaning "only that".

Verb participles:

Past Participle: uses the same form as the past tense in regular verbs;
e.g. *-ed: helped, looked, marvelled.*
Irregular verbs vary; e.g. *caught, become, chosen*
Function as adjectives describing nouns;
e.g. The <u>chosen</u> people.

Present participle: adds *-ing* to the infinitive form to function as an adjective or as a **noun** (**= gerund**);

Pres. part. as adj. The woman <u>laughing</u> is a friend.

Gerund: <u>Laughing</u> is infectious.

The gerund in French is simply an infinitive:
<u>Le rire</u> est contagieux.

APPENDIX VII

English Translations

In the following translation key, certain symbols have been used to facilitate a comparison of the English with the original French. These are not recommended for use in formal translations; they are only meant to aid the student who is learning. [Square brackets] indicate any editorial comment or word which would be better omitted from a finished translation. <Diamond brackets> indicate words which have been added to the original French. (Parentheses) provide alternative translations. Translations of Biblical passages are not always provided, since they can be checked against authoritative English translations. An element of aesthetic judgement is involved in any translation, depending upon the context and audience.

CHAPTER ONE

Exercise A
 1. after the conversation
 2. with the merchandise
 3. in the research
 4. out of the question
 5. under the government of
 6. in the publishing house <of>
 7. at the post office
 8. behind the tower
 9. between the structures
10. before the unknown
11. against the critique of truth
12. towards a liberation theology
13. about the theory
14. without energy
15 under the eyes of
16. out of context

17. by the critic
18. under a communist government
19. a [female] friend's question
20. among friends
21. to the nation
22. against secularism
23. in the face of danger
24. before the question
25. for the lecture
26. on <one's> knees _or_ kneeling
27. in front of the castle
28. with the nails
29. in the newspaper
30. towards the bookstore

Exercise B

1. a new edition
2. a charitable individual
3. an old man
4. a generous person
5. the new style
6. the correct address
7. an interesting library
8. a bad attitude
9. a little fault
10. another subject
11. a long prominent nose
12. a high tower
13. a good poem
14. the new theory
15. a bad poem
16. an intelligent author
17. charming eyes
18. an old apartment
19. a deadly woman
20. Dear friend (m.)

CHAPTER TWO

Exercise A

1. good (m., f.sg.)
2. good (m., f.pl.)
3. public (m., f.)
4. bad (m., f.)
5. Greek (m., f.)
6. obvious (m., f.)
7. favourite (m., f.)
8. anxious (m., f.)
9. powerful (m., f.)
10. Christian (m., f.)

Exercise B

1. to write
2. to belong
3. to give
4. to come
5. to go out
6. to reign
7. to keep
8. to be
9. to know
10. to deliver
11. to believe
12. to have
13. to forgive
14. to offend
15. to sanctify
16. to accomplish

Exercise C

1. gives (3sg.), given (pp.)
2. keeps (3sg.), keep (3pl.)   S
3. thinks (3sg.), think (3pl.)   S
4. accomplish (2sg.), accomplish (3pl.)
5. deliver (imp), delivered (pp.)   S
6. examines (3sg.), examined (pp.)
7. accomplished (pp), accomplish (2sg.)   S
8. reign (3pl.), reigned (pp.)
9. believe (2sg.), believes (3sg.)   S
10. prohibit _or_ defend (2sg.), prohibit _or_ defend (3pl.)

Exercise D

1. temptation, temptations
2. human world
3. the (sg., pl.)
4. human beings
5. offense, offenses
6. this, these
7. of/from (sg.), some _or_ of the (pl.)
8. century, centuries

Exercise E

1. quiche (a cheese dish)
2. four
3. tea
4. Thomas
5. when?
6. what?
7. theatre
8. theologian (m., f.)
9. theory
10. someone
11. who?
12. theological
13. which (m., f.)
14. sometimes
15. theology
16. theme
17. question
18. to qualify
19. thesis
20. that, which (direct object)

Exercise F
1. glory
2. you (disjunctive pronoun)
3. me/ I (disjunctive pronoun)
4. far away
5. be it (used as a correlative conj)
6. way (nf.)
7. may be (3pl.)
8. itself (refl.pr.)
9. care
10. history _or_ story[FF]

CHAPTER THREE

Exercise A

1. We are going out.

2. Faith brings glory.

3. They are calling the theologians.

4. I am finishing the newspaper.

5. We are giving a choice.

6. The son is asking for the truth.

7. We are studying translation.

8. I am losing the fear of confession.

9. Are you (sg.) asking for salvation?

10. You (pl.) are finishing the translation.

11. We call love as a witness.

12. You fear God, but not man.

13. I am taking the newspaper.

14. The son is watching television without any real interest.

15. She is showing the fault to the theologian.

16. The doctor is teaching medicine.

17. We are learning French.

18. The priest endures poverty.

19. Money helps to get out of poverty.

20. A friend does not lose faith.

Exercise B

1. We are preparing the Easter feast.

2. The power of God is made manifest in the Bible.

3. The French toast [Quebec] or lost bread [France] is on the table.[1]

4. The little effort is appreciated by the old woman.

5. Absolute poverty.

6. The translation is finished.

7. French literature is diverse.

8. In Europe, the cathedrals are often Gothic.

9. The library is air-conditioned.

10. A chosen people.

---

1 In Quebec, French toast is called 'gilded' bread, but in France it is 'lost bread' because baguettes (long sticks of fresh bread) dry up very quickly. The baguette is recovered by soaking slices in egg for frying.

Exercise C

1. in/by finishing the work

2. in/by speaking French

3. in/by giving an example

4. in/by invoking faith

5. In abandoning their work, they are giving a bad example.

6. By considering goodness in itself, he is learning to think.

7. By offering a choice, she manifests a sense of freedom.

8. Opening one eye, she looks at the theologian.

9. In studying, he makes poverty bearable.

10. The teacher speaks all while looking at poor Charles.

Exercise D

1. It was out of the question to suspect the church.

2. I went to see the priest.

3. We lost the books.

4. She entered ahead.

5. They (f.) climbed up among the trees.

6. You (pl.) stayed in poverty.

7. We have always given a choice.

8. We lost the original translation.

9. The new style is used in the newspaper.

10. They came before the nation.

11. She gave a choice.

12. The man defined a new theory.

Exercise E

1. Am I a theologian?

2. Are we artists?

3. Do I not have the right to be ill?

4. Why does he have a very high intellectual level?

5. How many Christians are practising?

6. Are you Catholic or Protestant?

7. Where do these Muslims come from?

8. Does the priest have the power to forgive?

9. Don't Christians have a living faith at Christmas?

10. Confessions are not heard today.[2]

11. We suffered from materialism and secularism.

12. Did you find the exit in the corridor?

13. At what hour are you leaving? <u>or</u> What time are you leaving?

---

2 This is a passive constuction in the present tense. If it were a compound past tense, *entendre* would be conjugated with *avoir*.

14. And if he died for nothing? ["Jesus Christ died for nothing, I suppose", Leonard Cohen].

15. Are you suffering?

16. What is love? It is a dangerous passion.

17. Does one have the right to succeed without making an effort?

18. May I name the successor?

19. What is preferable?

20. What are you thinking?

CHAPTER FOUR

Exercise A

1. some new developments

2. some lyrical poems

3. in fashion

4. some practical theories

5. I do not know any interesting long stories.

6. I am giving the book to the teacher.

7. The *Journal of Current Theology* fell under the chair.

8. I went to the store.

9. In the United States, they are often unfamiliar with Canadian political principles.

10. In Canada the people are bilingual, in principle.

Exercise B

1. The newspaper which is on the desk is a French newspaper.

2. The journal for which you are asking is in the office.

3. I am looking for the book which the teacher recommended.

4. The person who seems perturbed is the chair of the conference.

5. The book which I am reading is entitled *The Art of Smoking without Dying*.

6. The man who is entering is a teacher of French literature.

7. He is introducing the woman at whom you are looking *or* (less correctly) who you are looking at.

8. The beginning of the Gospel according to St. John is a biblical passage which is often cited.

9. The lawyer who is asking the question is my friend.

10. The hope [which one] lost yesterday returns today.

Exercise C

1. She has her book.

2. She loves her enemy.

3. He has his thesis.

4. The mother gave her forgiveness to her son.

5. We have our faith.

6. Edward? I am his sister.

7. They are their guides.

8. We are their friends.

9. They are your enemies.

10. Mary? Where is her brother?

Exercise D

1. I am thinking about my brother. I am thinking about him.

2. I am thinking about my sister. I am thinking about her.

3. I am suffering without you.

4. He is working for us.

5. I sang with them yesterday.

6. *I* don't have any books.

7. Are you calling Paul or me? Him?

8. My husband and I are planning to travel this year.

9. The fear of God is the beginning of wisdom.

10. The families here are poor. I am praying for them.

11. Not to us, oh Eternal One, not to us we give the glory, but to your name (Ps. 115:1).

12. We need them in order to finish the work.

13. According to them, man proposes, God disposes.

14. The heart has its reasons that reason knows not (Pascal).

15. According to him, she is learning quickly.

Exercise E

1. I have your book and that of John (*or* and John's).

2. Your mother and Mary's celebrate their birthdays today.

3. These events and those of yesterday are unbelievable!

4. We are studying the reign of Henry VIII and that of Elizabeth I.

5. We are considering these circumstances and those of yesterday.

6. My lawyer and that of my wife are friends.

7. The young child of Nazareth, in his twelfth year, at last takes himself to the Temple of Jerusalem. The latter is the centre of the world for the Jews (cf. Aron, p.127).

8. Those children need a father.

9. We are contesting the truth of his speech and that [*i.e.* the truth (f.sg.)] of his response to the questions.

10. The Sadducees do not share the aversion of the Palestinians for the language and Greek culture; the latter is despised by the Jews at the time of Jesus (cf. Aron, p.134).

CHAPTER FIVE

Exercise A

1. Ask Phillip if he kept his faith.

2. Let's finish in an hour!

3. Do not lose the key!

4. Come in before midnight!

5. Go out with your sister!

6. Think of me tomorrow.

7. Do not suffer without them.

8. Pray that God may help his son.

9. Ask Martin the question.

10. Let us pray together.

Exercise B   "Resurrection and Retribution"

A great number of those who sleep in the land of dust will wake up, some for eternal life, others for disgrace, eternal horror. The learned will shine like the splendor of the firmament, and those who have taught justice to a great number <of people will shine> like the stars, for all eternity.

You, Daniel, lock away these words and seal the book until the End-time. Many will stray here and there, and iniquity will increase.

Exercise C

1. If you can find the time, go to see this film.

2. We wish to consider the question in detail.

3. I am going to read this book tomorrow.

4. She is making a salad for this evening.

5. He knows how to philosophize.

6. We ought to leave immediately.

7. One ought to know the names of the students.

8. She cannot become a priest in the Catholic Church.

9. They (f.) ought to study the great philosophers.

10. I want to lose the fear of death.

11. We are going to continue after the meal.

12. We know that he is not coming.

Exercise F

Dedication to Leo Werth

I ask the children's forgiveness for having dedicated this book to a grown-up. I have a serious excuse; this grown-up is the best friend that I have in the world. I have another serious excuse; this grown-up can understand everything, even books for children. I have a third excuse; this grown-up lives in France where he is hungry and cold. He really has need of being consoled. If all these excuses do not suffice, I willingly dedicate this book to the child that this grown-up once was. All grown-ups were at first children. I therefore correct my dedication:

TO LEO WERTH WHEN HE WAS A LITTLE BOY

§48. The dialogues are for in-class oral practice only.

CHAPTER SIX

Exercise A

1. They died yesterday.

2. She is already dead.

3. They died during the Second World War.

4. Follow me, please.

5. We will drink and live right up to the end.

6. They often drink.

7. I sometimes write to James' brother.

8. I will read your letters to Paul from now on.

9. First of all, will you see the film?

10. We will see the film soon.

11. At times, it lasts a long time.

12. When one has experienced a war, one does not forget quickly.

13. In writing to Peter today, I am following my custom.

14. They will laugh for a long time.

15. They write often, almost always, to his family.

16. At last we are reading the passage which came to mind.

17. He will say tomorrow if he will be able to come from now on.

18. We do not drink during readings.

19. He will die tomorrow.

20. The sinner will receive the fruit (or the wage) of his sin.

Exercise B

1. She was born on April 2 in the year 2000.

2. In the evening, the students go to the library.

3. We can sleep in on Saturdays.

4. It is the feast of St. John the Baptist on June 24.

5. He plays hockey in the mornings.

6. That day, a brilliant idea came to us.

7. This sudden inspiration illuminated the mind.

8. In the morning of April 3rd, we went to the market.

9. Starting with Monday, we are going to begin again.

10. The work will be finished on May 15.

Exercise C

1. It is I who have made this mistake.

2. There will be three days of peace this weekend.

3. It is you who are always reading, not her.

4. They (f.) are the ones who demanded the right to vote.

5. There is a dog in front of the house.

6. It is the beginning of the passage which we point out as important.

7. They are the ones who know Canadian history.

8. There was a week of peace before the collapse.

9. It is a policy which may save the country.

10. If we insist upon this point, it is to suggest a correct understanding of forgiveness.

Exercise D

1. He arrived two hours ago.

2. We have been reading this passage for three months.

3. She has been reading this newspaper for four days.

4. She began to study four days ago.

5. We have been waiting for an hour!

6. They already left an hour ago.

7. She has not been on a diet for a year.

8. There are some unresolved theories advocated by this teacher.

9. They (f.) have not been working since the summer.

10. She went out early in the morning.

11. They lived five hundred years ago.

12. Canada has existed for nearly one hundred and fifty years.

13. He has been in Canada since the First World War.

14. There are some hypotheses to explain this phenomenon.

15. Have you been ill since yesterday?

Exercise E

1. It is up to her to choose the preferable translation.

2. This is the enumeration of the actions to be accomplished.

3. The function of silence will have to be analysed in detail.

4. It is fair to say that the Bible may allude to a time period established by Yahwe for the accomplishment of a precise goal.

5. Yesterday, I began to doubt.

6. We have not been able to think about anything else for a week.

7. Beginning next week, I will be ready to travel.

8. It is not yet time to gather the flocks together.

9. He is beginning to read slowly.

10. We will speak out loud.

CHAPTER SEVEN

Exercise A

1. Nothing. No-one. For the past two days that I have been home again, nothing has been happening, no-one has been coming.

2. He is never free in the evening, neither on the weekend, nor on holidays.

3. <He is> an adorable friend, always smiling, obliging, ready to help, giving without ever asking for help <in return>.

4. Do not blame before first having investigated <and> reflected, then express your reproach (Ec. 11:7).

5. It is said, "Give to the pious man and do not come to the aid of the sinner," but we are all sinners.

6. They (f.) suffer neither hunger nor exhaustion, and never abandon their tasks (Ec. 16:27b).

7. No-one has ever offended the other, and they have never disobeyed his word (Ec. 16:28).

8. Our ancestors have sinned: they are no longer; and <as for> us, we bear their faults (Lm 5:7).

9. Slaves rule over us, <and> no-one delivers our children from their hand (Lm 5:8).

10. Jesus says, "No-one has condemned the woman" and Marie-Magdalene agrees with him saying, "No-one." Jesus speaks again and says, "Go and sin no more."

Exercise B

1. I can only think of his visit _or_ I can think of nothing but his visit.

2. My friend never comes to the university any more.

3. This egotist (_or_ selfish person) never gives anything to anyone.

4. She lives in an appartment which scarcely affords any comfort.

5. I will never see Peter any more.

6. We no longer give to the word "charisma" the meaning of exceptional talent which someone has received from birth.

7. In the history of ideas and religious movements, nothing ever grows out of an entirely virgin (_or_ unspoiled) soil.

8. From a Christian point of view, there can be only one theology of the insurmountable scandal of the cross: that which comprehends the cross as a crisis.

9. He only wants to go to the cinema when she wants to read.

10. In the evening, there is no longer anyone at the university.

Exercise C

1. Nothing, neither the old gardens reflected in her eyes, nor the brightness of this lamp will hold this heart (Mallarmé, *Poetry*).

2. One must either believe or deny, or doubt (Pascal, *Thoughts*).

3. He is accompanied both by his sister and his mother (Gambetta).

4. He has neither father nor mother.

5. He neither drinks nor eats.

6. I do not wish to, neither must I, nor can I obey.

7. He speaks to no-one about either his business or his plans.

8. No-one is so eloquent, nor so profound.

9. There is nothing astonishing or rare in that.

10. Neither gentleness nor force can <do> anything.

Exercise D

1. I am looking for the text which the teacher recommended.

2. Students who study regularly are certainly going to succeed.

3. The friend to whom I am writing is in Paris right now (*or* at this time).

4. I cannot buy the books which I want (*or* lit. of which I have a desire).

5. The man to whom I spoke in the train is an archeologist.

6. Do not take the papers which we need.

7. The teacher explained to us the method by which he studied the prehistoric art of this region.

8. Peter is a friend with whom I cannot work easily.

9. I want the book, the critique of which I read in the newspaper.

10. Proust is an author whose style one easily recognizes.

11. The French course is a course to which the students go willingly (*or* with pleasure).

12. Teachers ought to speak about books in which the students have an interest.

13. Fontainebleau Castle, to which the history teacher referred, is <located> to the south of Paris.

14. Stephen Hatfield is a composer whose genius Canadians admire.

15. Catastrophes which one fears occur only rarely.

16. Here is a book which I will never need again.

17. Here is a document whose authenticity is not yet certain (*or* is still uncertified).

18. Films about which one often speaks are not always good.

19. I read Camus' book about which the teacher spoke in class.

20. Let's only buy the books which we need.

Exercise E

1. I know what you mean.

2. We know what the doctor will say.

3. He will be up-to-date on what is happening in the street.

4. It is Jacques Cartier who, in 1534, claimed possession of Canada in the name of France.

5. What makes the defeat of Montcalm so tragic is the mortal wound which he received on September 13, 1759.

6. That which we profess is the truth.

7. That which the theologians are teaching does not go against logic for all that.

8. What goes straight to the heart of the problem may be shocking.

9. There is what is extraordinary.

10. What is striking is the lack of compassion at the heart of the current government.

11. What I love in life is sleeping (Saint-Exupéry).

12. What moves me so strongly about this little prince <who has> fallen asleep is his fidelity to a flower, is the image of a rose which radiates in him like the flame of a lamp, even when he is sleeping (Saint-Exupéry).

Exercise F

Dominus Jesus, analysis in the Parisian newspaper *Le Monde* (Sept.6, 2000) before Cardinal Ratzinger was elected Pope Benedict XVI.

The German Cardinal Josef Ratzinger, prefect (since 1981) of the Congregation for the Doctrine of the Faith, is the author of this document approved by the pope. Reaffirming the superiority of the Catholic religion, the document is a cold shower for all those who profess œcumenism – the reconciliation between the separated Christian denominations – and dialogue with the non-Christian religions.

To the pope belong symbolic gestures, the kisses of peace with Protestant, Anglican or Orthodox *"separated brethren"*, the visits to synagogues or mosques, the handshakes with Buddhists or Hindus. To Cardinal Ratzinger, "guardian" of the doctrine, <belongs> the duty to defend the Catholic faith, according to him threatened by the dangers of relativism, subjectivism and a false idea of pluralism.

Cardinal Ratzinger reaffirms the plenitude of the Christian revelation: *"The words, the works and the historic existence of Jesus... bear within them the complete and definitive character of the ways of God's salvation."* He adds that only the Old and New Testaments are *"inspired texts"*. Only Christianity deserves to be qualified as *"faith"*, the other religions being mere *"beliefs"* which, if they may be treasures of wisdom, only arise from *"religious experience"* alone.

According to the cardinal, Jesus Christ is not *"a particular historic figure"* on the model of a Buddha, a Socrates or a great "sage" of humanity. He is *"the unique mediator between God and humankind, and the universal saviour"*. There is no way of salvation other than Christianity. That is a *"definitive"* truth. *"The salvific will of God is made manifest and accomplished, once and for all, in the mystery of the Incarnation, death and Resurrection of the Son of God."* All the other experiences of the divine *"may draw their meaning and their value only from that [experience] of Christ. They may not be considered parallel and complementary"* <experiences>.

CHAPTER EIGHT

Exercise A

1. I was wanting to ask the doctor a question.

2. I was going to answer your question.

3. If you were me, what would you do? Me? I would go to Quebec.

4. We would like to begin by considering reconciliation to be a completely reasonable solution.

5. In spite of the disadvantages, the elderly would say that old age brings wisdom.

6. Could we begin again? That would be preferable!

7. We could hardly glimpse the bell-tower in the distance.

8. Now Jesus loved Martha and her sister and Lazarus; and when he had learned that the latter was ill, he remained two days longer in the place where he was (John 11:6).

9. "Our friend Lazarus is resting, but I am going to go and wake him up" (John 11:11).

10. "Lord, if he is resting, he will be saved". Jesus had spoken of his death, but the disciples believed that he was speaking of the repose of sleep (John 11:12-13).

Exercise B

1. We have just arrived.

2. We had just arrived.

3. They have just received their diplomas.

4. They had just received their diplomas.

5. Have you just learned to read?

6. Had the doctor just written a book?

7. Mr. and Mrs. Stuart come from Scotland.

8. She has just been born ten minutes ago!

9. He had just been born when she died.

10. The art book which I have just received is a gift from my colleague.

Exercise C

1. She would have read the newspaper before leaving.

2. I will not go out before having asked my wife for forgiveness.

3. They will encounter another difficulty.

4. In considering the problem, they are hesitating without really coming to a decision.

5. He will be in England before the new year.

6. One must stay for three days after having met the president.

7. We had just said the same thing.

8. After having read the text, I changed my mind.

9. A little food remains in the bag.

10. It is too late to begin to read this evening.

11. It was necessary to stop his speech.

12. Once upon a time, there was a superstitious people who refused all belief in God.

13. Two sentences remain to be translated.

14. We listen without understanding anything.

15. It would have been necessary to be interested in theology.

Exercise D

1. If you had come, I would have been happy.

2. Could you keep today's newspaper?

3. If he had said something, I would have heard.

4. If I had been prepared to die for peace, like Gandhi, my prayers would have been granted.

5. The philosopher swore that he would not write any more.

6. If the woman had spoken, she would have been abandoned.

7. If they became (*or* were to become) rich, they would go around the world (*lit.* do a world tour).

8. If I were in Paris, I would visit Montmartre.

9. The protestant churches knew that they would be excluded!

10. We would like to look at your book.

11. If I were able to fall asleep, I would not be ill.

12. I knew that he would succeed.

13. If you came, I would be happy about it.

14. I would like to finish before noon.

Exercise E

If I were Marilyn <Munroe>, I would be very beautiful, but so fragile!

If I were God, I would really be annoyed...

If I were a flower, it would not be the forget-me-not.

If I were Groucho Marx, I would be rather happy. Jerry Lewis too, that could suit me as well.

If I were Madame Curie, I would be on postage stamps.

If I were Voltaire, I would be on bank notes.

Stop. I can't go on! (*lit.* I can <do> no more of it!)

If I were a man, I could not be a woman.

If I were Calamity Jane or Anny of the Far West, I would have some fine pistols. Oh la la!

If I were Joan of Arc, I would look after my sheep instead of going to chat with these English who are not worth so much. Ah no!

If I were Mitterand, I would not have gone to the Pantheon.

If I were young, I would not make the same blunders again. I would make others [of them].

If I were a fisherwoman of pearls, I would keep them for myself.

If I were W.C. Fields, I would really love little children.

If I were Chandler, ah, if I were Chandler, I would drink less in order to write more, in the name of God!...

If I were a dream, I would wake myself up...

Stop. I can't go on!

Exercise F

"L'Aprentissage: Paris 1831-1833", by Madeleine Des Rivières, *Ozanam un savant chez les pauvres* (Montréal, Bellarmin, 1984), pp. 227-8.

Using the verb tenses as written in French, i.e. the historic present, to assure an accurate recognition of them.

...[Louis-Philippe has been ruling France for one year.] A great number of monarchists are still convinced that he usurped the throne at the expense of the grandson of Charles X, the Duke of Bordeaux... Sporadic riots will erupt in Paris as in the outlying regions in the course of the years which will follow. The Congregation, a controversial religious organization which brings the most determined Christians together - not necessarily the most authentic ones - has just been dissolved. The Catholic religion is no longer the State religion. The Chambers give up ensuring the security of the clergy. Some priests have been put to death. Certain others among the most courageous will continue, nevertheless, to clearly display their beliefs.

   The great writers are at work. Balzac is writing his *Human Comedy*. <Victor> Hugo has just finished *The Hunchback of Notre Dame*. The poet Lamartine chooses politics, while Chateaubriand, exhausted and ruined, is abandoning the latter (*i.e.* politics) in order to write his *Memoirs*. It is the period when George Sand is publishing *Lélia* and experiencing her great successive passions with Sandeau, Musset and Chopin. Liszt and Berlioz, these immortals of music, are at the peak of their glory. Montalembert and Lamennais have just founded, in 1830, the newspaper *l'Avenir* which was inaugurating a liberal catholicism, favourable to the separation of Church and State. Eloquence and the written word have a primordial importance in the nineteenth century. Let's not forget it. They are the golden nails which establish ideas. At the Sorbonne, there is even (oh paradox!) a chair of sacred eloquence.

Footnotes:

10. Charles-Forbes, the count of Montalembert: French journalist and politician (1810-1870); contributor to the newspaper *l'Avenir* [The Future] and an apostle of liberal catholicism.

11. Félicité de Lamennais (1782-1854), French writer and thinker, <who> founded *l'Avenir*, and <was> an advocate of democratic humanitarianism.

CHAPTER NINE

Exercise A

1. He is giving the books to Peter and me. He is giving them to us.

2. I am telling the story to Francis. I am telling it to her.

3. When they have the results, they will report them to me.

4. In spite of his old age, he gets the better of his enemies.

5. They think that you are sincere when you are deceiving them.

6. She is giving the books to the citizens. She is giving them to them.

7. Here, we are recalling the theological vision of St. Ireneus. We are recalling it here. Let us recall it here.

8. The mission of the Church derives from its nature (_or_ her nature), such as Christ willed it.

9. The Second Vatican Council recalled to us the mystery of the priestly, prophetic and royal dignity of all the People of God.

10. The pastoral responsibility of the Church? Each priest exercises it in the heart of a particular Church <parish>.

11. Give him (_or_ her) the opportunity to exercise it, please!

12. He showed that this tradition was much more widespread at the beginning of Christianity than one would have thought (_lit._ could think it <to have been>) at first glance.

Exercise B

1. Are you going to Montreal? You have only to wait for me there.

2. I will be there this evening.

3. Please, answer my question. Me? I will respond to it.

4. If you wish to give up your vacation, give it up.

5. Then what good are the thorns of a rose? They are good for nothing (_or_ They have no use; they are useless; they serve for nothing).

6. I think as I breath, without thinking about it.

7. He has been keen to read it for a long time. He has been keen about it for some time.

8. Are you asking me a question about the exclusion of women from the ecclesial hierarchy? We are accustomed to it.

9. Will you accompany me? If you are keen on it.

10. Things are interesting to the degree that we are interested in them.

Exercise C

1. Have you enough money? Yes, I have enough [of it; *unnec.*].

2. The master sent the workers to the vineyard and then found some others [of them; *unnec.*].

3. He is intelligent and is very proud of it.

4. Philosophers of the nineteenth century? She has spoken a lot about them to me.

5. She is a member of the Society of Theologians, but he does not belong to it.

6. We have the texts, whereas they need them.

7. Let's not talk about it any more!

8. When the scholar enters, we are afraid of him.

9. In 1530, Holbein converted to the reform religion, asking - as the recruitment registers witness to it - for a better explanation of Holy Communion before committing himself.

10. His aesthetic activity triumphs over this latent melancholy (*lit.* melancholic latency), all while keeping an impression (*lit.* the trace) of it.

Exercise D

1. He is giving us worries. Is he giving you any?

2. Do not give any of it to him (*or* to her)!

3. I need some stamps. Yes, he told me that you need some [of them; *unnec.*].

4. There is not any money. No, there isn't any.

5. If you have found some money, give it to him (*or* to her).

6. What is the conclusion that you have drawn from the discussion? Do not hide it from me!

7. The woman is asking for the recently published book. Send it to her!

8. The whole document arrived yesterday. We are preparing it for you.

9. Think about it.

10. His/Her thesis directors (there are two of them) are not up-to-date on the situation. Explain it to them, please.

Exercise E

1. For every sin, mercy [*For:* dative of purpose].

2. All men are mortal.

3. All those who wish [it] may leave (**le: it** is pleonastic in English).

4. All that [which] sparkles is not gold.

5. All music is not suitable for praising God [*for* dative of purpose].

6. He refuses to participate in their study, all while announcing his own project.

7. He read the whole book in one sitting.

8. The pope can address all these churches.

9. Even the Protestants will listen to him.

10. The parish ought to be a house open to all and at the service of all.

11. My own method follows the same path.

12. He even destined them to be <made in> the image of his Son, in order to make of this Son the eldest of a multitude of brothers.

13. It is of this same unity which Jesus is speaking when using the image of the vine and branches (*or* vine shoots).

14. Laughter is the essence [*or* defining characteristic] of man [*or* humankind] (Rabelais citing Aristotle).

15. The weakness of God remains, in spite of everything, his (*or* her) strength.

Exercise F

Jean-Paul II, *Les fidèles laïcs* (Paris: Centurion, 1989), p. 110.

The Second Vatican Council proclaims it very loudly: «All that which is opposed to life itself, like every kind of homicide, genocide, abortion, euthanasia and even pre-meditated suicide; all that which constitutes a violation of the integrity of the human person, like mutilation, physical or moral torture or psychological constraints; all that which is offensive to the dignity of the individual, like subhuman living conditions, arbitrary imprisonments, deportations, slavery, prostitution, trafficing in women and children; or even degrading working conditions which reduce workers to the rank of mere instruments of profit without any regard for their free and responsible personality; all these practices and other analagous ones are, in truth, loathsome. While they corrupt civilization, they dishonour those who succomb to them still more than those who suffer them [i.e., they dishonour the perpetrators more than the victims], and they seriously demean the honour of the Creator.

Exercise G

Simone Weil, *Pensées sans ordre concernant l'amour de Dieu* (Paris: Gallimard, 1962), pp. 14-15.

Life, such as it is made for man is only bearable by the lie. Those who refuse the lie and prefer to know that life is intolerable, without for all that rebelling against their lot, end up receiving from without, from a place situated outside of time, something which permits <them> to accept life such as it is.

Everyone feels the evil, abhors it and would like to be delivered from it. The evil is neither the suffering nor the sin; it is both, for they are linked. Sin causes suffering and suffering renders <the person> bad, and this indissoluble mixture of suffering and sin is the evil in which we exist, despite ourselves, and in which we have a horror of finding ourselves.

We project a part of the evil which is in us onto the objects of our attention and our desire (*lit.* The evil which is in us, we project a part of it onto...) and they send it back to us, as if this evil was coming from them. It is for that reason that we assume a hatred and a disgust for the places in which we find ourselves overwhelmed by the evil. It seems to us that these very places imprison us in the evil. It is in this way that the infirm assume a hatred for their bedroom and their social milieu, even if this circle is made up of loved ones, and in this way that labourers, at times, assume a hatred for their factory, and so on.

But if by attention and desire, we project a part of our evil onto a perfectly pure thing, it cannot be tainted by it; it remains pure. It does not send this evil back to us. Thus we are delivered from it.

CHAPTER TEN

Exercise A

1. We still have a little wine (*lit*. There remains a little wine for us).

2. John has a lot of worries.

3. I am convinced that a great number of events happen to us which appear to be senseless (*lit*. appear to have no reason for being).

4. The majority of people are conservative.

5. She read a lot of historical novels.

6. This novel contains fewer characteristic elements.

7. If we had had enough time, we would even have read the text.

8. A collection of roman inscriptions (in Latin) tells me little.

9. Jesus poured out so much blood upon the cross.

10. Too many translations show too little sensitivity to the original language.

11. Few people have enough experience in this area.

12. I would like to welcome more people at my place.

Exercise B

1. I have as much estime for his prose as for his poetry.

2. God is the supreme question, encompassing and surpassing all the others, present to the most modest minds (<u>or</u> the simplest minds) as to the most sophisticated – sometimes without them knowing.

3. Thus in the same instance, God constitutes the most complex and demanding of challenges posed to human thought.

4. As many girls as boys were born.

276

5. The thing is all the more striking as the Emmaus episode is organized in a way identical to two other Lucan narratives.

6. This story develops more quickly than the other.

7. Our decision is all the more certain as it is taken after a few weeks of deliberation.

8. The Easter period is most appropriate for this reconciliation that readmits the penitent to the eucharistic communion.

9. After the peace of Constantine, the ancient system of penitence becomes more and more impractical, to such a degree that certain bishops only impose penance at the approach of death.

10. There no longer exists an exclusive alternative between the pair body-blood and the pair spirit-life, because the two aspects coincide in the eucharist in the most complete way.

Exercise C

1. The more one hurries, the less one advances (*Eng.* Haste makes waste).

2. He is busy with his affairs and we with ours.

3. We will cite the note from our book and you that from yours.

4. These passages and ours are very similar.

5. Here are the books which are hot off the press (*lit.* have just come out). Theirs are found on the highest shelf, his on the lowest.

6. These are the letters which I have just written. They are intended for the president, because he is more responsible for the poor than the vice-president.

7. Your letters seem good to me. I have not yet written mine.

8. Our prime minister is the head of our government, whereas a president is the head of yours.

9. My thesis and yours touch upon the same subject.

10. My faith and his do not lead in the same direction.

Exercise D

Reading: Lise Baroni, Yvonne Bergeron, Pierrette Daviau et Micheline Laguë, *Voices of Women; Rites of Passage: Pastoral Practices and Ecclesiastical Stakes* (Montréal: Paulines, 1995), pp.112-13.

Some women no longer tolerate being marginalized, in spite of their recognized competence and experience [...]. The Church of those who hold them in a minor station, all while preaching the natural equality of the sexes and justice for "all", cannot draw its authority from the Church of Jesus Christ. [...] Some, more exasperated, even attack the partriarchal law and theology head on, and see no future without substantial change on the anthropological, theological and ecclesiological levels. [...] They do not agree that the authorities call so little into question traditions which perpetuate inequality between the sexes. [...] They refuse the hermetic seal upon an outdated but still unshakable law. The extent of this institutional rigidity escapes them no more than it escapes organizations which defend human rights. Thus, by way of an example, Quebec's Council on the Status of Women, in referring to this absolute authority of the ecclesiastical institution, does not hesitate to mention violence in the Church:

> ... The subordination of women has been rooted in ways of thinking and institutions which are still stamped with the age-old sexism which has characterized them. The contribution of the Church to the inferiorization of women no longer has to be demonstrated. According to the most widespread version of creation, the woman was drawn from a rib of the man and was intended for him. According to Saint Augustine, the man's body is in the image of his soul, but not that of the woman.

And the text adds on the following page:

> ... In theory, the greater the inequality, the greater the potential for violence. Violence against women, like racial or religious violence, is rendered possible by the conviction that "the other", the woman, the black man, the Jew, is less valuable, less intelligent, less good looking and less useful to society than oneself, and not as close to God. Violence exists when there is scorn for the other and for his (or her) wishes, when there is a negation of his (or her) identity and his (or her) equality.[3]

---

3 *May the unacceptable cease*, op. cit., pp.25-29. Emphasis added. See also certain passages from pages 28 and 29 of this same text.

CHAPTER ELEVEN

Exercise A "Ananias and Saphira", Acts 5:1-11, TOB.

But a man called Ananias, whose wife was named Saphira, sold, in agreement with her, a plot of land which belonged to them. He kept a part of the money for himself and went to hand over the remainder to the apostles. His wife knew it. Then Peter said to him:

"Ananias, why has Satan been able to take possession of your heart in order to make you lie to the Holy Spirit and keep for yourself a part of the money yielded by this plot? Were you not able to keep it without selling it, or, if you sold it, to dispose of the price to your liking? Then how were you able to decide within yourself to commit such an act? It is not to human beings that you have lied, but to God.

In hearing these words, Ananias fell down and died. And all those who learned of it were seized with a great fear. The young people came to wrap up the body; then they took it away and buried it.

About three hours later, the wife of Ananias entered without knowing what had happened. Peter asked her:

"Tell me, have you sold your plot of land for that sum there? And she answered: "Yes, for that sum there." Then Peter said to her: "How then were you able to conspire (*lit.* decide together) to put the Spirit of the Lord to the test? Listen, those who buried your husband are already at the door and they are going to carry you away too (*lit.* you also).

In the same instant, she fell down at the feet of the apostle and died. The young people entered and found her dead; they carried her away and buried her close to her husband. The whole Church and all those who learned of these acts were seized by a great fear.

Exercise B Madeleine des Rivières, *Ozanam*, pp. 102-3.

In the month of July, Amelia, for whom the doctors again advised a stay at the seaside, regretfully leaves Frederic overwhelmed by the chance death of Professor Fauriel, for whom he is the substitute. Ozanam had a great esteem for this brilliant and wise man whom he considers a scholar.

Thus Claude Fauriel's chair falls vacant (*lit.* is found vacant). On might think that it would revert directly to Ozanam, but Frederic is only thirty-one years old; his titles are few (*lit.* thin) and his publications limited. The minister has his word to say. They even offer the position to Professor Jean-Jacques Ampère who teaches at the Collège de France. The latter refuses it to the benefit of Frederic. Ozanam is deeply touched by the gesture of his friend. Yet the game is not won for all that. He has to see the minister (*lit.* It is necessary <for him> to see the minister), then those who advise him, and he has to write asking for an audience, etc. For Frederic, it is <necessary> to resume the visits that he made several months earlier for the benefit of M. Soulacroix, to see the same influential people again, pleading this time his own cause. A frustrating and difficult process.

Ozanam escapes from time to time and runs to embrace Amelia in Dieppe, but immediately returns to Paris where his classes await him, along with his obligations at the Sorbonne and a work whose publication he wishes to hasten: *The Literary History of Germany.*

Frederic remains faithful to his daily letters and describes to his beloved how painful the separation is for him: "This house to which I return without hearing your sweet voice that used to call me, this living room where your place is empty, this silent piano, these little birds on the roof awaiting in vain your pretty hand which used to throw crumbs to them; all that saddens me."

Exercise C

1. I am my own person.

2. My former teacher gave me an old book.

3. We saw it (*f.*) last week.

4. She used to have a marvellous soprano voice.

5. He did it carefully.

6. My dear friend bought a very expensive bottle of wine for me.

7. The poor girl no longer wished to live.

8. An impoverished family was living in a clean house.

9. He looked carefully at his gold watch.

10. If we patiently consider this problem, we will resolve it.

Exercise D

1. We know that the Gospel is a re-reading of what Jesus said, did and was.

2. We would only like to state better what the aims and commitment of a Calvin were [i.e., someone like Calvin].

3. In their majority, the neo-Protestants prefer to follow the trail that their Genevan co-religionists have always blazed for them.

4. Here is the subject that Michel Foucault presented in his book, *A History of Madness in the Classical Age*.

5. The symphonies that Mozart composed possess (*lit.* are of < have) a musical genius which one easily recognizes.

6. Moreover, God begins by preserving and safeguarding a part of the unknowable and for that reason precisely without a name: "I am who I am" (Ex. 3:14).

7. The constant concern which the author manifests to disentangle erroneous from legitimate doctrines, to seek to know, for example, if the influence of Origen [...] was to transform Platonic thought or modify Christian doctrine [..], leads him, at times, to judge interactions between Platonism and Christianity.

8. "But God constitutes the most complex and demanding of challenges posed to human thought – in the manner, on another level, of this mountain summit ordinarily veiled by clouds," to which Karl Popper loves to compare the "objective or absolute truth" whose existence is not more affected by our ignorance, he says, than is the objective existence of the summit.

Exercise E   2 Chronicles 9: 1-7.

The Queen of Sheba learned of the renown of Salomon and came to Jerusalem to test him with riddles. She arrived with very great wealth, camels loaded with spices, and a large quantity of gold and precious stones. When she had arrived, she told him all that she had pondered. Salomon illuminated her on all her questions and none was a secret for him... When the Queen of Sheba saw the wisdom of Salomon..., her heart failed her and she said to the king: "What I have heard about you and your wisdom in my country was therefore true. I did not want to believe what they were saying before coming and seeing with my <own> eyes, but truly... you surpass the fame of which I have heard (*lit.* had had) the echo. Blessed are your people, blessed are your servants here, who wait upon you continually and who hear your wise pronouncements (*lit.* wisdom).

Exercise F Chateaubriand, *Le génie du christianisme*, 1802.

The Church under Emperor Julian was exposed to another persecution of the most dangerous kind. They did not use violence against the Christians, but they poured out scorn upon them. They began by stripping the altars; then they prohibited the faithful from teaching and studying literature. But the emperor, sensing the advantage of the Christian institutions, wished, by abolishing them, to imitate them. He founded hospitals and monasteries; and on the model of the evangelical worship, he tried to unite morality with religion, by having sermon-like speeches (*lit.* kinds of sermons) pronounced in the temples.

The Sophists, by whom Julian was surrounded, let loose against Christianity. Even Julian did not consider it beneath him to pit himself against the *Galileans*. The work which he wrote against them has not come down to us, but St. Cyril, Patriarch of Alexandria, cites some fragments from it in the refutation which he made of it, and which we still have. When Julian is serious, St. Cyril triumphs over the philosopher. But when the emperor has recourse to irony, the patriarch loses his advantage. Julian's style is lively, animated and witty. St. Cyril gets carried away. He is eccentric, obscure and convoluted. From Julian up to Luther, the Church in all its vigour no longer needed any apologists. When the Western Schism took form, new champions appeared with the new enemies. One must admit that the Protestants were at first superior to the Catholics (*lit.* had at first superiority over the Catholics), at least formally, as Montesquieu has observed [*lit.* present tense]. Even Erasmus was weak against Luther, and Théodore de Bèze had a lightness of style, which was too often lacking in his opponents.

CHAPTER TWELVE

Exercise A

1. Eternal God, you have fed us with your spiritual nourishment.

2. He suffered his passion and was placed in the tomb.

3. The character of Mary Magdalene has been associated, for all time, with the Easter event.

4. The little that we know of her is that she was exorcized by Jesus.

5. Mary Magdalene is linked, at least by her name, to Magdala in Galilee, whereas Mary, the sister of Martha, is established in Bethany in Judea.

6. Mary is declared happy, blessed, spirit-filled and pure.

7. The identity of Jesus, such as it is recounted by those who did not associate with him (_or_ hang around with him) may not be maintained; only that identity <recounted> by Jesus' table companions is considered true.

8. We know that Jesus was not followed around by a group of people who were noting down his words and actions.

9. Pure consciousness is currently considered the ultimate essence of the universe, including the physical universe.

10. Because of a bequest to an organization intended to prove, scientifically, the existence of the soul and the survival of the individual conscience after death, presentations were made by 133 organizations.

Exercise B

1. Behold! The two solitudes in Canada have just shaken hands.

2. We wondered what was happening in the street.

3. He is complaining of the noise that the neighbours are making.

4. She suspected that she had lost her book.

5. They looked at each other without saying anything.

6. He would really like to get along without smoking.

7. I promised to stop smoking.

8. Love each other.

9. We promised each other to see one another again.

10. That is <just> not done.

11. He is not succeeding in getting along without wine.

12. They talk to each other.

13. The newspapers are being sold down there.

14. You ought not to take it out on anyone but yourself
    (_or_ You ought to take it out only on yourself).

15. That is easily explained.

16. Political parties fight among themselves.

17. You are only hurting one another.

18. In Haggai 1:2 Yahwe takes it out on his people for their inactivity, faced with the
    rebuilding of the temple of Jerusalem (John Kessler).

19. The power of God is seen in nature.

20. Instruct and admonish one another with complete wisdom (Col.3:16).

Exercise C Marie-Paul Dion, «La recluse de Montréal, Jeanne Le Ber», Église et Théologie 22 (1991), 50-51.

Mr. Olier and Jerome Le Royer de la Dauversière had met and recognized each other providentially – miraculously? – in Paris. They had communicated to each other their reciprocal desire to work for the salvation of souls in New France by founding a colony there. Since their first encounter, they had always acted in harmony for the actualization of this great plan...

Nothing very precise allows us to know the names of the members of the Société Notre-Dame de Montréal. The impotence of researchers to find the names is perhaps an indication of the purity of the motives which animated them. They took pains to hide themselves from the eyes of men (_or_ humankind); almost all were only known by God alone, even if, among them, there were magistrates, counts, dukes, and ladies of high quality, of whom the majority were known and influential in Paris. The Associates, as associates, wished to leave to God alone the glory of the work which He himself had inspired in them. That, at least, is the opinion of the historian Fallion.

Exercise D   Paul Ricoeur, La métaphore vive (Paris: Éditions du Seuil, 1975).

Rhetoric died when the fashion for classifying figures of rhetoric had entirely supplanted the philosophical meaning, which used to animate the vast rhetorical empire, caused its parts to hold together and linked the whole to the organon and to first philosophy.

This feeling of an irreparable loss grows even more if one considers that the vast Aristotelian program itself used to represent, if not a reduction, at least the rationalization of a discipline which, in its place of origin, in Syracuse, had proposed to govern all usages of public speech. There was rhetoric because there was eloquence, public eloquence. The observation goes a long way: first of all, the word was a weapon intended to influence people before the jury, in the public assembly or even for eulogy and praise, a weapon invoked to give the victory in battles where speech is the deciding factor. Nietzsche writes: «Eloquence is republican.» The old definition received from the Sicilians – «rhetoric is the worker (or mistress) of persuasion» – reminds <us> that rhetoric was added as a «technique» to natural eloquence, but that this technique plunges into a spontaneous creativity. Among all the didactic treatises written in Sicily, then in Greece, when Gorgias had established himself in Athens, rhetoric was this *technê* which renders discourse conscious of itself and makes of persuasion a distinct goal to attain by means of a specific strategy.

Therefore, before the taxonomy (i.e. classification) of figures of speech, there was the great rhetoric of Aristotle; but before the latter, there was the untamed usage of speech and the ambition to capture its dangerous power by means of a particular technique.

CHAPTER THIRTEEN

Exercise A

1. He brought out the meaning of the text.

2. The philosopher will inform us of his subject tomorrow.

3. She got herself scolded by the publisher.

4. He has his suits made in Paris.

5. No-one in the world will make him change his mind (Cocteau, *Bacchus* III, 7).

6. He succeeded in making himself understood.

7. This young couple had a new house made for themselves.

8. They have their children do sports.

9. They made us wait.

10. She has her children read.

11. Before the believers, Nietzsche is more reserved, as if he feared making them suffer by making himself too well understood (Henri de Lubac).

12. If he had wished it, he could have had his wife send a letter.

13. The royal power will use the privileges as tools for making the faculty adhere to its ideas, according to the political opportunities or necessities.

14. In this way, it was more difficult for the faculty to promote their rights with the king (Lyse Roy).

15. You do nothing but complain _or_ All you do is complain.

Exercise B

1. He must be late on account of the bad weather.

2. That must be it!

3. She was to read the whole chapter this evening.

4. He should work!

5. He should have worked!!

6. You should share your knowledge with your friends.

7. They were supposed to come home sooner.

8. We were supposed to stop.

9. We will have to see them this evening.

10. One ought to love one's neighbours.

Exercise C

Lyse Roi, "Urban Space and a System of Representations: The Royal Entries of the Dauphin and King Francis I into Caen in 1532", *Memini* 5 (2001), pp. 51-2.

The entry leads the king to transgress a limit and restore it by taking possession of the city and recognizing the loyalty of his subjects. In this way, it makes of the limited spatial whole one part of a totality (one city among others in the realm) and this totality is summarized and condensed into one part (the whole realm in this city). The event of the entry also constitutes a defining moment of privilege in the confrontation of identities between those who receive and the one who is received. It structures the meeting of an urban identity and a princely identity. The urban community as well as the princely or royal power are defined and represented in a ritual whose motives (<u>or</u> the motives of which) are inscribed simultaneously in the short time of the event and the long time of history. The ceremonial structure, carved up into practically invariable sequences, imposed and controlled by the state power, and the diverse symbolic, festive and decorative programs imagined by the city are invested with an identifying function expressing the social existance and the recognition of a community and a power... In this sociological perspective, the struggles for identity are aimed at the monopoly of symbolic power (to cause to be seen and to be believed, to make known and cause to be recognized) and at the will to impose the legitimate definition of the divisions of the social world and a vision of the social world which gives meaning to the group. The analysis of the political field's performance leads Pierre Bourdieu to say that the ceremony is an act of dramatization for the social groups which give themselves first to themselves in the spectacle and then to the world.

Exercise D

Henri de Lubac, "Nietsche et la 'mort de Dieu'", *Le drame de l'humanisme athée.*

The meaning which Nietsche attaches to this expression, the 'death of God', is new. On his lips, it is not a simple statement. Neither is it a lamentation or a sarcastic remark. It expresses an option. 'Now', says Nietzsche, 'it is our taste (fashion) which decides against Christianity, not arguments.'[4] It is an act, an act as clean and as brutal as is that of a murderer. 'The death of God is not only a terrible fact for him, it is willed by him.[5] If God is dead, he adds in fact, 'it is we who have killed him'. 'We are the murderers of God.'[6]

Many people, the majority of them, do not notice it. They take the one who comes to

---

4. *Spirited Knowledge*. Bauemler is therefore deceived when he writes [that]... the decisive sentence 'God is dead' has the meaning of an historic fact (Niezsche, *Philosopher and Politician*, 1931, p.98). Nietzsche does much more than note a fact.

3. John Wahl, *The Nietzsche of Jaspers* in *Philosophical Research*, vol. 6, p.356.

6. *Spirited Knowledge*, n.125, *The Madman* (pp.104-5).

announce the news of it to them for a fool. There are two broad categories: believers and common atheists. The first, not comprehending anything by his words, are not even troubled by them. They keep up their dream in the middle of a world which is waking up. Their faith renders them blind and deaf, so to speak. The second, who have never believed in anything, greet it with a great laugh. Never have they suspected anything living beyond sensate life. Nietzsche would like to tear the latter out of their complacency; he would like to make them notice the void which has been hollowed out in them and he heckles them forcefully. In the face of the believers, on the contrary, if he feels them to be sincere and simple, his attitude is reserved, as if he feared to make them suffer by making himself too well understood... 'I arrive too soon', he says to himself, 'my time has not yet come'. It's that "the most significant events are also the slowest to command attention" (*lit.* to impose themselves).

CHAPTER FOURTEEN

Exercise A

1. Here is the best restaurant, that I know of, in this city [*connaisse* after a superlative adj.].

2. For a long time, De Gaulle seemed to be the only one able to save France.

3. In your opinion, who are the first Europeans to have arrived in America?

4. The best friend that a man can have is his dog [*puiisse* after superlative adj.]

5. She waited until the children would return [*reviennent* after *jusqu'à ce que*].

6. He left the country without the authorities knowing [*sachent* after *sans que*].

7. He is not more intelligent than she is [*n'* = **ne**; pleonastic in the second instance].

8. Although the situation may be difficult, you ought not to become discouraged [*soit* after *Quoique*].

9. They placed the most beautiful statues of Rodin in the museum so that they might not be damaged [*soient* after *afin que*].

10. Truly, truly, I tell you that[7] the rooster will not crow before you have denied me three times (John 13:38) [*aies*; aux. vb. in compound past after <*avant*> *que*].

---

7 *je te le dis*: I tell you it *or* I say it to you; the "it" (*le*) is converted to "that" in English. In both cases, these words receive the action of the telling or saying.

11. God said: "Let there be light!" and the light was (Gen.1:3) [*soit* after the jussive *que*].

12. May God wish to forgive me! <u>or</u> May God forgive me! [*veuille*; optative with *Que* implied].

13. May they rest in peace [*reposent* after *Qu'*; optative].

14. Not a week passes without an up-to-date professor taking up arms against the literature from before our time [*parte* after *sans qu'*].

15. [According to the Talmud] God wondered from what part of the male body he would form the woman. [He answered himself:] "I will not choose the head for this, so that she may not raise her own head up too proudly; nor <will I choose> the eye, so that she may not be too curious, nor the ear, so that she may not go around eaves-dropping at doors, nor the mouth so that she may not be too talkative, nor the hand so that she may not give in to prodigality, nor the foot so that she may not go out of her house continually. I am going to draw her from a part of the body which remains hidden, in order to make her modest (Robert Aron, *Les années obscures de Jésus*).
    [**N.B.** Here, *afin que* or *pour que* could also be translated as "lest" without the following negative; e.g. "lest she raise her own head up too proudly, lest she be too curious, lest she go around eaves-dropping, etc." The subjunctive verbs are: *élève, soit, soit, aille, livre, sorte.*]

16. Your son will not go out without having asked you for forgiveness [*ait*; aux. vb. in compound past after *sans qu'*].

17. It is the firm and persevering resolve for a commitment to the common good, in other words for the good of each and everyone <of us>, so that all of us may be truly responsible for everyone [*soyons* after *afin que*].

18. He fears that she may be deceiving him [*trompe* after a verb of fearing; ***ne*** is pleonastic].

19. Do you doubt [that] that is true? [*soit* after doubt]

20. Do not go there without anyone knowing [*sache* after *sans que*; *le* is pleonastic in English).

Exercise B

1. Remain calm! [plain imperative; no subunctive]

2. That requires the lay faithful to be continually finding more spiritual momentum, thanks to a real participation in the life of the Church, and to be illuminated by its [*or* her = the Church's] social doctrine.

3. The means and the way to actualize a policy which might aim at a real human developpment is solidarity [*puisse* expresses doubt].

4. May she be merciful!

5. I would like you to explain this passage to me (polite).

6. It seems doubtful that there might be beings on the other planets.

7. a. It is necessary that this child conquer his / her shyness.
   b. This child must conquer his or her shyness.

8. Sincerely yours, Pierre Trudeau (*lit.* Would you accept, dear Sir, the expression of my eminent feelings...).

9. I doubt that he is telling the truth (*or* may be telling the truth).

10. I am happy that you may be with us this afternoon.

11. It is possible that Jesus may have been raised from the dead!

12. It would be necessary for you to read the works of Rousseau.

13. I doubt that they will succeed in rediscovering the manuscript.

14. For her entire life, this woman has sought a man who would be perfect. That is why she has never married.

15. According to biblical Jewish thought, the universe is sacred. There is no distinction of any kind between the secular and the sacred. There is no atom of matter in which forces attached to the universal power do not reside. There is no gesture or act, apparently inconsequential, which in fact may not be attached to the cosmic destiny, and which might not influence its development (Robert Aron).

Exercise C

The question now to be asked is the following: may we, in the texts accessible to us, recognize the work of composition, and to what degree? Without a question, one notices numerous texts stitched together. "When the disciples <on the road to> Emmaus come to impart their experience of the Resurrection, the Eleven who joyously welcome them by informing them about Peter's vision, harmonize poorly with the disciples who, in the following pericope, are frightened when Jesus appears, and who are only convinced by numerous tangible proofs" (Luke 24: 33-42). The fact that the angels, in Matthew, command the women to tell the disciples to go into Gallilee where they will see the Lord harmonizes poorly with this other fact that the women themselves on the road, consquently to Jerusalem, benefit from an appearance of the Resurrected One. Moreover, it is unlikely that Jesus would repete to them simply the words that they have already heard from the angels (28: 7-10). It is difficult to accept that, in John, Mary Magdalene would twice linger near the tomb, that she would find it empty the first time and without any angel being there to interpret the event; that the second time the same angel interpreters would appear as in the synoptics, but without them having anything to announce to her, and finally that she would experience an encounter with Jesus.

CHAPTER FIFTEEN

Exercise A

1. He did not come, as far as I know.

2. We were doubting that he would write his history of Canada.

3. Let us ssume that a supernatural event might happen.

4. Arthur Rimbaud, an exemplary symbolist poet, wrote exquisite poetry until he left France, at the age of 19, to lead the life of an adventurer in Ethiopia.

5. I would really have loved him to finish his studies.

6. The poems of E.J. Pratt are numbered among the longest Canadian poems that I have ever read.

7. We deeply regret <the fact> that this author might wish to leave Canada; we doubt that he will come back from New York.

8. These newspapers are the best that one might find here here.

9. I feared that my thesis would be unacceptable (*ne*: pleonastic).

10. Rousseau doubts that children understand what they study.

11. Rouseau suspected that the previous teaching methods were not effective.

12. She wished him to finish his studies.

13. Few days passed without Paris, terrified, learning about some mysterious murder (*n'*: pleonastic).

14. Similar things used to happen every day without anyone dreaming of being shocked by them.

15. They pronounced his guilt before he might open his mouth.

Exercise B

1. Undoubtedly, farces and satirical skits played a great role in these 'mad festivities'.

2. They were permitted at Epiphany, but under certain conditions. They were only supposed to begin the evening before, or only after Vespers that very day, so that the divine office would not be interrupted.

3. As for comedies, they were not prohibited, but they were supposed to be examined by the principal "so that no biting or satirical characteristic might remain in them, nor anything improper which could offend a man of quality."

4. It was (*lit.* is) in 1683 and not in 1674 that the inscription was placed over the door. Father La Chaise would not have pointed out this case in the terms that we have just read, if it had been a deed accomplished nine years before (*or* a *fait accompli* of nine years; using the loan word).

5. The tragic output of the Jesuit Fathers is considerable... An unending production <of it> was necessary to meet this annual demand.

6. Although the Fathers, whose mission it was to feed the college theatres, would have known the ancient models better than anyone, yet they did not fail first of all to move perceptibly away from them.

7. Tragedy [...], according to Aristotle, is composed of three parts: the beginning, middle and end. If these three parts may be covered in three acts, without the action suffering from it, who then would have the right to complain about it?

8. The interruption, however momentary it might have been, of the link which unites Christ to his Father and life, introduces a fundamental and psychically necessary discontinuity into the mythical representation of the Subject (Kristeva, p.143).

142. Reading: Adolphe Gesché

"The Identity of the Individual before God"

When Moses questions God, whose dazzling <revelation> he has just experienced, and says to him: "If the sons of Israel ask me what your name is, what will I answer them?" (Ex. 3:13), he is asking the true question, a question of identity which alone is truly significant, when all is said and done. What is your name, so that I may know who you are, so that they may know who you are, and so that we <all> may know to which God we offer ourselves. The individual, in doing this, questions himself as much about God as about the future of his own identity. For it is not immaterial to the individual to know to whom he (or she) is going to give his (or her) faith. What am I and what will I become when I have[8] God face to face? As in every relationship, my identity is at play when the 'other' appears. It is important to know who he is, if I want to know what will come of it, for me.

Certainly, the whole question thereupon is not settled. Moreover, God begins by preserving and safeguarding a part of the unknowable, and for that reason precisely without a name: "I am who I am" (Ex. 3:14). In <all> that, furthermore, <there is> nothing which ought to offend us. It is important for the individual that God be what he is, and not an idol that I would have fashioned at the whim of my <own> needs, and in which I would do nothing but rediscover and serve myself. It is really by being, at first, what he is, and not what I want him to be, that God will then be this encounter for me, whose identity <and> whose name concern me in order for me to understand myself...

Still today, it is this question of Moses which the individual poses, indeed no longer merely that of the existence of God in itself, but much rather that more decisive one, in a sense, which concerns the relationship between the individual and God. Is this relationship constitutive or destructive of my being? Am I going to be annihilated in this relationship or come out of it magnified?

---

8. *j'aurai Dieu*: I will have God. After *quand* and similar temporal conjunctions, French uses the future tense, when English prefers the present. Cf. Parmentier, *Mise au point* (1993), p.174.

APPENDIX I: Literary Supplements

1. "The Secret of Master Cornille"

All that smacked of mystery and set everyone to gossiping a lot. Each one was explaining, in his <or her own> fashion, the secret of Master Cornille, but the general buzz was that there were even more bags of money than bags of flour in that mill.

In the long run, however, everything was discovered. Here is how:

In having the young people dance to my fife, one fine day I noticed that the eldest of my boys and little Vivette had fallen in love with one another. Deep down, I was not angry about it, because, after all, the name of Cornille was <held> in honour among us, and then seeing this pretty little sparrow [of a] Vivette scampering around my house would have given me pleasure.

<It was> only <that> , as our lovers often had occasion to be together, I wanted – for fear of accidents – to settle the affair immediately, and I went up as far as the mill to have a few words with the grandfather. Ah, the old sorcerer! You have to see how he received me <to believe it>! <It was> impossible to make him open the door. I explained my motives to him through the keyhole with great difficulty; and all the while that I was speaking, there was this wretch of a skinny cat that was hissing like <the> devil above my head.

2. A. Albert Camus, *The Outsider*

Today, mum died, or perhaps yesterday, I don't know. I received a telegram from the home: "Mother deceased. Burial tomorrow. Sincerely." That does not mean anything. It was perhaps yesterday...

I took the bus at two o'clock. It was very warm. I ate at Celest's restaurant, as usual. They all took great pains for me and Celest said to me: "You only have one mother." I was a little distracted, because I had to go up to Emmanuel's to borrow a black tie and armband from him. He lost his uncle a few months ago...

[The Trial of the Murder of the Algerian]

"Why did you wait between the first and the second shot?" he said then. Once more, I saw the red beach again and I felt the burning sun (*lit.* the burn of the sun) on my forehead. But this time, I did not say anything in response. Throughout the <long> silence which followed,

294

the judge seemed to be agitated. He passed his hands across his forehead and repeated his question with a slightly altered voice: "Why? You must tell me [it]. Why?" I still kept quiet.

Abruptly, he got up, paced with a great stride towards one end of his office and opened a drawer in a filing cabinet. He drew a silver crucifix out of it which he brandished about, returning towards me. And with a voice completely changed, almost trembling, he burst out: "Are you familiar with that?" I said: "Yes, naturally." Then he said to me very quickly and in an impassioned way, that *he* believed in God <and> that his conviction was that no man was so guilty that God would not forgive him, but that it was necessary, to that end, that the man should become, through his repentance, like a child whose soul is empty and ready to welcome everything. He had leaned his whole body over the table. He was waving his crucifix almost <right> above me. To tell the truth, I had followed him very badly in his reasoning, first because I was hot and there were some big fat flies in his office which alighted upon my face, and also because he made me a little afraid. At the same time, I recognized that it was ridiculous, because, after all, it was I <who was> the criminal. Nevertheless, he continued. I vaguely understood that, in his opinion, there was only one obscure point in my confession, the fact of having waited to fire my second gunshot. For the rest, it was very good, but that, he did not understand [it].

2. B. Proust, *In Search of Lost Time*

i. The Mystery of Memory

I find the Celtic belief very reasonable that the souls of those whom we have lost are <held> captive in some inferior being, in an animal, a vegetable, <or> an inanimate object, indeed lost to us, until <that> day, which never arrives for many, when we find ourselves passing nearby to a tree, entering into possession of the object which is their prison. Then they give a start, call out to us, and as soon as we have recognized them, the enchantment is broken. Delivered by us, they have vanquished death and return to live with us.

It is the same with our past. It is a waste of time [that we used] to seek to evoke it, <for> all our intellectual efforts are useless. It is hidden outside of its domain and its range in some material object (in the sensation that this material object would give to us) ... which we do not suspect. It depends upon chance for us to meet it, this object, or [for us] not to meet it before dying.

ii. Art and the Interpretation of Symbols

The year when we ate so much asperagus, the kitchen girl, normally charged with peeling them, was a poor sickly creature, in a state of pregnancy already quite advanced by the time we arrived at Easter, and we were even astonished that Françoise was allowing her to run so many errands and <do so many> chores, for she, each day more filled out, was beginning to carry the mysterious bundle (*lit.* basket) in front of her with difficulty, whose magnificent form one divined below her ample smock. The latter <folds> reminded <one> of the cloaks which clothe some of Giotto's symbolic figures, of which Mr. Swann had given me photographs. He himself made us notice it and when he used to ask us for news of the kitchen girl, he used to say to us: "How goes Giotto's Charity?" Moreover, the poor girl herself, fattened up to the face by her pregnancy, <nay> up to her cheeks which fell straight and square, indeed rather resembled these strong and mannish virgins, matrons rather, in whom the virtues are personified in the Arena Chapel. And I realize now that these Virtues and Vices of Padua resembled her even more in another way. In the same way that the image of this girl was heightened by the added symbol that she bore before her belly, without seeming to comprehend the meaning of it, without anything in her face conveying the beauty and the spirit of it, like a simple and weighty burden; so it is without appearing to suspect it that the powerful domestic who is represented at the Arena below the name "Caritas" and whose reproduction was hung up on the wall of my study in Combray, incarnates this virtue; that is without any thought of charity seeming ever to have been able to be expressed by her energetic and vulgar face. By a fine invention of the painter she tramples upon the treasures of the earth, but utterly as if she was stamping upon grapes in order to extract the juice from them...

These Virtues and Vices must have had a lot of reality in them, since they appeared to me <to be> as alive as the pregnant servant girl and since she herself did not seem much less allegorical. And perhaps this non-participation in virtue (at least in appearance) of the soul of a being... also possesses a reality beyond its aesthetic value, if not psychological, at least physiognomical, as they say. When later I had occasion to encounter, in the course of my life, in convents for example, some truly holy incarnations of active charity, they generally had the cheerful, positive, indifferent and gruff look of a surgeon in a hurry, this countenance in which no commiseration is to be read, no tenderness <when> confronted with human suffering, no fear of causing offense, and which is the unsweetened, dispassionate and sublime face of true goodness.

BIBLIOGRAPHY

I. Grammar Books

Booth, Maria Trudie. *French Phonetics: A Guide to Correct Pronunciation of French.*
  Lanham, Maryland: University of Maryland, 1997.

Carlut, Charles & Walter Meiden. *French for Oral and Written Review.*
  Toronto: Holt, Rinehart and Winston, 1968.

Dansereau, Diane M. *Savoir dire: cours de phonétique et de prononciation.*
  Toronto: D.C. Heath and Company, 1990.

Dietiker, S. *En bonne forme*, 4 ed. Toronto: Heath & Co., 1988.

Goosse, André. *Le bon usage* de Maurice Grevisse, 12me éd.
  Louvain-la-Neuve, Belgique: Éditions Duculot, 1993.

Léon, Monique & Pierre. *La prononciation du français.* Paris: Éditions Nathan, 1997.

Léon, Pierre R. *Prononciation du français standard.* Linguistique appliquée.
  Paris: Librairie Marcel Didier, 1966.

Olorenshaw, Robert & Rogers, Patrick J. *Les 100 pièges de l'anglais.*
  Alleur, Belgium: Marabout, 1985.

Parmentier, Michael A. *Mise au point: grammaire française, vocabulaire et textes,*
  2nd ed. Toronto: Harcourt Brace, 1993.

Stack, Edward M. *Reading French in the Arts and Sciences,* 4th ed.
  Boston: Houghton Mifflin Co., 1987.

Ziefle, Helmut W. *Theological German: A Reader.*
  Grand Rapids, Michigan: Baker Book House, 1986.

II. Bible Readings

La Bible de Jérusalem, nouv. éd., Paris: Éditions du Cerf, 1973.

Traduction Œcuménique de la Bible (TOB). Paris: Éditions du Cerf, 1982 and 1988.

III. Selections from Published Material

Aron, Robert. *Les années obscures de Jésus*. Paris: Desclée De Brouwer, 1960.

Baroni, Lise, Yvonne Bergeron, Pierette Daviau et Micheline Laguë.
    Voix des femmes; voies de passage: pratiques pastorales et enjeux ecclésiaux.
    Montréal: Paulines, 1995.

Bovon, François. "Le privilège pascal de Marie-Madeleine",
    New Testament Studies 30 (1984), pp.50-62.

Boysse, Ernest. *Le théâtre des jésuites*. Paris: Henri Vaton, 1880.

Camus, Albert. *L'Étranger*. Paris: Libraire Gallimard, 1957.

Chapsal, Madeleine. *Une soudaine solitude*. Paris: Librairie Arthème Fayard, 1995.

Chateaubriand, François-René. *Essai sur les révolutions: Génie du christianisme*.
    Texte établi par Maurice Regaud, Paris: Éditions Gallimard, 1978.

Daudet, Alphonse. "Le secret de Maître Cornille", *Lettres de mon moulin*.
    Paris: Presses Pocket, 1977. pp.80-81.

De Lubac, Henri. *Le Drame de l'humanisme athée*. 7me éd.
    Paris: Les Éditions du Cerf, 1983.

Des Rivières, Madeleine. *Ozanam un savant chez les pauvres*.
    Montréal: Bellarmin, 1984.

Dion, Marie-Paul. *La recluse de Montréal Jeanne Le Ber*.
    Église et Théologie 22 (1991), pp. 50-51.

Ellul, Jacques. *Politique de Dieu, politiques de l'homme.*
    Paris: Éditions universitaires, 1996.

Gesché, Adolphe. "L'identité de l'homme devant Dieu".
    Revue théologique de Louvain 29 (1998), pp. 3-28.

Jean-Paul II. *Les fidèles laïcs.* Paris: Centurion, 1989.

Kessler, John. `J (le temps) en Aggée I 2-4: conflit théologique ou "sagesse mondaine"?
    Vetus Testamentum 48.4 (1998), pp.555-557.

Kristeva, Julia. *Soleil noir: dépression et mélancolie.* Paris: Éditions Gallimard, 1987.

Onfray, Michel. *Traité d'athéologie: physique de la métaphysique.*
    Paris: Bernard   Grasset, 2005.

Proust, Marcel. *Du côté de chez Swann.* England: Parkstone Press, 1994.

Ricoeur, Paul. "Intellectual Autobiography", *The Philosophy of Paul Ricoeur.*
    The Library of Living Philosophers, 22. Chicago: Open Court, 1995.

———. *La métaphore vive.* Paris: Éditions du Seuil, 1975.

Rihoit, Catherine. "Ah, si j'étais...", *Le Monde,* 2 juillet 1982 quoted in *En bonne forme,*
    4th ed. S. Dietiker. Toronto: Heath & Co., 1988. pp. 302-4.

Roy, Lyse. "Espace urbain et système de représentations. Les entrées du Dauphin
    et de François Ier à Caen en 1532." *Memini. Travaux et documents publiés par
    la Société des études médiévales du Québec* 5 (2001). pp.51-52.

Saint-Exupéry, Antoine de. *Le Petit Prince.* 1946. France: Éditions Gallimard, 1999.

Tincq, Henri. "Le cardinal Ratzinger conteste la qualité d'églises aux confessions
    protestantes". *Le monde.* 6 Septembre, 2003. p.3.

IV. Secondary Sources

The Cambridge Dictionary of Philosophy. 2nd ed.
   Cambridge-New York: Cambridge University Press, 1999.

Dunaway, John M. *Simone Weil.* New York: Twayne Publishers, 1984.

The Encyclopedia of Philosophy. Supplement.
   New York: Simon & Schuster Macmillan, 1996.

CPSIA information can be obtained
at www.ICGtesting.com
Printed in the USA
LVOW02s0412150616
492674LV00010B/148/P